/ 00

# CREATED EQUAL:

## REFLECTIONS ON THE UNALIENABLE RIGHT TO LIFE

To my friend
Dr. James Dobson,

For Life,
Tom Glessner

## THOMAS A. GLESSNER

Copyright © 2016 Thomas A. Glessner
All rights reserved
First Edition

PAGE PUBLISHING, INC.
New York, NY

First originally published by Page Publishing, Inc. 2016

ISBN 978-1-68348-403-5 (Paperback)
ISBN 978-1-68348-404-2 (Digital)

Printed in the United States of America

# CONTENTS

*This book is dedicated to my grandchildren -- Patrick Joseph Goergen, his unborn brother James Thomas Goergen, and their unborn cousin Lincoln John Glessner. May you inherit a world where all life -- born and unborn -- is deemed precious and protected under the law.*

*Thank you to SaraLynn Goergen for her assistance in the editing process and to Brannan Glessner and Top Dawg Marketing for the creative design of the book cover.*

# FOREWORD

TWO DEAR FRIENDS I HAVE come to know in the course of my pro-life work are Norma McCorvey and Sandra Cano. They were, respectively, the plaintiffs in the 1973 landmark Supreme Court decisions legalizing abortion, Roe vs. Wade and Doe vs. Bolton. Technically, Roe and Doe both won their cases. Amazingly, neither of them understood or even sought the outcome that resulted. Neither of them had an abortion. Both of them simply wanted help with their own personal situations. Both of them were manipulated by aggressive attorneys who wanted to use the courts to change social policy on abortion.

As the years went on and they understood the implications of these decisions, they dedicated themselves wholeheartedly to working for the reversal of Roe and Doe and the end of abortion. I have prayed with them, lobbied with them, worked with them and wept with them. Sandra went home to the Lord in 2014.

Norma and Sandra represent America. They had a damaging policy imposed upon them by those who pretended it was what they wanted, and it turned their lives upside down.

In this book, my friend and colleague Tom Glessner probes the seriousness of the situation America faces with abortion. It is more than just a "bad policy." It is more than a mistaken court decision. Certainly there are plenty of both. But abortion policy in the United States today actually imposes on us a different kind of government.

The Court's abortion decisions do not say that the unborn child isn't human. They say that they do not know whether they are or not. But nevertheless, they take away protection from them. Now, if the court had said, "We have concluded that the unborn are not human, and thus we acknowledge your right to abort them," this would have still been a wrong decision, but at least it would have preserved in theory the principle that no government can authorize the killing of the innocent. But the justices did not preserve that principle. They subverted it. And when they subverted it, they established a different government than our Founding Fathers established.

We need to understand the seriousness of this reversal. What the Supreme Court said in Roe was, "We are now declaring that we the court, we the government of the United States, have the authority to remove some human beings from the protections of the Constitution. We have the authority to remove this protection not based on the humanity of the unborn, or lack thereof, but because we say so."

I don't think we as Americans have appreciated the absolutely radical break this decision represents. We tend to think that Roe was wrongly decided, and that because of Roe we will slide headlong down the slippery slope of evils that follow in its wake and end in a darker place than we can imagine. In fact, however, we are in that dark place. Roe put us there. It is hard to imagine much worse than the authorized killing of nearly 60 million children.

Where do we get totalitarian regimes? Where do we get holocausts? We get them from governments that somehow think they are the masters over life and death. When a government says that some people don't have to be protected, that is the stuff of which genocides are made. None other than Pope John Paul II made the same point when he wrote in The Gospel of Life in 1995 that a state which authorizes abortion "is transformed into a tyrant State," and that as a result, "the disintegration of the State itself has already begun" (n. 20)

Abortion is not just one of many issues. Because it attacks our nation at its foundations, it is the foundational issue. And because at the foundation of our nation is the sovereignty of God, those who work to end abortion are not only defending the rights of these children, but are defending the very rights of their Creator.

From this truth this book takes shape. Its message, like its author, carries the passion to correct the massive injustice of abortion. We need not only the truth this book contains; we need the urgency to act on it, and the readiness to make the sacrifices needed to implement it.

The Founding Fathers did no less to establish this nation on solid principles; we can do no less to restore those principles in public policy. That is why our national anthem concludes with a question. After relating the fact that the flag -- representing freedom and the principles of the Declaration -- was still standing amidst the battle waged by those who were defending it, the anthem asks, "Oh say, does that star-spangled banner yet wave, o'er the land of the free and the home of the brave?" In other words, are you still fighting for those same principles today, are you still fighting tyranny and defending life against its enemies today, are you still pledging your lives, your fortunes, and your sacred honor to stand up for the rights of the Creator? This is a question for us, for our children, for our grandchildren. Through the insight and urgency which this book conveys, may we ever answer that question with a profound Yes!

-- Fr. Frank Pavone, National Director, Priests for Life
President, National Pro-life Religious Council

# INTRODUCTION

I REMEMBER WELL THE COURSE I took on corporations while in law school. A corporation is a legally existing entity that has all of the rights and privileges under the law that a living, breathing human being has. To create a corporation, a lawyer must file articles of incorporation with the state agency empowered to grant a corporate charter. Once this corporate charter is granted, a corporation is brought into existence through a certificate of incorporation. After that the articles of incorporation require the corporation to establish, through its board of directors, the corporate bylaws, sometimes referred to as the corporate constitution. The articles of incorporation bring into existence the corporation, and the bylaws specify the rules under which the corporation must operate.

One critical point of corporate law was emphasized by my law professor concerning the relationship between the articles of incorporation and the bylaws. The two documents always must be interpreted to be consistent with each other. No contradiction between the provisions of these two documents can exist. If there is a contradiction between the two, then the provision(s) of the bylaws that contradict(s) the articles of incorporation are invalid and not legally binding upon the corporation.

The establishment of the American republic is analogous to the legal principles that form the legal powers and duties of a corporation. The document that brought our nation into being is the Declaration of Independence (U.S. 1776). This magnificent document created a new nation, which in the words of Lincoln was "conceived in liberty and dedicated to the proposition that all men are created equal."

Our United States Constitution was adopted and ratified to specify and enforce the rights of the people of this new nation as directed by the Declaration of Independence. These two documents must be interpreted as consistent with each other, and if there is a contradiction between the two which cannot be reconciled, then such provision(s) of the Constitution that conflict(s) with the Declaration of Independence are invalid and unenforceable.

On January 22, 1973, in *Roe v. Wade*, the United States Supreme Court interpreted our Constitution in a manner that denies to some human beings the unalienable right to life proclaimed in the Declaration of Independence. In doing so, the high court denied the proclamation that life is a self-evident and unalienable right which comes from the Creator and which no government can legitimately deny to some. The decision of *Roe* is perhaps the greatest example in American history where the inspired proclamations of our founding document were ignored and contradicted by a Supreme Court decision. Accordingly, the provisions of the *Roe* must be seen as invalid and unenforceable.

This is what the current political battle over abortion in America is all about. Does our nation really believe that all human beings are created equal and endowed by our Creator with the self-evident and unalienable rights of life, liberty, and the pursuit of happiness? If so, how can we tolerate the denial of the right to life to over one million unborn children a year?

*Life* is the first and foremost unalienable right mentioned in the Declaration of Independence. Without this right being secured in the law, all other rights are meaningless. If the right to life is not protected, then the right to liberty cannot be exercised by anybody with certainty. If the right to liberty is not secure, then the pursuit of happiness is impossible to achieve. Furthermore, if the unalienable right to life is denied to some, i.e., the unborn, because of social reasons then this precious right is not secure for any of us. (Indeed, the reasons for allowing abortion in *Roe* can easily and logically be used to justify the killing of those who are born.) The starting place, however, for the exercise of these God-given unalienable rights begins with the recognition that all human beings are created equal and, thus, deserve protection under the law of the right to life.

In 1857, the Supreme Court issued a decision, the *Dred Scott* decision, that denied the humanity of freed African American slaves, treating them as mere property as opposed to human beings created with unalienable rights. The Declaration of Independence proclaimed a standard by which our nation was to be bound, but the institution of slavery clearly violated that standard. Thus, there was a deep tension within the American culture, and the issue of slavery had to be addressed. Could America remain a free nation when it clearly was violating it principles through the denial to some human beings of their unalienable rights to life, liberty, and the pursuit of happiness? The Supreme Court gave credence to this great contradiction in its disastrous decision, and the repercussions quickly reverberated across the nation. America was launched into a brutal civil war where nearly seven hundred thousand Americans died—a blood bath unequaled by any other war in which our nation has been engaged.

What serious repercussions await America for its tolerance of the denial of the right to life of millions of human beings conceived since 1973? To date nearly sixty million unborn human beings have been killed by abortion in America in 1973. The destiny of this nation depends upon the final outcome of this struggle. Our nation must be brought into consistency with the great principles of its founding document.

This book discusses the foundational roots of America as set forth in the Declaration of Independence and how such foundational principles have been violated by the American tolerance for abortion on demand. America is a unique nation in the history of the world. At the time of the founding of our nation, the prevailing view throughout history was that personal rights and equality under the law are determined by the government and/or king and bestowed upon only those with whom the king has favor.

The American revolutionaries of 1776 believed otherwise. They founded their actions on the proclamation that our rights come from a Creator—not a king—and thus, all human beings are created equal. Every human being is equally valuable in the eyes of God because every human being is created in his image. Therefore, no government and/or king can legitimately deny to others the unalienable rights given to human beings by our Creator.

In denying this unalienable right to life to some Americans have denied the sovereignty of the Creator, who bestows upon his creation of humanity unalienable rights. Such rights come from the Creator and cannot be legitimately denied to anybody by government. In denying the unalienable right to life our nation has, in the words of Abraham Lincoln,

> We have forgotten God. We have forgotten the gracious hand which preserved us in peace, also multiplied, enriched and strengthened us. We have vainly imagined, in the deceitfulness of our hearts, that all these blessings were produced by some superior wisdom and virtue of our own. Intoxicated with unbroken success, we have become too self-sufficient to feel the necessity of redeeming and preserving grace, too proud to pray to the God that made us!" (Presidential Proclamation for a National Day of Prayer and Fasting, March 30, 1863)

I believe with all my heart that, one day, this nation will awaken and reaffirm its noble and founding principles for all human beings. Until that day arrives, however, I fear that much turmoil and heartache will fall upon America. A nation that ignores the sufferings and cries for life from its most vulnerable members is a nation on the verge of losing its soul.

Future historians will not judge modern-day America by its current military might or economic power. Rather, this nation will be judged by future generations by how we cared for our most vulnerable—the unborn, the infirm, the elderly, the handicapped, and the dying. If, however, our nation returns to the spiritual roots contained in its founding principles set forth in the Declaration of Independence, there is hope that once again America will be the champion of liberty and freedom for all, including the most defenseless of our human family.

Thomas A. Glessner, JD
President
National Institute of Family and Life Advocates (NIFLA)
Fredericksburg, Virginia

# CHAPTER 1

# A Day That Lives in Infamy

IN THE WORDS OF PRESIDENT Franklin Delano Roosevelt, certain historical dates "live in infamy."(1) January 22, 1973, was one of these. Virtually nobody I know remembers what they were doing on this day, but I do.

At that time I was a junior at the University of Washington in Seattle. My major course of study was political science, and my ambitions were to attend law school after graduation and, eventually, enter the political world, ultimately serving as a United States senator. As a student of politics and government, I was passionate about keeping up on current events.

On that day, I was walking across campus to go to my fraternity house and have some lunch when a fellow political science major came running up to me and rather excitedly blurted out, "Did you get the news today? President Johnson died."

Johnson had been out of office for four years, but his name still brought up strong emotions from political activists across the spectrum. To those who opposed the Vietnam War, his name was anathema. To conservatives who believe in limited government, his expansion of the welfare state through his Great Society program was also anathema. To students like myself who studied politics, he was a fascinating historical figure whose presidency had been marred by civil strife over the war and domestic issues. Thus, for me his death was a major event about which I needed to know more. So I hastened to return to my fraternity house for lunch and, hopefully, watch a special news broadcast about his death.

Twenty-four-hour cable television news was not then in existence, but I was fortunate to tune into a special midday report on the death of President Johnson. The report was concise and to the point, listing the causes of death and who was with him when he died. It then gave a brief synopsis and review of the highlights of his controversial presidency. In total, the report lasted no more than fifteen minutes.

At the very end of the report, the anchorperson made an interesting statement, saying, "In other news today, the United States Supreme Court rendered a decision finding the antiabortion laws in the states of Texas and Georgia unconstitutional and, thus, voiding the antiabortion laws in all fifty states." I remember very clearly my reaction to this news as one of apathy and indifference. In fact, my very distinct thought that raced through my mind upon hearing this report was, "Who cares?"

At that time I was a young evangelical Christian. I was raised in a minister's home where the responsibility for Christians to be socially involved in the issues of the day was always made clear. At the dinner table in our household, politics and religion were definitely topics of discussion, and I learned from an early age that one's religion did not end on Sunday evening after church. Rather, a true believer in Jesus Christ has a responsibility to address social evils and proclaim in the public arena an end to injustice. While Christ's salvation is free to those who believe it does not come without responsibilities to our fellow citizens.

The issue of abortion, however, was a novel one for me, and something that was quite foreign to most evangelicals at that time. My very first remembrance of the issue being discussed in my presence was when, at age fifteen, I was told after an evening church service that a young woman I had known as a child had become pregnant and had an abortion. Not knowing exactly what that meant, I immediately walked over to my mother who was having a conversation with another member of the church and asked her to tell me what abortion was.

I remember her shocked look and response. She quickly retorted, "If I ever hear you talk like that again in church, I will wash your mouth out with soap when we get home."

Abortion, however, soon would become a word that would be freely uttered from the mouths of many as it became a hot political issue that created intense discussion and debate, even within church circles. During the decade of the sixties, a crusade for the overturning of laws prohibiting abortion was accelerated throughout the nation. Led by Planned Parenthood, pressure was being mounted throughout our nation's cultural, religious, and political institutions to end legal bans on abortion.

The proponents of abortion cried out that abortion was an issue of women's rights. It was an issue of the right for women to control their bodies, and it was an issue of women's equality. On this latter point, they mockingly suggested that if men could become pregnant, then nobody would oppose abortion because, in their opinion, antiabortion laws are only a means to allow a chauvinistic society controlled by men to keep women in their place. Except for voices from the Catholic Church, few at that time challenged such views by asserting the obvious, that abortion kills another human being, who is the ultimate victim of such a violent act.

During the fall of 1970, my freshman year in college, the state of Washington had a popular referendum on the statewide ballot in November which, if approved by the voters, would liberalize the antiabortion laws of the state and open the door for abortion on demand. In my government class, this referendum was debated by the students, and I listened to both sides intently with a clear leaning to the prolife position. While I remained mostly silent during the debate, I did blurt out to those who supported abortion that it certainly appeared to me such an act was not trivial and was, contrary to their arguments, quite a bit different than removing a wart from one's finger. This comment brought forth laughs of scorn and ridicule. In response, I slid down in my seat, believing that I had embarrassed myself by speaking about something upon which I had little knowledge.

I thought little about the issue after that one uncomfortable scene during my freshman year until some years later. However, when on January 22, 1973, I heard the news about the Supreme Court's decisions of *Roe v. Wade* and *Doe v. Bolton*, my reaction was clearly benign and unconcerned. I remember my thoughts well, "This has nothing to do with me. This decision will have absolutely no impact on my life whatsoever." How clearly wrong I was.

After graduating magna cum laude and becoming a member of Phi Beta Kappa, I entered law school at the University of Washington to pursue my career aspirations, and in 1977 I graduated with my law degree ready to make my mark on the world. The plans that I had made for myself clearly had nothing to do with addressing the issue of abortion. I simply did not see this as an issue of concern.

When *Roe v. Wade* was issued few people, even the justices of the Supreme Court, realized the implications it had for future cultural change. Recently, during the congressional debate on the Affordable Care Act, more commonly referred to as Obamacare, Congresswoman Nancy Pelosi remarked that the Congress had to pass the act so that "we can know what is in it." (2) Time has shown that a truer statement has never been spoken by a political leader. The negative, unforeseen consequences of Obamacare appear in the news every day. In the very same manner, the impact and consequences of *Roe v. Wade* and its companion case of *Doe v. Bolton* were not fully comprehended by the Court when rendering its decisions. Indeed, Chief Justice Warren Burger specifically stated in his concurring opinion in *Roe* that the Court had not opened the door for abortion on demand. (3) Yet, Burger was sadly mistaken on this point. A careful reading of the language of both *Roe* and *Doe* clearly indicates that these decisions swung the door wide open for abortion on demand at any time during a mother's pregnancy.

Although most theologians, attorneys, philosophers, and cultural commentators did not realize this in 1973, the legal precedents set by *Roe v. Wade* (4) and *Doe v. Bolton* (5) were a radical departure from legal precedents and the established moral reasoning which had guided our republic from its beginnings. These two decisions voided the antiabortion laws in all fifty states, which protected the lives of unborn children and imposed criminal sanctions upon those whose felonious acts violated the laws.

Most of these states' antiabortion laws voided by *Roe* and *Doe* had been adopted between 1857 and 1874. The passage of such laws was influenced by a very important report issued by the American Medical Association (AMA). (6) This report proclaimed that medical science had established that human life begins at conception. Therefore, unborn human life must be protected by such laws. Around this time, the same state legislatures that passed these antiabortion laws also approved the passage of the Thirteenth, Fourteenth, and Fifteenth Amendments to the US Constitution, which granted personhood status and legal protection to former slaves.

The Court, in *Roe*, ignored this history and held that abortion is protected by the Constitution as a right to privacy under the Fourteenth Amendment. In doing so, it not only disregarded undisputed post–Civil War history, but it also opened up a Pandora's Box of unforeseen consequences that have unraveled the moral fabric of the nation.

The Fourteenth Amendment to the US Constitution states in part: "No state shall deny to any person life, liberty, or property without due process of law." In its argument before the Court, the state of Texas, the defendant in *Roe*, took this language seriously and stated that abortion cannot be allowed because it takes the life of a "person" without due process of law. Justice Harry Blackmun, the author of the Court's majority opinion, agreed that if this argument is correct then abortion cannot be allowed. (7) However, according to Blackmun, this only holds if an unborn child is a "person" under the Constitution. He then goes on to affirmatively state that unborn human beings are not "persons" within the meaning of the Fourteenth Amendment and, thus, are not protected by it(8).

The common dictionary definition of "person" is simply "a human being." (9) Blackmun's opinion does not deny the humanity of the unborn, it simply states that, human or not, unborn children are not "persons' under the Constitution. (10) This is a strange conclusion to arrive at in light of the responses by the states to the AMA report in both passing antiabortion laws and, at the same time, ratifying the Fourteenth Amendment.

Corporations, nonhuman beings, have long been held by the legal system to be persons with rights under the Fourteenth Amendment. (11) However, unborn children who are clearly human beings are not recognized as such under *Roe* and *Doe*. So now our legal system recognizes a great contradiction. Certain nonhuman beings, i.e., corporations, are persons under the Constitution and, thus, have protected legal rights, but some human beings, i.e., unborn children, are not persons and are denied the most basic Constitutional right of all—the right to life.

In denying legal protection to the unborn, the Court did say that after the point of viability in pregnancy (when the child can survive outside the womb albeit by artificial means), states could prohibit abortion unless the abortion is necessary to protect the life or health of the mother. (12) However, the line drawn of viability is arbitrary and nonsensical because the viability of an unborn child is not a measurement of its humanity.

Consider the concept of viability in another context. A person who is in a coma and kept alive through life support systems is clearly not a viable human being because he cannot live without artificial means. Yet such person is clearly a human being. Does his nonviability mean he has forfeited his right to live?

Viability is not a determining factor as to whether one is fully human or not. Rather, it is a measurement of the state of medical technology developed to keep human beings alive. In the abortion context, viability is determined simply by the current state of medical technology, which can keep a prematurely born infant alive. Medical technology is constantly changing and improving, so viability cannot be a measurement of the humanity of the unborn. The Supreme Court, however, failed to grasp this when issuing its ruling in *Roe*.

In 1973, the time of viability was estimated to be twenty-four gestational weeks. Today, because of the advancement of medical technology, many premature infants are born under twenty-four weeks gestational age and survive. Yet according to the Court's decision, their lives cannot be protected because they are not viable.

The Court also stated that it chose the time of viability as the critical time because the child then has "the capability of meaningful life outside the womb." (13) Thus, an undefinable standard of meaningful life was set forth to determine whether a human being has the right to live or die.

The implications of this statement are staggering. Presumably, the Court said this because the unborn child inside the womb is totally dependent upon her mother for continued existence, and thus, is not capable of "meaningful life outside the womb." However, is this also not true for newborns? For toddlers? If an unborn child's life is not "meaningful," and thus not protected, what about the lives of the handicapped? The paraplegic? The mentally handicapped? The comatose? The infirm? The dying? The elderly who are at the end of life?

Who defines what lives are meaningful and what lives are not? Previable unborn children are dependent upon the mother and are protected by the safe haven of the womb, a place where survival outside is impossible until viability. Is this what makes their lives meaningless? If so, since infants, small children, and for that matter, adolescents are also dependent upon their parents for survival, can their lives also not be considered meaningful and, therefore, can disposed of?

The Court's statement that abortions (even after viability) cannot be prohibited if the abortion is necessary to protect the health of the mother also is deeply troubling. Such language essentially means that abortions cannot be prohibited at any time during the nine months of a mother's pregnancy. In *Doe*, the Court defined the word "health" by stating, "The medical judgment may be exercised in the light of all factors—physical, emotional, psychological, familial, and the woman's age—relevant to the well-being of the patient. All these factors may relate to health." (14)

The word "health" is most commonly understood as the absence of illness. However, in the context of abortion, health factors, which justify an abortion, are defined by the Court as a variety of subjective feelings and factors that can most likely be found in any situation at any time during a mother's pregnancy. Because of this broad expansion of the definition of health, it is commonly accepted that abortion in America is virtually legal throughout all nine months of pregnancy.

In 1992, the high Court in *Planned Parenthood v. Casey* (15) revisited the correctness of its ruling in *Roe v. Wade* and *Doe v. Bolton* and upheld the central premise of these cases, stating that freedom to have an abortion is a liberty interest protected by the Fourteenth Amendment of the US Constitution. (16) In describing this constitutional liberty interest to have an abortion, Court said, "At the heart of liberty is the right to define one's own concept of existence, of meaning, of the universe, and of the mystery of human life." (17)

What an amazing statement! If this definition of protected Constitutional liberty is correct, then were not the jihadists attackers on 9/11 simply exercising a constitutionally protected right. After all, clearly these terrorists were sincerely acting out of their "own concept of existence, of meaning, of the universe, and of the mystery of human life."

The future consequences of *Roe* and *Doe* were not foreseen by the Court and others in 1973, but the results of these decisions and the negative impact they have had on the lives of millions cannot be denied. Since 1973, it is estimated that nearly sixty million abortions have occurred. Currently, more than one million abortions occur annually. The ethos of *Roe* and *Doe* has opened up the door for acts once believed to be unthinkable, such as assisted suicide, euthanasia, human cloning, fetal experimentation, and other actions taken in the name of medical science, which further advance the decline of respect for human life.

While I did not feel impacted by the abortion decisions when they first were rendered, my mind began to change in 1979 when consciousness regarding the issue of abortion began to sweep across the evangelical world. In 1979, Francis Schaeffer along with future Surgeon General, Dr. C. Everett Koop wrote a book entitled *Whatever Happened to the Human Race*. Francis Schaeffer, Dr. Koop and Dr. Mildred Jefferson (the first African American woman to graduate from Harvard Medical School) produced an accompanying film.

Schaeffer, Koop, and Jefferson toured the nation, showing the film in churches and on college campuses with the message that there is another life involved in the abortion decision and that life is killed by the procedure. Nobody has absolute rights, and when the exercise of a right results in the taking of the life of another, then such an act cannot be tolerated.

In response to this Schaeffer-Koop-Jefferson initiative, thousands of Protestant/Evangelicals were galvanized to stand with their Catholic brothers and sisters and speak out against abortion, which was occurring more than one million times a year. My wife Laura and I were among such evangelicals who answered the call. I particularly remember being appalled to learn that since *Roe v. Wade*, more than six million abortions had occurred. Today that number is nearly sixty million.

Christians, both Catholic and Protestant, began to organize to fight the edict of *Roe v. Wade* through political, social, and educational efforts. Organizations such as the Christian Action Council (now Care Net), Focus on the Family, Concerned Women for America, Heartbeat International, Family Research Council, Americans United for Life, and in 1993, the National Institute of Family and Life Advocates (NIFLA) were founded to provide opportunities and plans to reduce and end abortion in America.

Prolife pregnancy resource centers (PRCs) providing alternatives to abortion began to spring up in every American community, and later, such centers became medical clinics offering ultrasound to allow abortion-minded mothers to view images of their unborn children. Political organizations in every state began to work and educate the public about the candidates for office that would vote to protect unborn life. And sexual abstinence programs began to appear in the public schools to teach young people about the wisdom of chastity and delaying sexual involvement with another until marriage.

Today, forty-three years after *Roe v. Wade,* much progress has been made to turn the tide and change the cultural attitudes about abortion. Public opinion polls now show that a majority of Americans say they are prolife. (18) Recently, the Alan Guttmacher Institute, an agency with close ties to Planned Parenthood, reported that there was a 13 percent reduction in the number of abortions reported in 2011 since 2008. According to this report, abortions now number less than one million a year, which is a major reduction from the estimated high of 1.6 million a year in 1992. (19)

*Roe v. Wade* did more than radically change the law in our nation. It also radically changed the culture. What was once an unthinkable, felonious act prohibited by criminal laws became a constitutional right under *Roe*. Since that time, an entire generation has grown up to accept abortion as an acceptable choice regarding an unwanted pregnancy, and the devaluation of human life in American has escalated.

January 22, 1973, was clearly a day that "will live in infamy." Progress has been made to resist the impact of this decision, but there is much work to accomplish to bring about an end to abortion in America. Such efforts, however, must be rooted in the biblical grounds upon which the American public was established. This foundation can be found in a document whose truths are timeless – *The Declaration of Independence.*

## Moments of Reflection

1.  Reflect and meditate on Psalm 139, which says in part:

    For you created my inmost being; you knit me together in my mother's womb. I praise you because I am fearfully and wonderfully made; your works are wonderful, I know that full well. My frame was not hidden from you when I was made in the secret place. When I was woven together in the depths of the earth your eyes saw my unformed body. All the days ordained for me were written in your book before one of them came to be. (verses 13–16 New International Version [NIV])

    What does this verse say to you about the affection God has for his creation of each one of us when we were inside our mothers' wombs?
    What does this verse say to you regarding the sovereignty of God and his plan for you as a person with value?

2.  Think about your reaction when you first heard of abortion. Do you feel the same today? If not, what caused your change in thinking?

3.  What was your reaction when you first heard about *Roe v. Wade*? Did you understand the full implications of this decision? Do you have an opinion of this decision now?

4.  What factors must exist to render any human life "capable of meaningful life outside the womb?" Who makes such a determination? If any life is deemed to lack meaning, should such life be terminated as a common good for all of society?

5.  If an unborn child's life is not deemed meaningful because it is solely dependent upon the mother, can other lives already born also be deemed to lack meaning? Who should make such a determination?

## Endnotes

1.  On December 7, 1941 the nation of Japan attacked America at Pearl Harbor. The following day, December 8, President Franklin Delano Roosevelt addressed the Congress to ask for a declaration of war against Japan. Referring to the previous day as a "date which shall live in infamy," he gave the Pearl Harbor attack its most famous and enduring title (Franklin D. Roosevelt, Infamy Speech, December 8, 1941).

2.  "But we have to pass the [health care] bill so that you can find out what's in it." These words were uttered by then Speaker of the House Nancy Pelosi at the Legislative Conference for the National Association of Counties in March 2010.

3.  *Roe v. Wade*, 410 U.S. 113, (1973). In agreeing with the decision of the Court Chief Justice Warren Burger, in a concurring opinion states, "Plainly, the Court today rejects any claim that the Constitution requires abortion on demand" (410 U.S. 208).

4.   410 U.S. 113.
5.   *Doe v. Bolton*, 410 U.S. 179 (1973).
6.   The American Medical Association in 1857 issued a report on criminal abortion. A final version of the report was read at the AMA convention in Louisville in May 1859 and published later that year in the *Transactions of the American Medical Association*. The following are excerpts of the report:

The heinous guilt of criminal abortion, however viewed by the community, is everywhere acknowledged by medical men.

Its frequency—among all classes of society, rich and poor, single and married—most physicians have been led to suspect; very many, from their own experience of its deplorable results, have known. Were any doubt, however, entertained upon this point, it is at once removed by comparisons of the present with our past rates of increase in population, the size of our families, the statistics of our fetal deaths, by themselves considered, and relatively to the births and to the general mortality. The evidence from these sources is too constant and too overwhelming to be explained on the ground that pregnancies are merely prevented; or on any other supposition than that of fearfully extended crime."

The causes of this general demoralization are manifold. There are three of them, however, and they are the most important, with which the medical profession have especially to do.

**The first of these causes is a wide-spread popular ignorance of the true character of the crime—a belief, even among mothers themselves, that the fetus is not alive till after the period of quickening** (emphasis added).

The second of the agents alluded to is the fact that the profession themselves frequently supposed careless of fetal life; not that its respectable members are ever knowingly and intentionally accessory to the unjustifiable commission of abortion, but that they are thought at times to omit precautions or measures that might prevent the occurrence of so unfortunate an event. The third reason of the frightful extent of this crime is found in the grave defects of our laws, both common and statute, as regards the independent and actual existence of the child before birth, as a living being. These errors, which are sufficient in most instances to prevent conviction, are based, and only based, upon mistaken and exploded medical dogmas. (American Medical Association, "AMA Report on Criminal Abortion" in *Transactions of the American Medical Association* (1859))

7. *Roe*, 410 U.S. at 157. Justice Harry Blackmun, author of the decision, says, "The appellee and certain *amici* argue that the fetus is a "person" within the language and meaning of the Fourteenth Amendment. In support of this, they outline at length and in detail the well known facts of fetal development. If this suggestion of personhood is established, the appellant's case, of course, collapses, for the fetus' right to life would then be guaranteed specifically by the Amendment. The appellant conceded as much on reargument."

8. Id. at p.158. The Court said, "All this, together with our observation, *supra,* that, throughout the major portion of the 19th century, prevailing legal abortion practices were far freer than they are today, persuades us that the word "person," as used in the Fourteenth Amendment, does not include the unborn."

9. *Merriam-Webster's Dictionary* defines *person* as "a human being." Merriam Webster Online. Accessed September 24, 2014. http://www.merriam-webster.com/dictionary/person.

10. 410 U.S. at 158.

11. Corporate personhood is a legal concept that a corporation, as an entity made up of separate individuals, is recognized as having the same legal rights and responsibilities as flesh and blood human being. For example, corporations may contract with other parties and sue or be sued in court in the same way as human beings or unincorporated associations of persons. Since at least *Trustees of Dartmouth College v. Woodward*, 17 U.S. 518 (1819), the US Supreme Court has recognized corporations as having the same rights as natural persons to contract and to enforce contracts. In 1886 the Court reiterated this principle in *Santa Clara County v. Southern Pacific Railroad*, 118 U.S. 394 (1886). Under these legal principles corporations are classified as "artificial persons" having legal rights in the same manner that flesh and blood human beings possess.

12. *Roe*, 410 U.S. at 163. The Court said, "With respect to the State's important and legitimate interest in potential life, the "compelling" point is at viability. This is so because the fetus then presumably has the capability of meaningful life outside the mother's womb. State regulation protective of fetal life after viability thus has both logical and biological justifications. If the State is interested in protecting fetal life after viability, it may go so far as to proscribe abortion."

13. Id. at 163.

14. Id. at 192.

15. *Planned Parenthood v. Casey*, 505 U.S. 833 (1992).

16. 505 U.S. at 851.

17. Id. at 851.

18. The Gallup poll in its 2013 Values and Beliefs poll asked 1,535 national adults how they think most Americans feel about the abortion issue. Fifty-one percent thought that the public is mostly pro-choice, while 35 percent said pro-life. However, according to Gallup, this general perception contrasts with the fact that the same poll found that 48

percent of Americans call themselves pro-life and 45 percent pro-choice.

19. Induced Abortion in the United States." Guttmacher Institute. June 2014. Accessed November 2014. http://www.guttmacher.org/pubs/fb_induced_abortion.html.

# CHAPTER 2

# The Roots of the American Republic: "We Hold These Truths To Be Self-Evident"

AMERICAN FOUNDING FATHER THOMAS JEFFERSON penned these familiar and immortal words that brought into being a new nation: "We hold these truths to be **self-evident** that all men are **created equal** and **endowed** by their **Creator** with certain **unalienable rights** among these **life, liberty, and the pursuit of happiness**" (emphasis mine).

These famous words are followed by a methodical and detailed recitation of the complaints of the American colonists against King George of Great Britain and the bondage under which the Americans suffered. From this document a new nation was conceived in the concept of liberty, God-given natural rights, and the dignity of every individual. The world has never been the same.

Prior to the American Revolution, kings had absolute authority over their subjects, and the rights of individuals were granted arbitrarily by the king upon whomever he wished. Likewise, such rights could be denied by the king to whomever he wished. However, the American Revolution was based upon what was then a radical notion that human rights are not to be bestowed upon some by the government, which also has the authority to also take them away. Rather, natural rights that respect the dignity of every human being come from a Creator, and such rights cannot be denied to people by the king or government.

These natural rights are life, liberty, and the pursuit of happiness and are self-evident. A truth that is self-evident is one that is true in and of itself and does not need to be proved by further argument, reasoning, logic, or experimentation. For example, two plus two equals four and always will. This self-evident truth needs no further reasoning to establish its veracity. Likewise, the American nation was founded upon self-evident truths that need no further explanation in order to be established and proven.

## Created Equal

The first *self-evident* truth is that all men, i.e., all human beings, are created equal. This truth sets forth the proposition that there must be no society which has a ruling elite class that controls others who are deemed of inferior status. This is because humanity is created equal, and its Creator endows every human being with certain natural rights. In Christian terminology, this means that human beings are made in the image of God. Because of this, every human being is of equal value, and no human being is superior in status to others.

This first truth acknowledges that we are *created.* Modern academia and the intelligentsia scoff of this notion and proclaim that humanity is simply a higher form of animal life that has evolved to its current status of dominion over the rest of life on earth. However, if this is true, then no moral case can be logically made for the equal status of all human beings. If humankind is simply a higher form of animal life that has randomly evolved, then there is no foundation to proclaim the equality of every person. Rather, through the Darwinist philosophy of the survival of the fittest, some human beings will certainly evolve higher than others in intelligence, wealth, talents, etc., and thus achieve superior status.

The American Republic rejects this notion because it was founded upon the self-evident truth that all human beings are created equal. Accordingly, the Creator bestows upon his creation of humanity equal status to all and endows them with certain natural and unalienable rights.

Some who believe in a Creator also believe that he so created through the process of evolution. I call such proponents "theistic evolutionists." Others argue that evolution is an unproven theory not supported by true scientific inquiry, and that true science is consistent with the notion that life was created and did not evolve over a period of time. I choose not to venture into a discussion of this particular debate other than to say I heavily favor the latter position over the former. However, the space needed for a proper dissection of the arguments here is far more than allotted for this book. Since such a discussion will divert us from the topic at hand, this debate must be reserved for another forum.

There are those, however, who deny that humankind was created. These non-theistic evolutionists, i.e., atheists and agnostics, proclaim that belief in a Creator is simply a matter of faith and is contrary to science. Life, according to these voices, is simply a result of cosmic accidents that have randomly occurred over billions of years. Those who oppose this idea respond by saying the order of life and the universe clearly show an intelligent design that can only be explained by an intelligent Creator.

A few years ago, I entered into an intense discussion about this topic with a friend with whom I had grown up. He and I attended the same church as teenagers and were both very active in its youth group. Over the years, he had come to doubt his faith and eventually decided that he was at best an agnostic but most probably an atheist.

As we were sharing a meal and catching up, I inquired of him whether he had settled in his own mind the existence of God. He affirmed that he had done so and, in fact, was more convinced of the nonexistence of God than ever before. I wanted to challenge his thinking, so I laid out my argument why it makes sense to believe in a Creator, and in fact, faith in the existence of a Creator is the only logical conclusion one can come to if they deeply think about the alternatives.

My question to my friend was simply this, how did the universe come into being? I then laid out the only three possible explanations to this riddle.

One explanation says that millions of years ago out of a vast nothingness, something appeared; and through a serious of random cosmic accidents, the universe and life on earth came into being. When I used the word "nothing," I emphasized that it meant absolutely *no thing*. To explain further, I opened up my hand and asked him what I had in it. He responded, "Nothing." I responded, "You are wrong. In my hand is air which contains oxygen and other gasses that our eyes cannot see. Nothing means no thing."

I continued stating that this explanation for how the universe came into being is simply impossible to have happened because something can never come from nothing. Such a view clearly is contrary to the accepted laws of physics and thus, must be rejected as nonsensical. (1) Furthermore, since there is no scientific support for this view, if one believes it, he does so on *faith* in a theory that is contrary to accepted scientific fact.

As my friend began to look more uncomfortable, I then spelled out the second possible explanation for how the universe came into being. This view is the one gloried by that late scientist Carl Sagan when he said that the universe has always existed and always will exist. (2) According to Sagan, the universe is eternal and out of this nonpersonal, eternal universe through a series random cosmic accidents over billions of years life on earth resulted.

This view logically has some serious shortcomings. There is no scientific evidence to support the opinion that the universe is eternal, that it has always existed and always will exist. In fact, prevailing scientific thoughts say the opposite—that the universe had a beginning through what is commonly called the big bang theory(3). In addition, many scientists believe that there is evidence to support the theory that the universe is slowing down, dying, and one day will cease to exist. (4)

I was persistent in challenging my friend and said that he could choose to believe that the universe is eternal, that is has always existed and always will exist. However, to believe this means that he, like me, believes in an eternal something from which the world began.

To believe this, he must do so on faith because there is no scientific proof that establishes this possibility. Finally, to be a proponent of this idea is to ignore accepted scientific views on the origin of the cosmos.

The third explanation of how the universe came into existence is, of course, to accept the idea that it was created by a higher, intelligent being. This viewpoint requires faith. However, so do the other explanations given to this inquiry. I explained that this view makes more sense because it is supported by many things in the natural world that otherwise defy explanation. The order of the universe, the laws of physics, the miracle of human reproduction, the complexities of a single human cell, the beauty of nature, and other matters about our world that we take for granted clearly point to an intelligent design. They absolutely do not support the notion that the earth and life within it exists because of a series of random cosmic accidents over billions of year.

I asked. Can a random explosion in a paint factory somehow create a masterpiece such as the Mona Lisa? Or in the alternative, could the Mona Lisa somehow come into existence over billions of years of such random explosions in paint factories? What a silly notion! I further argued to my friend that even if this is possible, one is still left with the question as to what (or who) caused the explosion(s) in the first place.

I ended my argument by saying that my friend could deny the existence of a Creator and accept one of the other explanations on how the universe came into being. However, to do so requires faith in one of the other viewpoints. Yes, my belief in a personal eternal Creator requires faith. However, my faith is far more grounded in logic than his faith, which is grounded in unproven assertions rejected by science. In fact, I said that he frankly has more faith than I do to believe such things. I further stated that while he could hold on to the belief that there is no Creator, he would do so at great risk to his own peril. I then began to talk about a centuries old philosophical argument for the existence of God known as Pascal's Wager—a philosophical argument devised by the seventeenth-century French philosopher, mathematician, and physicist, Blaise Pascal (1623–1662). (5)

Pascal's Wager can be explained by starting with the proposition that belief in God the Creator is a matter of faith. (However, as already discussed, so is belief in the alternatives that say there is no Creator.) Therefore, if one believes, as a matter of faith, that the Creator exists, lives his life upon this belief but is wrong, he is in the same boat as the one who does not believe. Nothing is lost. In the words of C. S. Lewis, all that has happened is that one has given a compliment to the universe that is undeserved. (6)

On the other hand, the one who does not believe in God and is wrong losses everything, i.e., eternal life, peace of mind, etc. Given such a risky position to be placed in by unbelief and given that all belief propositions regarding the origin of life require faith, it is far more logical to place such faith in the existence of a Creator. This is not to say that placing faith in the existence of God when one has lived his life otherwise is an easy thing to do. However, I believe, and scripture verifies, that when a doubter sincerely and simply prays to God saying, "I believe. Help me, Lord, with my unbelief," God will reveal himself to such person. In scripture, God the Creator promises that he will not cast away those who honestly come to him. (7)

My conversation with my longtime friend ended abruptly and somewhat uncomfortably. His response to all of this was to say rather defensively, "You cannot claim that something cannot come from nothing. We simply do not know this!"

Such resistance to honest inquiry about truth made me sad, but such resistance to the idea of a Creator who bestows upon his creation of humanity special rights and privileges is quite common in certain circles of American culture. To believe otherwise is anathema to such an intellectual elite. However, the American republic was founded upon the idea that all human beings are, first and foremost, *created* by an intelligent Creator and, thus, are afforded natural rights of life, liberty, and the pursuit of happiness.

America was not founded only upon the idea that humanity is created, but rather, it is also based upon the belief that every human being is created equal. (8) This equality stems from the truth taught in scripture that God created mankind in his own image. From this truth flows the equality of value of every person as well as a bestowment of natural rights upon humanity made in the image of God.

Since such rights come from God alone, they cannot be legitimately taken away by any government.

This God-given equality does not mean sameness. It means equality of value and, hence, equal opportunities in life for every human being. While not everybody will achieve the same level of success or wealth in life, everybody should be given the same equal opportunity to achieve because everybody is created equal with equal value. Any government that denies such equality to its subjects has violated the natural law of God

Such divinely granted equality must not be confused with egalitarianism, which is a political philosophy that says that equality of people means sameness in social, political, and economic affairs. Egalitarianism is the pursuit of the sameness for all. This is particularly so in the economic sphere where it argues for wealth distribution from the wealthy to the less fortunate.

Equality of value and opportunity comes from the fact that all are created equal by a Creator. Egalitarianism, on the other hand, proclaims that it is government which grants and denies rights to people and, thus, has the power to make people equal. Such equality achieved under an egalitarian philosophy is not an absolute right because the government has the power to define what it means by equality and to modify and change its definition at a whim.

## The Unalienable Right to Life

Because humanity is created equal it is also *endowed* by the Creator with certain unalienable rights. To endow means to bestow upon another a gift that cannot be taken away. The Creator endowed his creation of humanity with the natural rights of life, liberty, and the pursuit of happiness as gifts which are unalienable. That is because they come from the Creator; they cannot be transferred from one to another or legitimately taken away by a government of men. Such unalienable rights belong to human beings because every person is created equal in the very image of the Creator.

The first of these unalienable rights listed in the Declaration of Independence is the right to life. Thomas Jefferson is credited with authoring these words, which specify the unalienable rights of life, liberty, and the pursuit of happiness. However, these concepts were not his original ideas. Jefferson was a lawyer who studied the legal commentaries of Sir William Blackstone (1723–1780), the English jurist who wrote the epoch legal work, *Commentaries on the Laws of England*. The *Commentaries on the Laws of England* are an influential eighteenth-century treatise on the common law of England originally published between 1765–1769. The work is divided into four volumes: on the rights of persons, the rights of things, of private wrongs, and of public wrongs.

The *Commentaries* were long regarded as the leading work on the development of English law and played a major role in the development of the American legal system. The *Commentaries* were influential largely because they were, in fact, readable and because they met a need. The *Commentaries* are often quoted as the definitive source of common law by courts in the United States and by the US Supreme Court whenever the court desires to engage in historical discussion of the development of American law. They are particularly helpful in understanding the intent of the Framers of the US Constitution and also help us understand the meaning behind the words chosen by Jefferson in writing the Declaration of Independence.

In the *Commentaries*, Blackstone begins with an eloquent discussion of natural rights of humankind emanating from the Creator. He equates the natural law of science and creation with natural moral laws that govern mankind. Just as God created the universe and, in so doing, established the natural laws of physics under which it is to operate, God likewise created moral laws under which his creation of humanity must operate. Blackstone writes,

> Thus when the Supreme Being formed the universe, and created matter out of nothing he impressed certain principles upon that matter, from which it can never depart, and without which it would cease to be. When he put that matter into motion, he established certain laws of motion, to which all moveable bodies must conform. And, to descend from the greatest oper-

ations to the smallest, when a workman forms a clock, or other piece of mechanism, he establishes at his own pleasure certain arbitrary laws for its direction; as that the hand shall describe a given space in a given time; to which law as long as the work conforms, so long it continues in perfection, and answers the end of its formation.

Man, considered as a creature, must necessarily be subject to the laws of his creator, for he is entirely a dependent being. A being, independent of any other, has no rule to pursue, but such as he prescribes to himself; but a state of dependence will inevitably oblige the inferior to take the will of him, on whom he depends, as the rule of his conduct: not indeed in every particular, but in all those points wherein his dependence consists. This principle therefore has more or less extent and effect in proportion as the superiority of the one and the dependence of the other is greater or less, absolute or limited. And consequently as man depends absolutely upon his maker for everything, it is necessary that he should in all points conform to his maker's will.

This will of his maker is called the law of nature. For as God, when he created matter, and endured it with a principle of mobility, established certain rules for the perpetual direction of that motion, so when he created man, and endured him with freewill to conduct himself in all parts of life, he laid down certain immutable laws of human nature, whereby that freewill is in some degree regulated and restrained, and gave him also the faculty of reason to discover the purport of those laws.

This law of nature, being coeval with mankind and dictated by God himself, is of course, superior in obligation to any other. It is bind-

ing over all the globe, in all countries, and at all
times; no human laws are of any validity, if contrary to this; and such of them as are valid derive
all their force, and all their authority, mediately
or immediately, from this original. (9)

The first right emanating from this natural law is, according to
Blackstone, the right to life. He says, "Life is the immediate gift of
God, a right inherent by nature in every individual; and it begins in
contemplation of law as soon as an infant is able to stir in the mother's womb. (10)

Blackstone's reference to the right to life beginning in the
womb is instructive as to what is meant by an unalienable right
to life as mentioned in the Declaration of Independence. First, it
should be pointed out that Blackstone's reference to life in the womb
is clearly to the point of what was then referred to as quickening—
the moment when movement of the unborn child is first felt by the
mother. However, this is not a statement that life begins at quickening. Rather, it is a statement which reflects the legal understanding
at that time that before quickening, before the mother can feel the
baby move, there is no evidence of life. Thus, such a view is a legal
evidentiary point in the law that long has been abandoned due to the
development of scientific medical evidence, which proves that life
begins conception even though the mother may not have any physical awareness of this life until she feels the baby move. (11)

What is very significant about Blackstone's statement, however,
is that it recognizes that unborn human life has an unalienable right
to life and thus, has rights under the law. Blackstone expounds on
this point: "An infant *in ventre fa mere*, or in the mother's womb, is
supposed in law to be born for many purposes. It is capable of having
a legacy, or a surrender of a copyhold estate made to it. It may have
a guardian assigned to it; and it is enabled to have an estate limited
to its use, and to take afterwards by such limitation, as if it were then
actually born". (12)

In *Roe v. Wade* the United States Supreme Court was confronted
with the argument from the state of Texas, the defendant in the case,
that an unborn child is a person under the Fourteenth Amendment

to the US Constitution and, thus, the taking of its life through abortion amounts to the denial of the life of a person without due process of law—an act prohibited by the language of the Amendment. The Court said, "If this suggestion of personhood is established, the appellant's case, of course, collapses, for the fetus' right to life is then guaranteed specifically by the Amendment." (13)

The Court, however, goes on to conclude that the meaning of the word person in the Fourteenth Amendment can only be applied "postnatally," and that it could not find legal authority or references that would apply the term to prenatal life. (14) Apparently, the Court did not bother to consult the words of Blackstone when making this dramatic and tragic conclusion.

Since natural rights are the gifts of the Creator, this natural right to life is unalienable (i.e., it cannot be legitimately denied to some by government) and it is self-evident (i.e., it is true as a matter of principle and no further reasoning or logic is needed to establish its truth.) However, while the right to life, which begins in the womb, is self-evident, modern medical technology shows beyond any reasonable doubt that life itself within the womb is self-evident.

The National Institute of Family and Life Advocates (NIFLA) is a nationwide legal network of more than 1,370 pro-life pregnancy resource centers (PRCs) and pregnancy medical clinics (PMCs). Of this membership, nearly one thousand operate as PMCs, providing ultrasound confirmation of pregnancy to mothers who are seriously considering abortion. The vast majority of these mothers who see an ultrasound image of their unborn children will choose life. (15) Clearly, the technological miracle of ultrasound provides self-evident proof that life exists in the womb.

A few years ago, NIFLA teamed up with a few congressmen to promote federal legislation that, if passed, would have provided funds for pro-life PMCs to purchase ultrasound equipment. To promote this bill, a luncheon meeting was sponsored by the Congressional Pro-Life Caucus where I spoke, and we did a live ultrasound demonstration for those in attendance. While every member of Congress was invited, the meeting was attended mostly by young staff members.

I spoke about the power of the ultrasound exam to provide to a mother considering critical abortion information about the baby within her. As I spoke, I noticed in the back of the room a few young congressional staffers who were smirking at what I was saying, and they were clearly mocking my message under their breaths to each other. I assumed that they most likely were staff members of a congressman who was an abortion supporter, and their attendance over their lunch hour was simply for their own amusement.

After I finished speaking, we proceeded with the ultrasound demonstration, and the demeanor of these young staffers dramatically changed. The ultrasound image was projected onto a large screen in the front of the auditorium, and the baby, about twelve weeks gestational age, did a wonderful job of moving, dancing, sucking her thumb, and showing what prenatal life was all about. The congressional staffers, who were amused at my words, were speechless at what they saw projected onto the screen. The intense gazes coming from their eyes told the story of how modern medical technology has made the truth of unborn life self-evident.

Later on in his commentaries, Blackstone makes this dramatic pronunciation:

> This natural life being, as was before observed, the immediate donation of the great creator, cannot legally be disposed of or destroyed by an individual, neither by the person himself nor by any other of his fellow-creatures, merely upon their own authority. . .[T]hat whenever the constitution of a state vests in any man, or body of men, a power of destroying at pleasure, without the direction of laws, the lives or members of the subject such constitution is in the highest degree tyrannical. (16)

These words from Blackstone are clear. A more accurate and succinct description of the impact of *Roe v. Wade* upon our nation has not been given. The decision in *Roe* has empowered a few to take the lives of millions of unborn human beings at their own whim and pleasure. This decision is lawless because it denies to the unborn the unalienable right to life and, in so doing, mocks the Creator who gives this right to those he makes in his own image. This decision, as an interpretation of our Constitution, renders it, in the words of Blackstone, "the highest degree tyrannical."

## The Unalienable Right to Liberty

*Liberty* as referenced in the Declaration of Independence and the Constitution is a natural unalienable right from the Creator. It is a gift bestowed upon humanity because humanity is made in the image of God. Life is the first of such natural rights because without it all other rights are meaningless. After the right to life comes the right to liberty, which also is a self-evident and unalienable right, bestowed by the Creator upon humanity made in His image.

Since childhood, most of us have sung those inspiring words, "Our fathers' God to Thee, author of liberty, of Thee I sing." We refer to America as the "land of the free and the home of the brave," and the word liberty is entrenched in our national consciousness as a foundational American value. Yet the erosion of cultural values in American society over the last few decades has turned our understanding of the meaning of liberty into something that would be considered quite foreign to our nation's Founding Fathers.

The Declaration of Independence speaks of the inalienable right to liberty endowed upon mankind by our Creator, and our Constitution, in the Fifth and Fourteenth Amendments, speaks of prohibiting government from taking away a person's liberty without due process of law. What did the Founders mean when they declared liberty to be such a cherished value and right of American citizenship?

Blackstone writes that after the unalienable natural right to *life* comes the unalienable right to liberty. He says, "[T]he law of England regards, asserts, and preserves the personal liberty of individuals. . . Of great importance to the public is the preservation of this personal liberty for if once it were left in the power of any, the highest, magistrate to imprison arbitrarily whomever he or his officers thought proper... there would soon be an end of all other rights and immunities." (17)

This natural right of liberty, referred to in the Declaration of Independence and the Constitution, is a right to be free from oppressive and illegal physical restraint by the government. Hence, the constitutional and legal requirement of due process before one's liberty can be denied is the foundational cornerstone to American criminal jurisprudence.

Blackstone further writes, "A natural and regular consequence of this personal liberty is, that every man may claim a right to abide in his own country so long as he pleases; and not to be driven from it unless by the sentence of the law. (18)

This traditional understanding of liberty, as stated eloquently by Blackstone, is the freedom from being restrained by the government, i.e., arrested and imprisoned without the protection of due process of law where formal charges are made and the accused has an opportunity to confront the charges against him. However, this view of liberty was abandoned long ago by the federal judiciary and was replaced by the view that constitutional liberty also includes the right to engage in self-indulgence without constraint from the law. This perversion of the historical understanding of constitutional liberty was gradual and took place over many decades during the twentieth century.

In the early 1900s, the US Supreme Court began to expand the legal understanding of constitutional liberty to include not only protection from illegal physical restraint but also to include substantive legal rights, such as the right to enter into contracts, the right to direct the education of one's child, and the right to procreate. The legal doctrine invoked by the high court in doing this is known as substantive due process.

Government is prohibited by the Fifth and Fourteenth Amendments to the Constitution from denying to any person liberty without due process of law. Traditional procedural due process requires that before a person is deprived of his personal liberty, he must receive notice of criminal charges against him, a right to confront the evidence and witnesses, protection against self-incrimination, and have guarantees of a fair and speedy trial. Substantive due process, on the other hand, is not concerned with procedural matters but instead uses the due process clauses in the Fifth and Fourteenth Amendments to define the very substance of liberty.

As a matter of expressing the political and cultural values of American society, such an expansive view of liberty is hardly controversial. As a constitutional republic, the American government, both at state and federal levels, can (and in some cases should) define and expand the rights of citizens. However, a republican form of government such as ours requires that an expansion of such rights be done through the legislative process where elected officials, subject to accountability from the public, adopt such expanded rights after a full and exhaustive political debate in the public arena. It is indeed a dangerous scenario to allow for new understandings of the meaning of constitutional liberty to come from unelected federal judges, who are appointed for life and are not subject to accountability from the public at large through the political process.

The Supreme Court further expanded the concept of constitutional liberty in the latter part of the last century to include the right to procreate and the right to purchase contraceptives. While the acknowledgment of such rights may have merit to some, it is clear that they do not have their genesis in the liberty acknowledged in the foundational documents of the nation—the Declaration of Independence and the Constitution. Rather, these new rights of liberty relate to changing sexual mores of an increasingly secular society. Whether or not the public desires such rights is clearly a matter to be decided in the political arena after robust debate. It is quite another matter to have such rights imbedded into the meaning of the Constitution through judicial fiat. Such judicial activism elevates such rights to an exalted constitutionally protected status, and thus, it becomes virtually impossible for the public to challenge such a recognition through the political process.

The ultimate expansion of the meaning of constitutional liberty came in 1973 when the Supreme Court, in *Roe v. Wade*, held that the constitutional liberty enjoyed by Americans includes the right to have one's unborn child killed prior to birth. At the time of this ruling, all fifty states had criminal laws prohibiting abortion as an assault against both a pregnant mother and her unborn child. However, because of this ruling, political debate on this emotional and volatile topic became moot, and in a single monumental political moment in American history, a felonious act became a protected right of constitutional liberty.

Since 1973, the nation has been divided over the issue of abortion in a manner not seen since the issue of slavery separated the nation. However, the Supreme Court did not complete its distorted view of constitutional liberty with *Roe*. After two decades of ruling and adjudicating on legislative efforts to curtail abortion, the Supreme Court further expanded the meaning of liberty in 1992 with its decision in *Planned Parenthood v. Casey*.

In *Casey*, the Court appeared to be modifying its decision in *Roe* to allow for some state regulation of abortion. However, the Court also attempted to enlighten the public as to what it considers to be protected liberty under the constitution. In discussing liberty, the *Casey* decision boldly proclaims, "At the heart of liberty is the right to define one's own concept of existence, of meaning, of the universe, and of the mystery of human life." (19)

If we are to take the Court at its word, then it would appear that now any state regulation that infringes upon a person's ability to define his concept of existence and of meaning can be found unconstitutional. Under this new, "enlightened" understanding of liberty, virtually any state law can now be rendered unconstitutional if the judiciary is persuaded that the law in question hinders an individual's understanding of the universe, and of the mystery of human life.

Could not the actions of Osama bin Laden and the 9/11 terrorists now be constitutionally protected under this expansive view of liberty? After all, were not these murderers merely attempting to sincerely define their own concept of existence, of meaning, of "the universe, and of the mystery of human life?"

It is abundantly clear where this evolving and unrestrained reasoning of the federal judiciary has taken us. Constitutional liberty, as understood by the Founding Fathers, has now been replaced with an unrestricted license to do as one pleases. Can the republic survive such an ethos? The issues of abortion, assisted suicide, euthanasia, same-sex marriage, and unrestrained genetic research all bear down upon the moral fabric of the nation and, when finally resolved, will determine the ultimate destination of America.

Scripture tells us that "where the Spirit of the Lord is there is liberty." (20) It also tells us that a fruit of the Spirit of the Lord is "self-control."(20) Constitutionally protected liberty cannot be mistaken for an unrestricted license for individuals to do whatever pleases them. Such an unrestrained lack of self-control not only will end in the destruction of the individual engaging in such behavior but in the ultimate and complete erosion of the societal values that have kept the nation strong and vibrant over the decades of its existence.

America is at a crossroads. Our singing of the patriotic words, "Let freedom ring," will ring hallow if we further corrupt ourselves and allow license to replace liberty as a foundational constitutional value. When license replaces liberty, then virtue becomes corruption. Benjamin Franklin stated, "Only a virtuous people are capable of freedom. As nations become more corrupt and vicious, they have more need of masters." (22)

The greatness of this nation lies in the fact that our love of liberty was founded in our love of virtue and goodness. Alexis de Tocqueville is quoted as saying, "America is great because she is good, and if America ever ceases to be good, America will cease to be great." (23)

If our traditional values continue to be corrupted and true liberty becomes mere license, then our nation will cease to be good; and with the cessation of goodness, we will have lost our claim to greatness.

We cannot end this discussion of the meaning of liberty without mentioning the obvious contradiction that existed at the time of the founding of the Republic between the words of the Declaration of Independence and the institution of slavery. At that time, slavery existed in America and supported the economies of a number of the colonies. Some critics of America point this out to show that either our Founders were hypocrites who did not practice what they preached, or worse, they saw African slaves as less than fully human and thus not covered by the meaning of the words "life, liberty, and the pursuit of happiness." Is this a fair criticism?

Slavery was an institution that had existed for centuries prior to America's founding. It was practiced worldwide. While in America and in other British colonies it had a racial component with whites enslaving blacks, racial discrimination was not always the foundation of the practice. Black African tribes also enslaved members of other African tribes and sold them to white slave traders.

In America, as part of the British Empire, many colonies adopted the practice because it was an economic foundation for the international British rule. The economies of the southern colonies were primarily agricultural, and thus, the practice of slavery was highly advantageous to many southern plantations for the growing and harvesting of certain crops such as tobacco and cotton.

It was this kind of world and culture in which the Founders lived. The abominable practice of slavery was simply a part of life in much of the world at that time and had been for centuries. Thus, for the Founders to proclaim liberty as an unalienable right from the Creator bestowed upon all of humanity was, indeed, a bold and radical notion.

It should first be noted that not all of the Founding Fathers owned slaves. John Adams, Samuel Adams, Alexander Hamilton, and Thomas Paine, among others did not. George Washington, Thomas Jefferson, Patrick Henry, and James Madison, among others did. John Quincy Adams, our sixth president and son of John Adams, was politically aligned with a growing abolitionist movement that advocated the immediate end to the practice of slavery in America. Both Benjamin Franklin and John Jay owned slaves but later freed their slaves and served as officers in their respective state's antislavery societies. The prestige they lent to these abolitionist organizations gave them credibility and contributed to the gradual abolition of slavery in each of the Northern states.

While some of the Founders owned slaves the pages of history are full of statements from many of them, even those who owned slaves, as to their aversion to the practice of slavery. The following quotes are just a sample of many such comments:

> "I believe a time will come when an opportunity will be offered to abolish this lamentable evil." (Patrick Henry in a letter to Robert Pleasants, January 18, 1773)

"Nothing is more certainly written in the book of fate than that these people are to be free." (Thomas Jefferson, *Autobiography*, 1821)

"[The Convention] thought it wrong to admit in the Constitution the idea that there could be property in men." (James Madison, from *The Records of the Constitutional Convention of 1787*, August 25, 1787)

"There is not a man living who wishes more sincerely than I do, to see a plan adopted for the abolition of it." (George Washington, letter to Robert Morris, April 12, 1786)

"Every measure of prudence, therefore, ought to be assumed for the eventual total extirpation of slavery from the United States. . .I have, throughout my whole life, held the practice of slavery in abhorrence." (John Adams in a letter to Robert Evans, June 8, 1819)

"It is much to be wished that slavery may be abolished. The honor of the States, as well as justice and humanity, in my opinion, loudly call upon them to emancipate these unhappy people. To contend for our own liberty, and to deny that blessing to others, involves an inconsistency not to be excused." (John Jay in a letter to R. Lushington, March 15, 1786)

While they proclaimed liberty as a core founding principle of a new nation, the Founders lived in a transitional time of upheaval in the existing status quo in regard to the rights of the people versus the legitimate power that monarchies should be allowed to exercise over their subjects. Their proclamations of liberty and equality, expressed in the Declaration of Independece, clearly defied the existing acceptance by many of the institution of slavery and their views. The Declaration clearly set forth principles, which challenged this existing state of affairs. At the same time, however, day-to-day life in the American colonies served as an example that such principles, while nobly held, were not practiced consistently.

Slavery was simply an ugly fact of life in colonial America. For one living in a society where it was the norm, developing a conscience to oppose it would require deep thinking and conviction from the Holy Spirit. It appears that the Founders did indeed cultivate such a conscience while still living in a day-to-day world where slavery was accepted. Advancing an opposition to slavery at this time actually shows a radical departure from the accepted norms with a commitment to the new view that life is a gift from God, upon which is bestowed the unalienable right to liberty.

The noble principles of life, liberty, and the pursuit of happiness set forth a new standard upon which the rights and treatment of all human beings are to be based. However, for the Founders to set forth in writing such principles to guide this new nation was one thing while bringing the new American nation into complete consistency with such principles was something else. As history has shown, the centuries old institution of slavery that was deeply imbedded into the economic system of the colonies would not die overnight. Yet the seeds of its eventual abolition were implanted in the proclamation of the Declaration of Independence, which set in motion a chain of events that eventually tossed slavery into the ash heaps of history where it belonged.

The institution of slavery and its abolition served as the first and most formidable hurdle for the Founders to clearly achieve, as the Constitution would say in its preamble, "to form a more perfect union." At the constitutional convention in 1787, a debate raged regarding the census to be taken in the United States and whether or not slaves should be counted in it. The census was vitally important because, under the Constitution, each state is apportioned representation in Congress according to its population. Thus, to count each slave as one person would increase the population of the slave-holding states in the South and thus increase their representation in Congress. To not count slaves at all in the census would decrease the voting representation and political influence of the slave-holding states in Congress. Abolitionists wanted the latter while pro-slavery forces wanted the former.

To keep the states unified, a compromise was reached which counted slaves as three-fifths of a person for census purposes. This provision in our original Constitution has been misunderstood and unfairly criticized by some to poorly argue a case that the Founders were racists who did not consider black slaves fully human. To the contrary, this compromise decreased the political power of the slave-holding states by reducing their representation in Congress and thus increased the political power of the Northern states that had banned slavery. Its passage was a victory for anti-slave forces and kept the state delegations to the convention unified in its task of drafting our Constitution. As a compromise on the issue of slavery, it was, in fact, the first anti-slavery piece of legislation adopted in our constitutional history.

One Founding Father who has received harsh criticism and accusations of hypocrisy in regards to slavery is Thomas Jefferson, the author of the Declaration of Independence. To understand the situation regarding Thomas Jefferson, we need to look at his specific situation at his Monticello estate where he lived near Charlottesville, Virginia. He inherited his slaves and did not purchase or sell them, and the law in Virginia at that time made it virtually impossible for a slave owner to emancipate his slaves without dire economic consequences. (24)

Despite being the owner of slaves, Jefferson's words and actions throughout history show that he was a man deeply troubled by the institution of slavery. For instance, as a young lawyer and member of the House of Bourgeois in Virginia in 1769, he proposed legislation that would emancipate the slaves in that colony. Since the agricultural economy of Virginia relied upon the work of slaves the passage of such legislation was not practical and it did not go far. (25)

Jefferson's opposition to slavery is also clearly shown in his initial draft of the Declaration of Independence, which contained the following language regarding the British king:

> He [George III] has waged cruel war against human nature itself, violating its most sacred rights of life and liberty in the persons of a distant people who never offended him, captivating and carrying them into slavery in another hemisphere, or to incur miserable death in their transportation thither. This piratical warfare, the opprobrium of infidel powers, is the warfare of the Christian king of Great Britain. Determined to keep open a market when men should be bought and sold, he has prostituted his negative for suppressing every legislative attempt to prohibit or to restrain this execrable commerce; and that this assemblage of horrors might want no fact of distinguished die, he is now exciting those very people to rise in arms among us, and to purchase that liberty of which he has deprived them, by murdering the people upon whom he also obtruded them; thus paying off former crimes committed against the liberties of one people, with crimes which he urges them to commit against lives of another.

This language was deleted from the final draft of the Declaration because of opposition from the colonies of South Carolina and Georgia which threatened to withhold support until such language was omitted.

Jefferson eventually accepted the reality that the abolition of slavery was going to happen over a period of time and in incremental steps, but he was aware of the evil of its continued existence as he later declared in reference to slavery: "God who gave us life gave us liberty. Can the liberties of a nation be secure when we have removed a conviction that these liberties are the gift of God? Indeed, I tremble in fear for my country when I realize that God is just and His justice cannot sleep forever." (26)

God's justice and judgment upon America came as Jefferson predicted in the horrendous War between the States where nearly seven hundred thousand Americans died. Abraham Lincoln acknowledged in his second inaugural address that this terrible war was God's judgment upon America for its tolerance of slavery. (27) He further stated that America could not continue to exist "half slave and half free" and that the abolition of this practice was necessary to bring our nation into full consistency with its founding principles. (28)

I have resided in Fredericksburg, Virginia, since 1994 and have had the privilege of living close to several battlefields from this tragic war. One such battlefield is commemorative of the Battle of the Wilderness and lies just five miles away from my home. On occasion, my wife and I like to drive to this battlefield and causally stroll among the trees and reflect upon what happened on this land so many years ago. It is a peaceful and reflective stroll at the present, but upon it, in 1863, war and bloodshed raged.

Periodically during these strolls, I will reflect upon what happened years ago in the very place I am walking. The Battle of the Wilderness was fought over a period of about four days. During this time, more than seventeen thousand men on both sides of the conflict were killed. One bullet chamber was fired every seven seconds for fourteen hours until darkness came, and the armies ceased fire until the light of morning. This firepower was so great that the trees and the brush of the surrounding forest caught fire. When the troops pulled back due to darkness, they were unable to remove all of their wounded with them. Thus at night, during the darkness, both sides of the battle could hear the screams of terror from the wounded who were left and were being consumed by the fires. (29) Such is the face of judgment upon a society that denies to fellow human beings made in the image of God their unalienable rights to life, liberty, and the pursuit of happiness.

America paid a heavy price for its denial of these God-given unalienable rights to African American slaves. Jefferson's haunting prediction of God's justice awakening became reality and, as President Lincoln acknowledged, the blood of hundreds of thousands of young Americans was shed as the ultimate price for a nation to pay when God is mocked and the unalienable rights he bestows upon humanity made in his image are denied to some.

The Founding Fathers struggled greatly with the issue of slavery, and America ultimately paid the price for this atrocity. Yet it was, in fact, the ideals of the Founding Fathers and the Declaration of Independence that guaranteed the eventual abolition of this evil and the recognition that all human beings, regardless of race or color, have been given these unalienable rights by the Creator. In doing so, America has paved the way for the rest of the world to follow. Sadly, the history of the world indicates that the lessons America learned have not been heeded as nation after nation in the twentieth century have committed atrocities and bloodshed of the innocent in pursuit of political power.

Were the Founding Fathers hypocrites by proclaiming the unalienable right to liberty while at the same time tolerating and even participating in the institution of slavery? I don't believe so when one looks at the definition of "hypocrisy." The *Merriam-Webster Dictionary* defines this to be "the feigning to be what one is not or to believe what one does not." The very words of the Founding Fathers, including those who owned slaves, indicate that they did not accept slavery as consistent with their ideals, and their actions showed that they anticipated its eventual abolition. This clearly does not fit under the definition of hypocrisy. Rather, the Founding Fathers' proclaimed ideals that laid the groundwork for the eventual abolition of slavery.

Frederick Douglass, former slave and abolitionist, understood the contradiction and conflict that the Founders faced in dealing with slavery. Yet he also understood that their ideals mandated the eventual end to slavery and bondage. In speaking of the Founding Fathers, he stated:

> I am not wanting in respect for the fathers of
> this republic. The signers of the Declaration of
> Independence were brave men. They were great
> men too—great enough to give fame to a great
> age. It does not often happen to a nation to raise,
> at one time, such a number of truly great men.
> The point from which I am compelled to view
> them is not, certainly, the most favorable; and yet
> I cannot contemplate their great deeds with less
> than admiration. They were statesmen, patriots

and heroes, and for the good they did, and the principles they contended for, I will unite with you to honor their memory.

They loved their country better than their own private interests; and, though this is not the highest form of human excellence, all will concede that it is a rare virtue, and that when it is exhibited, it ought to command respect. He who will, intelligently, lay down his life for his country, is a man whom it is not in human nature to despise. Your fathers staked their lives, their fortunes, and their sacred honor, on the cause of their country. In their admiration of liberty, they lost sight of all other interests.

They were peace men; but they preferred revolution to peaceful submission to bondage. They were quiet men; but they did not shrink from agitating against oppression. They showed forbearance; but that they knew its limits. They believed in order; but not in the order of tyranny. With them, nothing was "settled" that was not right. With them, justice, liberty and humanity were "final;" not slavery and oppression. You may well cherish the memory of such men. They were great in their day and generation. Their solid manhood stands out the more as we contrast it with these degenerate times.

How circumspect, exact and proportionate were all their movements! How unlike the politicians of an hour! Their statesmanship looked beyond the passing moment, and stretched away in strength into the distant future. They seized upon eternal principles, and set a glorious example in their defense. Mark them!

Fully appreciating the hardship to be encountered, firmly believing in the right of their cause, honorably inviting the scrutiny of an

> on-looking world, reverently appealing to heaven to attest their sincerity, soundly comprehending the solemn responsibility they were about to assume, wisely measuring the terrible odds against them, your fathers, the fathers of this republic, did, most deliberately, under the inspiration of a glorious patriotism, and with a sublime faith in the great principles of justice and freedom, lay deep the corner-stone of the national superstructure, which has risen and still rises in grandeur around you. (30)

This unalienable right to liberty is a gift from God that no government can legitimately deny to some. The fact that America did deny this to African slaves meant that it would pay a heavy price down the road of history, and indeed, it did. This self-evident truth is part of the foundation of the American Republic, and it cannot be called in question simply because our nation has not been consistent in its history in acknowledging it as a principle that guides us. The price our nation has paid for this inconsistency is, in fact, proof that such unalienable rights come from God, who will not be mocked and will not ignore a nation that denies such rights to human beings made in his image.

## The Unalienable Right to the Pursuit of Happiness

I believe that the most misunderstood of the three self-evident and unalienable rights mentioned in the Declaration of Independence is the right to the pursuit of happiness. This self-evident right is not (what some would say) a pursuit of self-indulgence. It is not a pursuit to do anything one desires. As stated previously, divinely ordained liberty is far different from a license to do whatever one pleases. Likewise, the self-evident, God-ordained pursuit of happiness is not the right to pursue whatever one pleases to the detriment of others.

A good reference point in understanding what is meant in the Declaration of Independence concerning the pursuit of happiness is, again, Sir William Blackstone. In his *Commentaries on the Laws of England*, Blackstone writes:

> Considering the Creator only as a being of infinite power, he was able unquestionably to have prescribed whatever laws he pleased to his creature, man, however unjust or severe. But as he is also a being of infinite wisdom, he has laid down only such laws as were founded in those relations of justice that existed in the nature of things antecedent to any positive precept. These are the eternal, immutable laws of good and evil, to which the Creator himself in all his dispensations conforms; and which he has enabled human reason to discover, so far as they are necessary for the conduct of human actions. Such among others are these principles: that we should live honestly, should hurt nobody, and should render to everyone their due. (31)

Based upon these eternal laws of justice ordained by the Creator for humanity, Blackstone continues to annunciate what the true pursuit of happiness is.

> As therefore the Creator is a being, not only of infinite power, and wisdom, but also of infinite goodness he has been pleased so to contrive the constitution and frame of humanity, that we should want no other prompter to enquire after and pursue the rule of right, but only our own self-love, that universal principle of action.
>
> For he [the Creator] has so intimately connected, so inseparably interwoven the laws of eternal justice with the happiness of each individual, that the latter cannot be attained but by observing the former; and, if the former be punctually obeyed, it cannot but induce the latter.

> In consequence of which mutual connection of justice and human felicity, he has. . . graciously reduced the rule of obedience to this one paternal precept, "that man should pursue his own true and substantial happiness" demonstrating, that this or that action tends to man's real happiness, and therefore very justly concluding that the performance of it is a part of the law of nature; or, on the other hand, that this or that action is destructive of man's real happiness, and therefore that the law of nature forbids it. (32)

According to Blackstone, the pursuit of happiness is absolutely connected with the divine laws of eternal justice and, thus, cannot be obtained unless such laws are obeyed. Obedience to the laws of eternal justice, i.e., treating one's neighbors as himself, obeying the Golden Rule, etc., means that one is living in the manner for which he is created. In doing so, he is in a relationship with his Creator who bestowed upon him these unalienable rights and, therefore, is experiencing true happiness. This is a self-evident natural law under which mankind was created. Being at one with the Creator guarantees happiness and the purpose for which every human being is created is to pursue such happiness with all vigor and energy one has. Therefore, such a right does not allow one to act in any manner desired. Consideration of the rights of others is a foundational maxim for the exercise of the pursuit of happiness. Liberty is not license and the pursuit of happiness is not the right to do whatever one wishes. Rather, such unalienable rights, when exercised, acknowledge the rights of our fellow human beings and are not valid if used to injure and destroy others.

Related to this right to pursue happiness are our fundamental Constitutional rights of the freedom of religion, the freedom of speech, the freedom to peacefully assemble, the freedom to petition our leaders for a redress of grievances, the freedom to vote, the freedom to travel and many other Constitutional rights which we as Americans enjoy. Indeed, such rights are ours to exercise because we are granted by the Creator the unalienable right to pursue happiness.

It should be noted that the pursuit of happiness is the last of the three unalienable rights mentioned in the Declaration of Independence, and I believe there is a reason for this. The first right listed is the right to life. Without such a right being secured under the law, no other rights have meaning. If one does not have the right to live, then he surely cannot exercise the other two rights with any assurance that they will not be denied to him. Because of this, when a government denies the right to life of some human beings, such as the unborn, then the rights of all human beings are not secure. If the right to life is not protected, then certainly, the right to liberty and the pursuit of happiness are not secure and mean very little. If a government determines that it can take away the foundational right to life although it cannot do so legitimately, then it can also deny to its citizens the other unalienable rights granted to us by our Creator.

Since January 22, 1973, a day that lives in infamy, nearly sixty million unborn human beings have been killed by abortion. Because of *Roe v. Wade*, the law has refused to protect the unalienable right to life of these innocent human beings. As in the days when this nation tolerated slavery, America today tolerates and condones the intentional denial to some of God-given unalienable rights. Perhaps the prophetic words of Thomas Jefferson should be brought to mind, and we should all tremble in fear for our nation when we realize that "God is just and his justice will not sleep forever."

## Moments of Reflection

1. The Declaration of Independence lists unalienable rights in the specific order of life, liberty, and the pursuit of happiness. Is the order in which these rights are listed significant? In what way?

2. If, as stated by Blackstone, the right to life begins in the womb is there ever a justification for the taking of unborn life? Do exceptions for abortion legitimately exist? If so, why?

3. What is the difference between liberty and license? Are the two essentially the same? Did the American Founding

Fathers believe that the unalienable right to liberty mean one has the constitutional freedom to do whatever he pleases? If not, what limitations can legitimately exist in the law upon the exercise of liberty?

4. Does it make a difference on how society values each human being if there is a Creator who created each human being with unalienable rights? Would such a viewpoint on the value of humans be different if no Creator exists?

5. What does the pursuit of happiness mean to you? What did it mean to the Founding Fathers? Does the exercise of this right bring with it responsibilities to others? In what way?

6. How do you explain (or reconcile) the fact that some of the Founding Fathers owned slaves yet they proclaimed liberty to be a gift from God to all humankind? Were the Founders hypocrites?

7. What future ramifications, if any, does the denial of the right to life to the unborn have for
   a. The elderly?
   b. The handicapped?
   c. The dying?
   d. The mentally disabled?
   e. The American nation?
   f. The World?

# Endnotes

1.  The laws of thermodynamics define fundamental phys-
    ical quantities (temperature, energy, and entropy) that
    characterize thermodynamic systems. The first law of
    thermodynamics says that energy cannot be created or
    destroyed. The British scientist and author, C. P. Snow,
    had an excellent way of stating this law. He said, "You can-
    not win (that is, you cannot get something for nothing,
    because matter and energy are conserved)." Hence, some-
    thing simply cannot come from nothing (Boundless, "The
    Three Laws of Thermodynamics," *Boundless Chemistry*,
    Boundless, December 1, 2014), https://www.boundless.
    com/chemistry/textbooks/boundless-chemistry-textbook/
    thermodynamics-17/the-laws-of-thermodynamics-123/
    the-three-laws-of-thermodynamics-496-3601/).

    In his popular 1980 television documentary, *Cosmos*,
    Sagan said, "The Cosmos is all that is or was or ever will
    be. Our feeblest contemplations of the cosmos stir us—
    there is a tingling in the spine, a catch in the voice, a faint
    sensation, as if a distant memory, of falling from a height.
    We know we are approaching the greatest of mysteries."
    Cosmos: A Personal Voyage. Performed by Carl Sagan.
    USA: PBS, 1980. Television Mini-series.

2.  The night sky presents the viewer with a picture of a calm
    and unchanging universe. So the 1929 discovery by Edwin
    Hubble that the universe is in fact expanding at enormous
    speed was revolutionary. Hubble noted that galaxies out-
    side our own Milky Way were all moving away from us,
    each at a speed proportional to its distance from us. He
    quickly realized what this meant—that there must have
    been an instant in time the entire universe was contained
    in a single point in space. Hence, Hubble and other sci-
    entists proposed that the universe must have been born in
    this single violent event, which came to be known as the
    big bang.

Astronomers combine mathematical models with observations to develop workable theories of how the universe came to be. The mathematical underpinnings of the big bang theory include Albert Einstein's general theory of relativity along with standard theories of fundamental particles. Today, NASA spacecraft such as the Hubble Space Telescope and the Spitzer Space Telescope continue Edwin Hubble's work of measuring the expansion of the universe. One of the goals has long been to decide whether the universe will expand forever, or whether it will someday stop, turn around, and collapse in a big crunch.

3.  Adams, David. "Universe Is Fading Away, Say Astronomers." The Guardian. August 18, 2003. Accessed September 7, 2014. https://www.theguardian.com/science/2003/aug/18/universe.sciencenews.

4.  The lamps are going out all over the universe. Astronomers have found that not enough bright young stars are emerging to take the place of the old stars burning out, so, in the ultimate retirement crisis, the cosmos is simply fading away."

And we shall not see them lit again in our lifetime—by the time our swollen sun is expected to swallow the Earth in the dim and distant future, the light from the stars could be down to around half of what it is now. In time, there will be no stars left shining at all.

"The age of star formation is drawing to a close," said the appropriately named Professor Alan Heavens from Edinburgh University's Institute for Astronomy, who helped to carry out the new study.

It's not suddenly going to get very dark, but it's been getting dimmer over the last few thousand million years and that will continue.

The great galactic dimmer switch is being turned down because the universe just can't make stars like it used to.

"Stars are formed in galaxies and there was a peak in the rate at which galaxies formed, and that time has passed and been and gone," Prof Heavens said.

The number of stars being created has been in decline for about the last 6bn years, and there is little chance of a surge in productivity in the future. The conditions for making stars are less favourable now and most of the ingredients required, including hydrogen and helium, have already been used up.

Although some stars hurl material back into space for recycling as they age and begin to expand, much of it remains locked away. All of this means that, as the stars formed billions of years ago begin to lose their twinkle one by one, the universe will eventually be made up of nothing but the dark and cold corpses of white dwarfs, neutron stars and black holes.

5.  Pascal's Wager posits that humans all bet with their lives on the presupposition that either God exists or he does not. Given the possibility that God actually does exist and assuming the infinite gain with belief in God or infinite loss with unbelief, a rational person should live as though God exists and seek to believe in God. If God does not actually exist, such a person will have lost nothing.

6.  "But supposing one believed and was wrong after all? Why, then you would have paid the universe a compliment it doesn't deserve. Your error would even so be more interesting and important than the reality. And yet how could that be? How could an idiotic universe have produced creatures whose mere dreams are so much stronger, better, subtler than itself?" C. S. Lewis, *Mere Christianity* (San Francisco: Harper One, 2001).

7.  Luke 11:9: "And I say unto you, ask, and it shall be given you seek, and ye shall find: knock, and it shall be opened to you."

The argument being put forward simply is for the existence of a Creator. It is not attempting to make the case for the deity of Christ and the truth of Christianity.

Once one has arrived at the conclusion that God does exist, their journey of faith has begun, and the next steps must be to confront the claims of Christ who said that he is "the Way, the Truth, and the Life" (John 14:6).

In considering these remarkable claims of Jesus, one must be confronted with the obvious—either they are true and Jesus is, indeed, God incarnate as he claimed to be, or they are false and Jesus is a deceiver and a liar. Simply calling him a great moral teacher is not an option.

C. S. Lewis put it this way:

I am trying here to prevent anyone saying the really foolish thing that people often say about him: "I'm ready to accept Jesus as a great moral teacher, but I don't accept His claim to be God." That is the one thing we must not say. A man who was merely a man and said the sort of things Jesus said would not be a great moral teacher. He would either be a lunatic—on the level with the man who says he is a poached egg—or else he would be the Devil of Hell. You must make your choice. Either this man was, and is, the Son of God: or else a madman or something worse. You can shut Him up for a fool, you can spit at Him and kill Him as a demon; or you can fall at His feet and call Him Lord and God. But let us not come with any patronizing nonsenses about His being a great human teacher. He has not left that open to us. He did not intend to. (*Mere Christianity*, 52)

8.  The American Revolution was centered on this concept of equality among all human beings and that in the order of nature God did not create some superior to others. Thus, the concept of a monarchy where one man is anointed as ruler over others simply because of his birth into a royal family was repugnant to the Founders. Patriot Thomas Paine writes of this in his pamphlet *Common Sense* as follows:

As the exalting one man so greatly above the rest cannot be justified on the equal rights of nature, so neither can it be defended on the authority of scripture; for the will of the Almighty, as declared by Gideon and the prophet Samuel, expressly disapproves of government by kings. All anti-monarchical parts of scripture have been very smoothly glossed over in monarchical governments, but they undoubtedly merit the attention of countries which have their governments yet to form. (Thomas Paine, *Common Sense* (Applewood Books), 13)

9.  Sir William Blackstone, "Introduction on the Study of Law," *Commentaries on the Laws of England,* vol. 1, sec. 2 (The Legal Classics Library, 1983), 38–41.

10.  Sir William Blackstone, *On the Rights of Persons,* vol. 1, bk. 2, *Commentaries on the Laws of England* (The Legal Classics Library, Special Edition, 1983), 125.

11.  The view that legal rights are granted to the unborn upon quickening, or when movement of the child is first felt by the mother was not a statement of the moral status of the baby prior to quickening. It was simply an evidentiary standard for the law to follow.

On this point, Attorney Clark Forsythe comments:

The law could not protect what it did not know existed, so the enforceability of abortion law was always tied to evidence of pregnancy. Until the twentieth century quickening—which does not typically occur until sixteen to eighteen weeks of pregnancy—was the most reliable evidence. The American colonies adopted the English common law, which prohibited abortion after quickening.

In the nineteen century, the American states updated the English common law by passing specific statutes to eliminate the quickening distinction, prompted by the developments in medical science that produced a new understanding of fetal development. The AMA strongly endorsed these legal changes in the 1860s. By the 1860s, many states had prohibited abortion after conception, except to save the life of the mother. (Forsythe, Abuse of Discretion: The Inside Story of Roe v. Wade, (Jackson, TN: Encounter Books, 2013))

12. Blackstone, -*On the Rights of Persons*, 125.

13. *Roe* , 410 U.S. at 156–157.

14. 410 U.S at 157.

15. The National Institute of Family and Life Advocates (NIFLA) currently has more than 1,350 members , which are prolife pregnancy resource centers that supply needed resources and counseling to mothers who are seriously contemplating abortion. Of this membership, over one thousand operate as medical clinics, providing ultrasound confirmation of pregnancy to these mothers. In 2014, NIFLA undertook a survey of its members that operate as medical clinics to assess the effectiveness of ultrasound in the choice of a mother seriously thinking about abortion. The survey results show that more than one hundred thousand ultrasound examinations were provided in 2013 by NIFLA members and over 70 percent of all women receiving the ultrasound service chose life.

16. Blackstone, *On the Rights of Persons*, 125.

17. Blackstone, *On the Rights of Persons*, 130–131.

18. Blackstone, 133.

19. *Planned Parenthood v. Casey,* 505 U.S. 833, 851 (1992).

20. 2 Corinthians 3:17.

21. Galatians 5:22.

22. Benjamin Franklin to Messrs- the Abbes Chalet and Arnand. April 17, 1787. (*Pondering 1420 Principles*, Alan Snyder, Ph.D, Professor of History at Southeastern University, Lakeland, Florida).

23. Alexis de Tocqueville was the famous nineteenth century French statesman, historian, and social philosopher. He traveled to America in the 1830s to discover the reasons for the incredible success of this new nation. He published

his observations in his classic two-volume work, *Democracy in America*. He was especially impressed by America's religious character.

24. William Cohen, "Thomas Jefferson and the Problem of Slavery," Institute of Advanced Studies, July 1, 2011, http://www.iea.br/iea/english/journal/38/cohenjefferson.pdf.

25. Jefferson began his political career at the age of twenty-six as a member of the Virginia legislature. Early in his career, he proposed to Col. Richard Bland, a fellow legislator, the together they attempt to emancipate the slaves in Virginia. The failed attempt caused Jefferson to conclude that as long as Virginia remained a colony of Great Britain, such an effort would fail (Thomas Jefferson, *The Writings of Thomas Jefferson,* ed. Paul Leicester Ford, vol. 1 and vol. 11 (The Thomas Jefferson Memorial Association, 1903).

26. Thomas Jefferson, *Notes on the State of Virginia,* "For in a warm climate, no man will labor for himself who can make another labor for him. This is so true, that of the proprietors of slaves a very small proportion indeed are ever seen to labor. And **can the liberties of a nation be thought secure when we have removed** their only firm basis, **a conviction** in the minds of the people **that these liberties are the gift of God?** That they are not to be violated but with his wrath? **Indeed I tremble for my country when I reflect that God is just: that his justice cannot sleep forever**" (emphasis added).

27. Abraham Lincoln, Second Inaugural Address, Appendix E.

28. Lincoln, Second Inaugural Address.

29. At the Wilderness Battlefield, outside Fredericksburg, Virginia, a placard describing the horrors of this battle contain the following account by Union Staff Officer Lieutenant Robert Robertson: "Hell Itself. The woods would light up with the flashes of musketry, as if with lightning, while the incessant roar of the volleys sounded like the crashing of thunder-bolts. Brave men were falling

like autumn leaves, and death was holding high carnival in our ranks."

30. Frederick Douglass and Philips S. Foner, *Pre–Civil War Decade 1850–1860*, vol. 2, *The Life and Writings of Frederick Douglass*,
(New York: International Publishers Co., 1950).

31. Blackstone, *Commentaries*, 40.

32. Blackstone, *Commentaries*, 40–41.

# CHAPTER 3

# The Declaration of Dependence

> It is the duty of nations as well as men to own
> their dependence upon the overruling power of
> God. (1)
>
> Abraham Lincoln

THE WORDS AND THE MESSAGE of the Declaration of Independence are inspiring and set forth the foundation of the American republic. We are a nation that was conceived under the self-evident biblical truth that all human beings are created equal and are granted by our Creator certain precious rights that cannot be legitimately taken away by others. The recognition of the unalienable rights of life, liberty, and the pursuit of happiness is what has made America unique in the history of the world.

Unfortunately, since the issuance of *Roe v. Wade*, these unalienable rights have become endangered. The constitutionally protected right to life is no longer a protected right for those human beings who still reside in the womb. Furthermore, with the growing acceptance of infanticide, euthanasia, and assisted suicide, this right to life is not clearly a protected right for others who have been born but are deemed to be a burden on society. Because of the current tenuous nature of the right to life the legal protection of the other unalien-

rights of liberty and the pursuit of happiness lacks stability and puts the existence of these rights in jeopardy.

With the basic right to life not firmly protected under the law, can we as American citizens be confident that our right to liberty and right to the pursuit of happiness will remain? Indeed, current events clearly indicate that the protection of religious liberty in America is being eroded and with the further erosion of this unalienable right will come the loss of the right to the pursuit of happiness.

The loss of these rights and their protection under the law means that our nation will have completely rejected the Creator, who bestows such rights upon every human being because every such person in made in his image. When this rejection comes (I don't believe we are there yet), the end of America as we know it will be complete. In the spirit of Thomas Jefferson, we should "tremble in fear" for our country.

Over the years, many leaders in the prolife cause have emphasized that the movement to protect the lives of the unborn is primarily a civil rights movement, not a religious one. Of course, the prolife movement exists to protect the most basic of all human and civil rights—the right to life—and, as such, is a civil rights movement of the noblest of ideals. Yet I would challenge those who proclaim that this movement is not also, at its heart, a religious movement.

In the wonderful movie *Chariots of Fire* the true story is told of Eric Liddell, a Scottish Christian pastor and missionary who was blessed with extraordinary athletic ability and was the odds-on favorite to win the gold medal at the 1924 Olympics in the one-hundred-yard run. However, because of his religious convictions, he refused to participate in the trial heats for the one hundred because they were being run on a Sunday, and to him, Sunday belonged solely to the Lord. He was mocked in the media and pressured by many to violate his conscience for the sake of his country.

The movie has a scene (which apparently did not actually happen) where Eric Liddell is confronted and pressured by the prince of Wales and other British dignitaries on the Olympic committee to renege on his commitment to honoring the Lord's day. As he refused to succumb to the pressure, eventually, an acceptable compromise was reached that allowed him to run another day in another event.

At the end of the scene, one member of the committee remarked to another that it was a good thing Liddell had not given in to the pressure because what they actually sought to do was to sever him from the very source that gave him the power to run fast.

The power source for the pro-life cause is faith in the Creator of the universe and his sovereignty. To sever ourselves from this truth is to sever ourselves from the very source of power upon which we rely for our day-to-day strength and effectiveness. Without the power of God in our lives and ministries, we will fail miserably in the mission to restore the sanctity of human life in our nation.

We believe that all human beings are made in the image of God, and because of this, as Christians, Christ was sent into the world to redeem fallen humanity. Because of the value of each human being to the Creator, we have been endowed with the unalienable rights of life, liberty, and the pursuit of happiness.

This is the fundamental basis of our commitment to restore protection for innocent human life and is clearly part of our religious faith. To deny this in any way or to downplay the religious nature of our work is to sever ourselves from the very power which can bring about success to our efforts. Yes, the pro-life movement is a civil rights movement. However, it is also a religious movement that seeks the blessings of God upon its efforts to end the vicious onslaught of a death ethic, which has engulfed our nation and society.

Abraham Lincoln stated that "it is the duty of nations as well of men to own their dependence upon the overruling power of God." It is time that all leaders of our nation—political, religious, corporate, and educational—pronounce their dependence upon the sovereign God who has bestowed upon us the unalienable rights of life, liberty, and the pursuit of happiness. By declaring our dependence upon God for our very existence, we are also submitting the success of our efforts to his will and "overruling power."

As a tool to enable Americans of all religious persuasions to proclaim this dependence upon God, a document has been prepared entitled The Declaration of Dependence. This important document sets forth the life principles that come from the Declaration of Independence and is a statement upon which all Americans who seek a restoration of the sanctity of life can agree. It is a statement of unity to bring together thousands of Americans to declare their dependence upon God the author of life and to seek an end to the destruction of innocent human life under the life principles set forth.

The Declaration of Dependence can be read and signed by going to www.declarationofdependence.org. (2) As thousands of citizens read and sign this document, the names of the signatories will be periodically delivered to Congress as a show of unity from concerned American citizens who want to see the sanctity of life restored in our laws and public policies.

## The Declaration of Dependence

Human history undeniably demonstrates that when a nation becomes divided on the fundamental issue of the value of human life, it is a nation that has placed its future in jeopardy. Whenever a culture accepts the idea that the lives of some human beings are inferior, and thus, disposable, it has embarked upon a dangerous journey down a slippery slope which in the last century brought a once great nation to accept the death camps of Auschwitz and Buchenwald.

The value of human life in America has been significantly degraded from the issuance by the United States Supreme Court of *Roe v. Wade* on January 22, 1973. Since this decision, nearly 60 million unborn children have died from abortion in the United States. Currently, more than one-fourth of all pregnancies in America annually end in abortion.

This devaluation of human life has opened the door for the societal acceptance of euthanasia, assisted suicide, human cloning, embryonic and fetal experimentation, and other serious practices undertaken in the name of medical science.

When a nation is confronted with such a diminution in its moral foundation, the nation's spiritual, religious, political, and cultural leaders must issue a warning of impending peril. The devaluation and destruction of the lives of some human beings through abortion requires that we declare the foundational principles of life upon which our nation was birthed and, in so doing, issue a warning to our fellow countrymen.

This prevalent and callous disregard for innocent human life indicates that America has, in the words of Abraham Lincoln, "forgotten God. We have forgotten the gracious hand which preserved us in peace, also multiplied, enriched and strengthened us. We have vainly imagined, in the deceitfulness of our hearts, that all these blessings were produced by some superior wisdom and virtue of our own. Intoxicated with unbroken success, we have become too self-sufficient to feel the necessity of redeeming and preserving grace, too proud to pray to the God that made us!"

We proclaim that in order to heal our nation, we must humbly submit to our Creator and His gracious hand that has preserved us. We must declare our dependence upon Him and His overruling and sovereign power.

In reference to slavery, Thomas Jefferson said, "I tremble in fear for my country when I realize that God is just and that his justice will not sleep forever."

In the spirit of Thomas Jefferson, we declare that God is just and that unless the lives of innocent human beings in America are once again protected by the law, His justice will awaken to bring judgment upon our nation.

In reference to slavery, William Wilberforce, British abolitionist and Member of Parliament, said, "You may choose to look the other way, but you can never say again that you did not know."

In the spirit of William Wilberforce, we declare that this nation cannot continue to look the other way regarding the destruction of innocent human life by abortion and pretend that it does not know of its devastating impact.

In reference to slavery, President Abraham Lincoln proclaimed that this nation cannot continue to exist "half slave and half free" because a "house divided against itself cannot stand."

In the spirit of Abraham Lincoln, we declare that abortion, once again, has made America once again a nation that is "half slave and half free." We cannot continue to exist when the lives of some human beings are deemed inferior and thus, can be destroyed.

In reference to slavery, Frederick Douglass, abolitionist and former slave, quoted scripture stating that "righteousness exalteth a nation."

In the spirit of Frederick Douglass, we reaffirm this principle and proclaim that a righteous nation must protect the lives of all within its boundaries, both born and unborn.

In reference to the holocaust, Dietrich Bonhoeffer, Lutheran pastor and martyr, said, "Silence in the face of evil is itself evil. God will not hold us guiltless. Not to speak is to speak. Not to act is to act. The test of the morality of a society is what it does for its children."

In the spirit of Dietrich Bonhoeffer, we commit ourselves to speak for the innocent unborn children in our nation who cannot speak for themselves.

In reference to segregation and the Jim Crow era, Martin Luther King Jr. said, "He who passively accepts evil is as much involved in it as he who helps to perpetrate it."

In the spirit of Martin Luther King Jr., we declare that we cannot remain silent and passively accept the destruction of innocent human life through abortion.

In reference to abortion, Mother Teresa said, "The greatest destroyer of peace is abortion because if a mother can kill her own child, what is left for me to kill you and you to kill me? There is nothing between. It is a poverty to decide that a child must die so that you may live as you wish."

In the spirit of Mother Teresa, we declare that we stand unified in the name of peace to oppose the spiritual poverty that abortion has brought upon our nation.

In response to this moral breakdown of our nation, we, the undersigned, stand in unity to assert a firm, foundational, and unwavering belief in the sanctity of human life and in the legal personhood of all human beings. In doing so, we declare the following:

- The foundational principle of our nation is the Declaration of Independence, which acknowledges that every human being is created equal and endowed by our Creator with the unalienable rights of life, liberty, and pursuit of happiness. These self-evident truths form the bedrock upon which the American republic was built and are the basis of the Judeo-Christian ethic upon which our nation was conceived.
- The unalienable right to life is the first of such natural rights given to us by the

Creator, and without its protection in law, all other rights are meaningless.

- Every human being, born and unborn, is made in the image of God, the Creator and thus, is granted these unalienable rights that no government can deny.

- Because every human being, born and unborn, is made in the image of God, every human being is a "person" accorded value. The value of every person exists not because of race, ethnicity, condition of dependency, circumstances surrounding conception, physical attributes, talents, or societal position but rather, exists because each person is made in the image of God. Accordingly, the life of every innocent person must be protected under the law.

- The term "person" applies to all living human beings from the beginning of their biological development, regardless of the method of reproduction, age, race, sex, gender, physical well-being, function, size, level of development, environment, and/or degree of physical or mental dependency and/or disability.

- *Roe v. Wade* denied personhood to the unborn, and in so doing, stated that such humans are not capable of "meaningful life outside the womb." Such language from our Supreme Court has opened the floodgates for abortion on demand and the further destruction and manipulation of human life.

- The restoration of the protection of innocent human life shall not be completed until the personhood of all human beings, born and unborn, is recognized under the law, and the principles of *Roe v. Wade* are rejected by the American nation and its leaders.

- Strategies to achieve personhood and legal protection for all human beings will differ, and there will be differences of opinion on the actions we take to achieve this goal. However, such differences do not indicate a lack of unity on the foundational principles set forth herein.

Therefore, in agreement that "righteousness exalteth a nation," and in reliance upon an unshakable faith in our Creator and in His sovereign will that governs the affairs of mankind, and in pursuit of the restoration of the legal protection of every human being made in His image, we, the undersigned, pledge to one another our sacred honor, our mutual respect, and our mutual cooperation to achieve the restoration of the sanctity of human life in our nation.

In pursuit of these principles we further declare our dependence upon our Creator who sustains all life according to His sovereign will. And in the words of Abraham Lincoln, we commit ourselves to work toward this common cause "with malice towards none, with charity for all, with firmness in the right as God gives us to see the right" and in so doing, we strive to "bind up the nation's wounds" as we achieve a just society where all human beings, born and unborn, are cherished and protected under law.

**IF YOU BELIEVE IN THE DECLARATION OF DEPENDENCE, SIGN NOW! GO TO WWW.DECLARATIONOFDEPENDENCE. ORG**

## Moments of Reflection

1. What does it mean to be, in the words of Abraham Lincoln, dependent upon the "overruling power of God?"
2. What changes in America do you envision happening if its cultural, religious, educational, and corporate institutions became dependent upon the "overruling power of God?"
3. Would a renewed dependency upon God from our nation's leaders in all areas of the culture bring about an end to abortion? Would such a situation bring about a renewed respect for human life in all stages?

## Endnotes

1. Proclamation Appointing a National Fast Day, March 30, 1863, (see appendix D).
2. Author Thomas A. Glessner was interviewed by Dr. James Dobson in July 2014 for two broadcasts regarding the Declaration of Dependence. Dr. Dobson became a signer of the document on the second broadcast. You can listen to a podcast of the broadcasts by going to www.nifla.org and going to the Wilberforce Forum.

# CHAPTER 4

## The Wilberforce Forum Reflections on the Unalienable Right to Life

You may choose to look the other way, but you can never again say that you did not know. (1)
William Wilberforce

ONE OF THE GREATEST HEROES in history is William Wilberforce. Wilberforce was a member of the British Parliament in the late eighteenth century and served into the nineteenth century. During this time period, his was the leading voice against the institution of slavery in the British Empire.

Wilberforce's mission to end slavery and emancipate slaves throughout the British Empire was daunting and clearly appeared impossible to most. Slavery was an institution that fueled the economy of much of the British Empire. For Wilberforce to stand against it was not only unpopular in many circles of his society but also appeared to be a hopeless cause. At times, he had allies who worked with him. At other times, he acted alone. At all times, he placed his trust and dependence upon God for the results of his labors.

The mission to end the institution of slavery is virtually the same as the mission to end the abortion of unborn children. To justify slavery, proponents of it had to exercise twisted logic and proclaim that African slaves were not fully human and, thus, could be owned as property and treated as such by their masters. Likewise, to justify abortion, those who support such a practice must engage in the twisted dehumanization of the unborn. The slavery issue of the past and the current abortion issue are virtually the same issue. They both deny the full humanity of a class of people in order to exploit this class. Furthermore, to justify such exploitation past proponents of slavery and current proponents of abortion must deny the proclamations of the Declaration of Independence that all human beings are created equal and endowed by the Creator with the inalienable rights of life, liberty, and the pursuit of happiness.

William Wilberforce opposed slavery because he believed that every human being is made in the image of God. His actions to end the practice serve as an inspiration to those who work to end the institution of abortion. Wilberforce relied upon his unshakable faith in God who values all human beings equally. He refused to accept the status quo of English society, which accepted slavery as part of its culture. He persevered for fifty years in standing against this great evil, fighting against it with all of his might. Three days before his death in 1833, his efforts succeeded as the British Parliament formally ended slavery and emancipated all slaves within its jurisdiction.

Wilberforce is perhaps the greatest example of a political leader who remained true to principle, which was founded firmly upon the truth of scripture. He is today honored throughout the world as a great man of principle who stood for the oppressed and the disenfranchised. His example is an inspiration to all who are standing firm in the battle for the sanctity of human life and to end the destruction of the unborn.

It appears that sometimes Hollywood really does get it. The movie *Amazing Grace* exemplifies this. *Amazing Grace* chronicles the story of William Wilberforce and also touches on the relationship between Wilberforce and John Newton, a former captain of a slave ship who, after his conversion to Christianity, authored the famous hymn "Amazing Grace."

The movie deals primarily with the struggles of Wilberforce, who initially questioned whether he could be totally devoted to God and at the same time devote himself to the political war to abolish slavery. He concludes that, indeed, his devotion to Christ requires him to be committed to ending the ugly moral blight that slavery cast over the English empire.

The movie also touches on Wilberforce's relationship with Newton but gives little detail on the life of Newton and what events transpired to bring about his dramatic change of heart and the writing of the beloved hymn. An understanding of the influence of John Newton on Wilberforce is crucial if we are to fully understand that it is only through God's amazing grace that individuals can achieve societal changes, which have eternal implications.

Facets of Newton's life are exemplary of the power of God's amazing grace to change men's lives. (2) John Newton was born over three hundred years ago into a seafaring English family. His mother died when he was seven, and he left school at age eleven to join his father at sea. He quickly adopted the vulgar life of a seaman, and his life grew coarse and harsh. In talking about this time period, he stated, "I was capable of anything. I had not the least fear of God, nor the least sensibility of conscience. I was firmly persuaded that after death, I should merely cease to be."

John eventually locked arms with the skipper of a slave ship bound for West Africa. His captain befriended John and took him to his plantation where he lived with his wife, a beautiful and cruel African tribal princess. She grew jealous of her husband's friendship with Newton. When her husband went to sea and left John at the plantation due to an illness, she seized her opportunity. Her husband's ship was barely over the horizon when she apprehended John and threw him into a pigsty. She temporarily blinded him and left him in a delirious state to die.

Newton was kept in chains in a cage like an animal and did not die. When word spread through the country that a black woman was keeping a white slave, many came to observe and taunt him. They threw stones at him and mocked him in his misery. He would have starved to death except for black slaves waiting for a ship to take them to America, who shared their meager scraps of food with him.

After five years, Newton's captain friend returned but called him a liar when John told him how he had been treated. When they set sail, Newton was treated more harshly and allowed to eat only the entrails of animals butchered for the crew's mess. During this time, he was involved in the slave trade. Of this he said, "I never had the least scruple to its lawfulness."

As Newton became more entrenched in the slave trade, he became a decadent blasphemer and mocker of faith. He eventually became the captain of his own slave ship, transporting thousands of black slaves to the plantations where they were exploited, tortured, and even killed for economic gain. Thousands of these humans never completed the initial voyage as they died in wretched conditions on the slave ship that were unfit for animals.

On one voyage, Newton's ship crashed upon shoreline rocks. Newton was despondent and cried out to the God, whom he had ignored his entire life. He was amazed that God's mercy remained on him after a life of hostile indifference to the gospel. He said of this: "My prayer was like the cry of ravens, which yet the Lord does not disdain to hear."

Newton was miraculously rescued and went back to England to reflect upon the mercies of God in his life. He fell under the influence of Methodist preacher George Whitefield, a compatriot of John Wesley, and entered into a new life with Christ as his captain and the slave trade as his regretted past.

In the movie, John Newton talks of his slave trading days to his friend Wilberforce with intense contrition and brokenness, noting that he had twenty thousand ghosts haunting him, an obvious reference to twenty thousand slaves he had tortured in his ships over the years. Physically blind at this time, he references to Wilberforce the words he had penned in his hymn, "Was blind, but now I see" and acknowledges that he was experiencing the truth of those precious words.

Newton died two days short of Christmas 1807 at the age of eighty-two and left a spectacular testimony to the miracle of God's amazing grace. On his deathbed he proclaimed, "I commit my soul to my gracious God and Savior, who mercifully spared and preserved me when I was an apostate, a blasphemer, and an infidel and delivered me from that state on the coast of Africa into which my obstinate wickedness had plunged me."

Newton's life impacted the life of William Wilberforce who, in turn, impacted the entire world by his devotion to the claims of Christ. The true message of the lives of both Newton and Wilberforce tells us that none of us, as fallen individuals, have the capacity to impact the world for eternal good, but each of us can make an eternal impact when we experience God's true amazing grace offered free to all who will accept it.

As in Wilberforce's time we live in a society today where life is cheapened and degraded. Sensuality and pleasure cost millions but don't bring happiness while the value of human life is at an all-time low. One out of every three pregnancies is aborted today for convenience, and the death toll of the unborn killed continues to mount at a rate of over one million a year.

Where are the William Wilberforces of our time to speak out?

Individuals across our nation today need to experience that amazing grace that transformed the lives of Wilberforce and Newton. This is a grace undeserved but offered freely to those who will accept it. While it is free it is not cheap. It does not allow one to live a life of callous indifference to the plight of others. Rather, when experienced, it transforms and empowers us to live our lives as change agents for the eternal kingdom that is coming and which will end once and for all the oppression and killing of the innocents across the globe.

We all need a dose of that amazing grace which changed the lives of William Wilberforce and John Newton. These two men changed the world because they experienced this amazing grace in their lives. May we all experience this grace every day in our own lives so we can also change our nation and the world. Give me more of that amazing grace!

Over the years I have written many Commentaries regarding the sanctity of life and have published them online at www.nifla.org in a section entitled *The Wilberforce Forum*. For the convenience of the reader these Commentaries are published in this book on Appendix J.

# Endnotes

1.  Wilberforce's famous speech on the floor of the English
    Parliament regarding the slave trade. May 12, 1789:

    I mean not to accuse any one, but to take the shame
    upon myself, in common, indeed, with the whole par-
    liament of Great Britain, for having suffered this horrid
    trade to be carried on under their authority. We are all
    guilty—we ought all to plead guilty, and not to exculpate
    ourselves by throwing the blame on others; and I there-
    fore deprecate every kind of reflection against the various
    descriptions of people who are more immediately involved
    in this wretched business.

    [I]n this very point (to show the power of human
    prejudice) the situation of the slaves has been described by
    Mr. Norris, one of the Liverpool delegates, in a manner
    which, I am sure will convince the House how interest can
    draw a film across the eyes, so thick, that total blindness
    could do no more; and how it is our duty therefore to trust
    not to the reasonings of interested men, or to their way of
    coloring a transaction.

    The slaves who are sometimes described as rejoicing
    at their captivity, are so wrung with misery at leaving their
    country, that it is the constant practice to set sail at night,
    lest they should be sensible of their departure . . .The truth
    is, that for the sake of exercise, these miserable wretches,
    loaded with chains, oppressed with disease and wretched-
    ness, are forced to dance by the terror of the lash, and
    sometimes by the actual use of it.

    It will be found, upon an average of all the ships of
    which evidence has been given at the privy council, that
    exclusive of those who perish before they sail, not less
    than 12½ percent perish in the passage. Besides these, the
    Jamaica report tells you, that not less than 4½ percent die
    on shore before the day of sale, which is only a week or
    two from the time of landing. One third more die in the
    seasoning, and this in a country exactly like their own,

where they are healthy and happy as some of the evidences would pretend.

When first I heard, Sir, of these iniquities, I considered them as exaggerations, and could not believe it possible, that men had determined to live by exerting themselves for the torture and misery of their fellow-creatures. I have taken great pains to make myself master of the subject, and can declare, that such scenes of barbarity are enough to rouse the indignation and horror of the most callous of mankind.

From every consideration I shall deal frankly with the House, by declaring, that no act of policy whatever will make me swerve from my duty and oblige me to abandon a measure which I think will be an honor to humanity.

Having heard all of this you may choose to look the other way but you can never again say that you did not know.

# CHAPTER 5

# How Did It Ever Come to This?

> This [the Holocaust] must never happen again
> . . . Be vigilant about your rights. Care about
> the rights and human dignity of others. When
> the rights of any group, no matter how small,
> no matter how marginal, are violated, your lib-
> erty, your freedom is put at risk. Let there never
> be a day when we cast about in horror and have
> to ask the question, "How did it ever come to
> this?"
>
> *Thomas Childers, Ph.D., Professor of*
> *History, University of Pennsylvania*

IN 2013, THE NATION WAS shocked to learn the gruesome details concerning the abortion practice of Dr. Kermit Gosnell in Philadelphia, Pennsylvania. The facts concerning this so-called practice of medicine read more like a curriculum vitae from a demon than they do of a physician sworn to practice the healing art of medicine.

Kermit Gosnell and several of his staff were charged and con-victed of numerous counts of homicide in connection with the deaths of a former patient via a botched abortion and multiple infants who were born alive and then murdered at Women's Medical Society, his West Philadelphia clinic. According to the evidence at trial, Gosnell frequently delivered viable babies and then snipped their spinal cords with scissors, leaving them to die. Gosnell even collected body parts in jars which were displayed openly when police raided the clinic to secure evidence of illegal prescription drug dealing. What makes the situation all the more stunning is that state Department of Health regulators deliberately avoided inspecting abortion clinics, such as Gosnell's clinic, during the administrations of pro-choice governors Ridge and Rendell to avoid putting up barriers to abortion.

As major news media sources reluctantly began to report about Gosnell's house of horrors, Americans were shocked to learn the details. Even those who adamantly proclaimed themselves to be pro-choice on abortion expressed outrage at the bloody details and joined a large chorus of the American public that asked, "How did it ever come to this?"

In the spring of 2015 an undercover investigation of Planned Parenthood was made by the Center for Medical Progress (CMP), a front organization set up to expose the gruesome abortion practices of Planned Parenthood. Indeed, CMP produced a shocking set of eleven undercover videos that caught Planned Parenthood officials selling body parts of aborted babies for medical research.

- In the first video Dr. Deborah Nucatola of Planned Parenthood comments on baby-crushing: "We've been very good at getting heart, lung, liver, because we know that, so I'm not gonna crush that part, I'm gonna basically crush below, I'm gonna crush above, and I'm gonna see if I can get it all intact."
- In the second video Planned Parenthood's Dr. Mary Gatter jokes, "I want a Lamborghini" as she negotiates the best price for baby parts.
- In the third video Holly O'Donnell, a former employee who worked inside a Planned Parenthood clinic, details first-hand unspeakable atrocities and how she fainted in horror over handling baby legs.

- In the fourth video Planned Parenthood's Dr. Savita Ginde states, "We don't want to do just a flat-fee (per baby) of like $200. A per-item thing works a little better just because we can see how much we can get out of it." She also laughs while looking at a plate of fetal kidneys that were "good to go."

- In the fifth video Melissa Farrell of Planned Parenthood-Gulf Coast in Houston boasts of Planned Parenthood's skill in obtaining "intact fetal cadavers" and how her "research" department "contributes so much to the bottom line of our organization here. You know we're one of the largest affiliates. Our Research Department is the largest in the United States."

- In the sixth video Holly O'Donnell of Planned Parenthood describes technicians taking fetal parts without patient consent: "There were times when they would just take what they wanted. And these mothers don't know. And there's no way they would know."

- In the seventh and perhaps most disturbing video Holly O'Donnell describes the harvesting, or "procurement," of organs from a nearly intact late-term fetus aborted at Planned Parenthood Mar Monte's Alameda clinic in San Jose, CA. O'Donnell says her supervisor asks her: "'You want to see something kind of cool.' And she just taps the heart, and it starts beating. And I'm sitting here and I'm looking at this fetus, and its heart is beating, and I don't know what to think."

- In the eighth video Cate Dyer CEO of Stem Express, a company that purchases fetal remains from abortions for medical research, admits that Planned Parenthood sells "a lot of" fully intact aborted babies.

- In the ninth video a Planned Parenthood medical director discusses how the abortion company sells fully intact aborted babies — including one who "just fell out" of the womb.

- In the tenth video Planned Parenthood is exposed selling specific body parts — including the heart, eyes and "gonads" of unborn babies .The video also shows the shocking ways in which Planned Parenthood officials admit that they are breaking federal law by selling aborted baby body parts for profit.

- In the eleventh video a Texas Planned Parenthood abortionist is shown planning to sell the intact heads of aborted babies for research. Amna Dermish of Planned Parenthood is caught on tape describing an illegal partial-birth abortion procedure to terminate living, late-term unborn babies, which she hopes will yield intact fetal heads for brain harvesting.

- Unreleased videos from CMP also show Deb Vanderhei of Planned Parenthood caught on tape talking about how Planned Parenthood abortion business affiliates may "want to increase revenue [from selling baby parts] but we can't stop them." Another video has a woman talking about the "financial incentives" of selling aborted baby body parts.

The release of these videos sent shock waves across the nation and were followed by calls from some for criminal investigations of Planned Parenthood. However, the only criminal indictments issued as of the time of this publication have been against the officials of CMP. CMP founder David Daleiden and his colleague Sandra Merritt have been indicted by a Houston grand jury for tampering with a governmental record. Daleiden was also indicted for violating a legal prohibition on the purchase and sale of human organs. (Which, of course, he did not do as his offers for purchase were bogus and intended to expose the illegal practices of Planned Parenthood.) No indictments were issued against Planned Parenthood for its vile practices. Planned Parenthood officials promptly crowed in the media that it had been vindicated and that justice was being served for it being victimized by CMP.

So it appears that in America today those who expose evil are treated as criminals and those who do evil are seen as victims. It appears that right is now wrong and wrong is now right in the land of the free and the home of the brave.

We must repeat once again – "How did it ever come to this?

History shows that when a nation and culture devalues and dehumanizes a certain group of people in order to control them, such nation inevitably slides down a slippery slope where the eventual abuse, manipulation, and killing of such people are accepted. In 1920, a German lawyer, Karl Binding, and a German physician, Alfred Hoche, published a book that was very influential upon the thinking of the German elite in academia, medicine, and the law. The ethic promoted by this book led to the holocaust and the murder of millions.

The book, *The Release of the Destruction of Life Devoid of Value,* argues that there is such a thing as a human life so disabled, handicapped, and defective that it is devoid of value. Hence, the most humane thing society can do to such a life is to end it. Therefore, the legalization (release) of mercy killing (destruction of life devoid of value) should be allowed by law and practiced as an exercise of medical ethics.

In this work, Binding asks, "Above all I want to pass on this preliminary most urgent question: 'Is there a human life that has to such a degree lost its legal rights that its continuation is of no value for itself or to society?" (1) Binding and Hoche go on to argue that there is such a condition of a human being. They make statements in regards to the handicapped as "incurable idiots—no matter if they have been born one or if they have become like one at the last stage of their suffering, as for example the paralytics." (2)

The work of Binding and Hoche deeply impacted the culture of the German nation during the 1920s and set the foundation for the acceptance of the Nazi death camps and the extermination of the Jews. In the German experience, the Holocaust came about gradually after first there was an acceptance of the notion that some human life is less valuable than others and the killing of such a life can be justified as a societal benefit. Once the handicapped, the infirm, and the dying were dehumanized in this manner, then the class of people to be further dehumanized enlarged to include the mentally retarded and certain races of people such as the Jews.

At the end of World War II, many German citizens were required to walk through the killing camps that were in their communities and see the horror that they allowed to be released against other human beings. They must have asked themselves, "How did it come to this?" The answer to that is simply—it started when your culture accepted the idea that there is such a life not worthy to be lived. It started when your culture violated the principles set forth in the American Declaration of Independence that every human being is created equal and given by the Creator an unalienable right to life.

While the principles of the Declaration of Independence are set forth in the founding document of America, they are not exclusively American principles. To the contrary, they reflect the natural law of God placed upon the heart of every human being and apply to all cultures and nations at all times. The German people learned that violation of these principles of the natural law results in disaster and destruction.

America's past history with slavery validates this as does the German experience under Nazi rule. Killings become justified when the dehumanization of a group of people is complete. Slaves were considered mere property and something less than fully human. Jews were considered subhuman by the Nazis. Having lost their humanity in the eyes of the ruling forces, both groups of people could easily be killed on a massive scale.

This was the end result of slavery which was tolerated by the rationalization that black slaves were not fully human. This was the end result of racist Nazi ideology, which proclaimed the superiority of one race over another. It will also be the end result of the rejection of the American ideal that all human beings are created equal and that some human beings, i.e., the unborn, are less than fully human and do not have "meaningful life."

The American experience with abortion parallels both its past concerning slavery and the German history concerning the holocaust. In both instances dehumanization of others was required to justify their exploitation and killing. The same is true for the acceptance of abortion. No better source exemplifies this than the spine-chilling editorial printed by the California Medical Association in its journal *California Medicine* 113, no. 3, September 1970.

At the time of the publication of this editorial, the topic of abortion was being intensely debated across the nation as the battle over this issue was being fought over the hearts and minds of the American public. The editorial states in part:

> The process of eroding the old ethic and sub-stituting the new has already begun. It may be seen most clearly in changing attitudes toward human abortion. In defiance of the long-held Western ethic of intrinsic and equal value for every human life regardless of its stage, condi-tion, or status, abortion is becoming accepted by society as moral, right, and even necessary. It is worth noting that this shift in public attitude has affected the churches, the laws, and public policy rather than the reverse. Since the old ethic has not yet been fully displaced it has been nec-essary to separate the idea of abortion from the idea of killing, which continues to be socially abhorrent. The result has been a curious avoid-ance of the scientific fact, which everyone really knows, that human life begins at conception and is continuous whether intra- or extra-uterine until death. The very considerable semantic gym-nastics which are required to rationalize abortion as anything but taking a human life would be ludicrous if they were not often put forth under socially impeccable auspices. It is suggested that this schizophrenic sort of subterfuge is necessary because while a new ethic is being accepted the old one has not yet been rejected.
>
> It seems safe to predict that the new demo-graphic, ecological, and social realities and aspi-rations are so powerful that the new ethic of rela-tive rather than of absolute and equal values will ultimately prevail as man exercises ever more cer-tain and effective control over his numbers, and uses his always comparatively scarce resources to provide the nutrition, housing, economic sup-

port, education, and health care in such ways as to achieve his desired quality of life and living. The criteria upon which these relative values are to be based will depend considerably upon whatever concept of the quality of life or living is developed. This may be expected to reflect the extent that quality of life is considered to be a function of personal fulfillment; of individual responsibility for the common welfare, the preservation of the environment, the betterment of the species; and of whether or not, or to what extent, these responsibilities are to be exercised on a compulsory or voluntary basis.

The part which medicine will play as all this develops is not yet entirely clear. That it will be deeply involved is certain. Medicine's role with respect to changing attitudes toward abortion may well be a prototype of what is to occur. Another precedent may be found in the part physicians have played in evaluating who is and who is not to be given costly long-term renal dialysis. Certainly this has required placing relative values on human lives and the impact of the physician on this decision process has been considerable. One may anticipate further development of these roles as the problems of birth control and birth selection are extended inevitably to death selection and death control whether by the individual or by society, and further public and professional determinations of when and when not to use scarce resources.

The established American ethic in how we treat other human beings is set forth in the Declaration of Independence. All human beings are to be treated equally under the law because all human beings are created equal by God and have unalienable rights given to them by the Creator. However, over the years this ethic has eroded to essentially mean today that some human beings are not to be considered equal. Yet, as stated in this editorial:

> "While a new ethic is being accepted the old one has not yet been rejected. Americans for the most part still support the concept of equality under the law for all. However, the acceptance of abortion on demand conflicts with this ethic and thus, our culture struggles with such a contradiction. To reconcile this inconsistency, as the editorial says, we must go through considerable semantic gymnastics to "rationalize abortion as anything but taking a human life."

The plain and undeniable truth, however, is that acceptance of abortion in the law and in the culture is a denial of the unalienable right to life to some human beings who are deemed not worthy of life. This hard truth about American culture must be acknowledged and corrected if we desire to save the soul of our nation. When the unalienable and self-evident truths of the Declaration of Independence are rejected, then there are no checks upon the actions of people like Kermit Gosnell.

Has American come to accept the idea that there is such a thing as a life not worthy to be lived? Have we like the German nation in the 1920s accepted the concept that there is such a thing as a life devoid of value?

The language from the Supreme Court in its *Roe v. Wade* says that there is such a thing as human life that is incapable of meaningful life because such lives reside within the wombs of their mothers. Furthermore, the acceptance in the law of a virtually unlimited constitutional right to abortion has led to the acknowledgment in the civil courts of causes of action against physicians for the wrongful birth and/or wrongful life of those whom would have been aborted if their mothers had only been given certain genetic information about them during pregnancy. (3)

I don't believe that we as a nation are quite yet ready to fully embrace this utilitarian ethic that promotes killing of others for the convenience of some. However, I do believe that we are heading down a pathway where the ideals of our Founders concerning the natural God-given rights of human beings are completely thrown asunder. If such a day ever arrives, then the prophetic words of Thomas Jefferson declaring that the justice of God will not sleep forever will once again be realized.

How did it ever come to this? We must honestly answer—it came to this when our nation rejected the self-evident and unalienable right to life and accepted the idea that there is such a thing as a human life not worthy to be lived.

## Moments of Reflection

1. How do you respond to the idea promoted by Binding and Hoche that there is such a thing as a life not worthy to be lived?

2. Is there such a life so devoid of value that the most merciful and humane way to treat this life is to end it? Why or why not?

3. How has the concept of abortion on demand contributed to the idea that some lives are less valuable or less meaningful than others?

4. What social factors in America led to the existence of Kermit Gosnell and his house of horrors? What can be done to eliminate such factors?

5. Do you agree with the commentary from the California Medical Association that "the very considerable semantic gymnastics which are required to rationalize abortion as anything but taking a human life would be ludicrous if they were not often put forth under socially impeccable auspices. It is suggested that this schizophrenic sort of subterfuge is necessary because while a new ethic is being accepted the old one has not yet been rejected"?

# Endnotes

1.  Karl Binding. and Alfred Hoche, The Release of the Destruction of Life Devoid of Value: It's Measure and It's Form, p.17. Originally published in German by Felix Meiner in Leipzig, 1920. English 5126 translation and comments by Robert L. Sassone, (1975), 17." With the following:

    Karl Binding and Alfred Hoche, The Release of the Destruction of Life Devoid of Value: It's Measure and It's Form, trans. Robert L. Sassone, (1975). 17. Originally published in German.

    Binding further states in his introduction: "There are undoubtedly living people whose death means a final release for themselves and at the same time a relief of a burden for society and for the country. This burden serves no useful purpose, except maybe to give an example of highest unselfishness" (18).

2.  Binding and Hoche, 20. Binding further states, "The second group is composed of incurable idiots—no matter if they have been born one or if they have become like one at the last stage of their suffering, as for example the paralytics . . . Because they need considerable care, they are the cause for new job creation, the aim of which is to completely support worthless life year after year" (20–21).

3.  Wrongful birth lawsuits occur when a mother gives birth to a child who has a handicap, such as Down syndrome or spina bifida, and which could have been detected in the womb through prenatal screening and genetic testing. If the mother is not advised of the possibility of her child having such a handicap and that she has the option to abort this child, then she has a legal right to sue her prenatal care physician for the "wrongful birth" of her child. The mother's legal claim says that had she known of the handicap she would have exercised her legal right to have an abortion. Hence, since she was not properly advised

of the handicapped condition of her child, the birth is wrongful and she is due compensation.

In a wrongful life law suit, a child who is born with a handicap that could have been detected in the womb is given the legal right to sue the mother's doctor for his wrongful life, arguing that he should have never been born. Hence, the doctor should be required to pay compensation to him.

In *Roe v. Wade*, the Supreme Court stated that only when one is capable of "meaningful life outside the womb" can his life be protected by the law. Now because of the legality of abortion, civil law recognizes that there are wrongful births and wrongful lives. Has American culture now come into agreement with Binding and Hoche that there is such a thing as a life not worthy to be lived?

# CHAPTER 6

# A Nation Ruled by "Men Without Chests"

"A silent, unavoidable revolution is taking place in society, a revolution that cares as little about the human lives it destroys as an earthquake cares about the houses it ravages. Classes and races that are too weak to dominate the new conditions of existence will be defeated."

Karl Marx (1)

CHRISTIAN WRITER AND PHILOSOPHER C. S. Lewis wrote about a cultural decline of the Western world in his classic work, *The Abolition of Man*. In this essay, Lewis foresaw the gradual coarsening of societal ethics to the point where human life is degraded and cheapened beyond recognition. According to Lewis, this future world is fueled by the redefinition of what it means to be human. Society, in such a state, changes the definition of humanity as traditionally understood by all civilizations since the dawn of time. In the words of Lewis, when this happens, the "abolition of man" has occurred.

Lewis describes each individual as being made up of three parts—the head, the chest, and the stomach. (Traditional theology refers to this as the body, the soul, and the spirit.) The head, says Lewis, represents the intellectual part of each human being. It is the rational thinking processes that distinguishes humans from animals. The chest is where the heart is and represents the spiritual nature of a person telling each of us what is right and wrong and giving us moral guidance. (This is what I refer to as the natural law of God placed upon the heart of every human being.) The stomach represents both good and bad desires that every human being has, i.e., sexual desires, lusts, desire for intimacy, physical needs, etc.

It is the chest that connects the stomach to the head. It provides the moral compass over individual behavior and, thus, applies the brakes to instincts that, without such a moral sense, are animalistic and destructive. Without the chest, a human being's intellect, i.e., the head, is controlled by the stomach and is free to release destructive actions that result in the control, manipulation, and killing of other human beings for the perceived benefit of society as a whole. This is the kind of future world envisioned by Karl Marx, Adolf Hitler, and other ruthless tyrants of history who have pursued control over the lives and destinies of others to obtain their own view of utopia, which relies upon the mass killings of those deemed inferior and inconvenient.

Lewis envisioned a future where nations are ruled by "men without chests." In such a world, vices once prohibited by society become commonplace and rampant because the chest no long exists to check the lusts of the stomach. In this future world, the lives of individual human beings are considered valueless and the rights of the controlling elite, i.e., men without chests, are considered supreme.

When human beings live without a moral compass they are, in fact, living in denial of the existence of a Creator. If no Creator exists then there are no absolute truths establishing right from wrong. If there are no absolutes of right and wrong then there are no absolute prohibitions against the taking of innocent human lives. If there are no absolute prohibitions against the taking of innocent human lives, then the killing of nearly sixty million unborn human beings by abortion can be justified. The slide down this slippery slope began with a denial that all human beings are "created equal and endowed by their Creator with certain unalienable rights, among these life, liberty, and the pursuit of happiness." This slide will end when we become ruled by men without chests, and the abolition of man will have become complete.

The foundation of the American republic proclaims that every human being is created with unalienable rights. There is a Creator who establishes the absolutes of right and wrong and grants to his creation of humanity unalienable rights. Life is the first and foremost of these rights. Without this unalienable right, no other rights matter. When this unalienable right is denied arbitrarily to some, then it belongs to nobody. When this occurs, our nation will have embarked upon a journey that will end with a small elite (men without chests) controlling the lives of the vast majority of humans.

In 1818, Mary Shelley wrote a remarkable novel entitled *Frankenstein*. Of course, when this book is mentioned, most of us smile and recall the silly horror movie of the 1950s starring Boris Karloff and featured an uncontrollable beast created by a mad scientist, Dr. Victor Frankenstein. However, I recently read this novel and, to my amazement, discovered that Mary Shelley's work was a serious, and prophetic, discussion of where science could lead if not controlled by a moral sense of right and wrong. In fact, the book sets forth a very clear example of what a society led by men without chests would look like.

In the novel, Dr. Victor Frankenstein, in the process of creating his humanlike creature, states,

> No one can conceive the variety of feelings which bore me onwards like a hurricane, in the first enthusiasm of success. Life and death appeared to me ideal bounds, which I should first break through, and pour a torrent of light into our dark world. A new species would bless me as its creator and source; many happy and excellent natures would owe their being to me. No father could claim the gratitude of his child as completely as I should deserve theirs. Pursuing these reflections

> I thought that if I could bestow animation upon
> lifeless matter, I might in the process of time
> (although I now found it impossible) renew life
> when death had apparently devoted the body to
> corruption. (2)

Dr. Frankenstein determines that he, not God, is the one who has the power over life and death, and in doing so, unleashes upon the world an uncontrollable monster who murders at will.

The fictional story of Dr. Frankenstein is a clear example of what happens when the intellectual part of each human being, i.e., the head, is not controlled by the spiritual side, i.e., the chest, which gives each person a moral foundation and sense of right and wrong. Dr. Frankenstein is clearly a man without a chest, seeking to claim for himself the role of the Creator God.

When a nation and culture accepts the idea that some human beings are not endowed by the Creator with an unalienable right to life, then the moral foundation upon which such nation rests has been damaged. Men without chests eventually emerge to lead such a nation and the path upon which they take the nation leads to its eventual destruction. Unless the moral foundation of the nation, i.e., the chest, is restored, such foundation will eventually crumble and the nation which it supports will collapse.

Is America now a nation led by men without chests, such as Dr. Frankenstein? One only needs to see how far America has come since the *Roe* decision in 1973 to begin to articulate an answer to this question. Simply consider the following:

- Since *Roe,* there have been nearly sixty million unborn children killed by abortion.
- *Roe* paved the way for civil medical malpractice law suits for the wrongful birth and wrongful life of handicapped babies, thus, acknowledging in the law that there is such a thing as a life not worthy to be lived.
- The philosophical basis for *Roe* is used to justify the growing acceptance of practices such as assisted suicide, eutha-

nasia, human cloning, and medical experimentation with the remains of aborted infants.

- A movement known as transhumanism has now emerged, proclaiming that through a blending of medicine and technology, the creation of a post-human being with superior physical and mental attributes is possible and should be pursued. (3)

The quest to redefine humanity began with the denial that all human beings are made in the image of God. It is a denial that all human beings are endowed by God with the self-evident and unalienable rights proclaimed in the Declaration of Independence. From this denial came the justification for medical experimentation on the remains of the unborn aborted and other actions undertaken in the name of medical science, such as human cloning, which exploit and manipulate some human beings for the perceived betterment of others.

In the end, if such actions are not opposed, the control of America by men without chests will be complete. In the end, Dr. Victor Frankenstein will have jumped out of the pages of the Mary Shelly novel and become alive in the persona of our nation's leaders. In the end, the abolition of man will have occurred.

## The Role of the Church

Abortion (and other related life issues) is, at its heart, truly a spiritual issue. The position one takes on this issue indicates that person's view of the nature of God and the nature of humanity.

Are all human beings created in the image of God? If so, have all human beings been endowed by the Creator with self-evident and unalienable rights of life, liberty, and the pursuit of happiness? The answers one gives to these two questions provide fully their view of who God is and what he requires of us.

While this is primarily a spiritual issue it, of course, is debated and fought in arenas outside of the church, i.e., academia, government, political parties, etc. However, because abortion and other life related issues are primarily spiritual they must be addressed and fought within the churches of America. A gospel that does not proclaim the sanctity of all human life and advocate for the protection of innocent human life is a gospel that denies the overruling sovereignty of the Creator God.

The only organized opposition to abortion after the issuance of *Roe v. Wade* came from the Catholic Church. Almost immediately after this decision came down Senator James Buckley (R-NY), a Roman Catholic, and Senator Mark Hatfield, an Evangelical Protestant, cosponsored a constitutional amendment that would overturn *Roe* and restore legal protection to the unborn. (The proposed amendment went nowhere in the Senate and did not even garner hearings.)

Despite the prolife advocacy of Hatfield, for the most part, Evangelicals were silent on the issue. It was not until 1979 that Protestants, and particularly Evangelicals, provided serious organized opposition to abortion. This was in the aftermath of the movie and book *Whatever Happened to the Human Race*, written by evangelicals Frances Schaeffer, a theologian, and Dr. C. Everett Koop, who later became surgeon general under President Reagan,

While some Protestant denominations, primarily evangelical in nature, have spoken out in defense of the protection of innocent unborn life, some mainline Protestant denominations have actually endorsed abortion as an issue of equal rights for women. A notorious pro-abortion advocacy group, the Religious Coalition for Abortion Rights, now known as the Religious Coalition for Reproductive Choice (RCRC), says on its website:

> The Religious Coalition for Reproductive Choice (RCRC) was originally founded in 1973 as the Religious Coalition for Abortion Rights (RCAR) to safeguard the newly-won constitutional right to privacy in decisions about abortion. RCRC founders were clergy and lay leaders from mainstream religions, many of whom had provided women with referrals to safe abortion services before the Supreme Court legalized abortion in

*Roe v. Wade.* The founders believed that there would be at most a ten-year struggle to secure the right to choose. In fact the struggle is far from over. It has changed and intensified, and the stakes are growing.

Today, our coalition comprises national organizations from major faiths and traditions, religiously-affiliated and independent religious organizations, Affiliates and grassroots communities across the country, Spiritual Youth for Reproductive Freedom (SYRF), and a religious leaders network that includes faith leaders, seminarians and ordained clergy. Additionally, we have thousands of individual supporters advocating from their pews and in their communities around the country. We are also present on Capitol Hill, and in coalition with other reproductive rights/health/choice/justice organizations in Washington, DC and in the states.

While our member organizations and individual supporters are religiously and theologically diverse, they are unified in the commitment to preserve reproductive choice as a basic part of religious liberty, and to be a collective voice for reproductive justice. For four decades, RCRC has been working where faith intersects with issues related to our reproductive lives.

When seeing someone who is clearly religious—whether they're wearing indicators of their faith such as a clerical collar, a crucifix, a kippah, or even a t-shirt with a religious message on it—you might assume that person does not believe a woman should have access to compassionate abortion care, or comprehensive sexuality education, or even contraception.

RCRC is proof that you would likely be mistaken. For over 40 years, RCRC has been a voice

103

for reproductive choice, and has been active in working with women and men—especially those at the margins—at the intersection of faith, policy and our reproductive lives. Supportive clergy have been giving sermons about the moral agency of women to make decisions about their lives for decades, as well as praying quietly with women when actually making those decisions. We have stood arm in arm with proponents of comprehensive sexuality education, worked for a version of the Affordable Care Act that included contraception with no co-pays, and were instrumental in bringing faithful voices of those at the pulpit, in pews and in communities across the country to issues such as the Violence Against Women Act, the approval of Plan B pills and telemedicine for abortions, and for the ability of servicewomen to access abortion care while serving our country. We believe in faith expressed in action.

Solidly grounded in a deep belief that our work should be sourced, implemented and led by the people it affects, we are building a grassroots movement of people who understand that it's time for religious people who believe in reproductive justice to stand up. (4)

RCRC has been a strong proponent of abortion on demand since its inception and lists on their website twenty-seven religious groups, including some Protestant denominations that support its mission to promote abortion. (4) One such denomination that has supported abortion and the mission of the RCRC is the Presbyterian Church USA. Claiming 1.8 million members nationwide the PCUSA is the nation's largest Presbyterian denomination.

In its 2014 General Assembly, the delegates of the PCUSA voted down a resolution that condemned the killing of babies born alive during abortions. Such was the practice of notorious abortionist Kermit Gosnell, yet the delegates of this mainline denomination did not seem to feel the need to condemn such actions. This gathering of PCUSA undertook further action to support the denominations pro-abortion stand by refusing to pass a resolution that simply urged a season of reflection for two years on the denomination's support for abortion.

Mark Tooley, a writer for *The American Spectator,* observed these actions of the PCUSA as follows:

> Mainline Protestantism, at least in its official curia, has been liberal for nearly 100 years. But for most of that century it was a thoughtful, dignified liberalism that still roughly adhered to historic Christianity's moral architecture, even if it no longer upheld the core doctrine. But the yonder years of stately Protestantism, at least in the old Mainline, are largely over.
>
> Getting far less attention was the PCUSA General Assembly's overwhelming rejection of legislation that urged a "season of reflection" on the denomination's support for abortion-rights, including its long-time membership in the Religious Coalition for Reproductive Choice (RCRC), which opposes any restrictions on abortion. Liberal Mainline Protestantism, starting in the 1960s, began its first major break with traditional Christian ethics by embracing abortion rights, discarding traditional notions about sacred human life in favor of radical autonomous individualism. The Mainline's support for abortion and implied hostility to large families, now compounded by its redefinition of marriage and divorcing of sex from marriage, have all helped to create a culture where the typical Mainline congregation is now largely gray headed and has few if any children.
>
> Of course, some media reports will hail the PCUSA's ostensibly courageous shift leftward as

> heralding the irresistible tides of history and rep-
> resenting Christianity's future. But after about a
> half century of continuous decline, neither the
> PCUSA nor any Mainline denomination can be
> seriously seen as any barometer of mainstream
> religious trends, not in the U.S., and even less
> so around the world. Reportedly many overseas
> Presbyterian churches, many of them now larger
> than the PCUSA, are prepared to break ties with
> the PCUSA over its abandonment of Christian
> sexual teaching. Some of them already have. (5)

The PCUSA is not the only mainline Protestant denomination that has been actively supportive of abortion and has refused to
support efforts to protect the unborn. Sadly, the United Methodist
Church, the Lutheran Church of America, the Disciples of Christ,
and other denominations have a history of support for abortion and
the work of the RCRC.

While certain mainline Protestant denominations clearly and
overtly support abortion others, including many evangelical churches,
either remain passively quiet about the issue or timidly mention it
periodically in passing. The timidity of pastors and church leaders
to actively and aggressively take a stand comes from fear of offend-
ing people and/or a misunderstanding of the IRS rules that prohibit
churches from endorsing or opposing candidates for political office.
They reason that because abortion is a political issue to speak out
might bring upon their congregation the wrath of the IRS. However,
such fears are not grounded in a correct understanding of IRS rules
and regulations. Such rules prohibit church endorsements of political
candidates. They do not prohibit speaking out about moral issues
from the pulpit. Furthermore, such a fear is misguided in that it is
based upon a belief that abortion is primarily a political issue and not
a spiritual one.

Lutheran pastor and Christian martyr, Dietrich Bonhoeffer said,
"Silence in the face of evil is itself evil. God will not hold us guiltless. Not to speak is to speak. Not to act is to act." (6) I believe that

Bonhoeffer's words are chilling and serve as a warning to Christian leaders and people of faith across America today.

I must also point out that although the Catholic Church has officially taken a strong stand against abortion and has spoken up eloquently for the unalienable right to life, many professing to be Catholics do not adhere to the teachings of their church. The polling data of the election of 2012 showed that a majority of Catholics supported Barrack Obama, the most pro-abortion president we have seen to date. (7) Clearly, the position of their church on this issue did not impact the way these voters cast their ballots.

Another example can be found in the current makeup of the United States Senate. The most common church affiliation listed among the current US Senate is Catholic. Currently, twenty-two US senators are so listed. If every Catholic currently serving in the Senate simply voted the dictates of their faith, then abortion could be severely restricted or even eliminated in the law.

Among the Catholic senators currently serving are intense supporters of abortion such as, Maria Cantwell (D-WA), Susan Collins (R-MA), Richard Durbin (D-IL), Kirsten Gillibrand (D-NY), Heidi Heitkamp (D-ND), Tim Kaine (D-VA), Patrick Leahy (D-VT), Edward Markey (D-MA), Barbara Milkulski (D-MD), Patty Murray (D-WA), and Jack Reed (D-RI). Perhaps the most influential Catholic in public office today is Vice President Joe Biden, who is a long-time supporter of abortion. Current secretary of state John Kerry is also Catholic. When he ran for president in 2004, his campaign mentioned that he had served as an altar boy in his youth at his local Catholic parish. Kerry, like those mentioned above, is also a strong supporter of abortion. Another prominent Catholic serving in the House of Representatives who is also pro-abortion is Nancy Pelosi (D-CA), the former Speaker of the House.

While certain Christian denominations have voiced opposition to abortion and support for the unalienable right to life it is clear that such message has not taken hold of the hearts and minds of many members of these churches. The experiences of prolife pregnancy resource centers (PRCs) verify this. PRCs collect initial data on the religious affiliations of their clients/patients and report that many such women considering abortion list a Christian church as their spiritual background. Indeed, I recall in my early days, speaking out on abortion as a guest speaker at a local church and being talked to in private after the service by a young pregnant woman who related to me that her father, a deacon in the church, was insisting that she obtain an abortion. He had made the appointment for her the next day and was going to personally take her to the clinic. The young lady sorrowfully told me that he was adamant that she was not going to disgrace her family and church by remaining pregnant and having a child out of wedlock.

The Alan Guttmacher Institute is a Planned Parenthood research affiliate, and it researches abortion statistics worldwide. It undertook a study on abortions performed in 2000–2001 by surveying more than ten thousand women who had abortions during that time period. The institute found that 43 percent of women over age seventeen said they were Protestant while 27 percent said they were Catholic. But Catholics were more likely to get an abortion: The abortion rate for Catholic women was 22 per 1,000 women; the rate for Protestants was 18 per 1,000 women, according to study author Rachel K. Jones. (8)

Overall, 78 percent of the women surveyed said they had a religious affiliation. (Besides those who marked that they were Catholic and Protestant, 8 percent said they belonged to other religions.) The remaining 22 percent said they had no religious affiliation. Thirteen percent said they were evangelical or born-again, and three-fourths of those had identified themselves as Protestant. (9)

Such statistics should awaken the community of faith. Seventy percent of women obtaining abortions claimed some allegiance to the Christian faith. We must ask some very troubling questions regarding this. Where was the community of faith when these women were struggling with their decision to terminate their pregnancies? What kind of teaching on the sanctity of life were these women hearing in their churches?

It is imperative that the Christian community, both Catholic and Protestant, speak in defense of life and educate the members of their churches on this vital issue. The Christian church has a prophetic role to play to call society to a higher standard, but we must first remove the log in our own eye before we demand that the speck of dust in our neighbor's eye be removed. The Christian community, led by the clergy, must be intimately involved in addressing this issue with their congregations by reaching out to those who are sitting in the pews and are suffering immensely from the burden of guilt and remorse imposed upon them by a choice they regret. Furthermore, clear biblical teaching on the sanctity of life in our churches will clearly help to end abortion within the community of faith.

Years ago, I was asked to speak at a church in Baltimore in commemoration of Sanctity of Life Sunday, an event honored by churches across the nation in January of each year. This church expressed an enthusiasm for the sanctity of life issue at an intensity level that I had not seen before. I asked a person who was a member of the church's pro-life committee where such commitment and enthusiasm came from. The response was inspiriting and instructive.

The person shared that a few years before the pastor's wife (with her husband's approval) confessed before the entire congregation that she had four abortions prior to marrying her husband. She shared that the Lord had convicted her to make her story known publicly because she knew that some women in the church were deeply hurting from an abortion in the past and did not know how to deal with it. The church's response was staggering. Women began to come forward to confess that they too had had an abortion and were suffering from guilt and depression. A post-abortion ministry came into being in the church. Furthermore, men who had been involved in abortion in the past began to come forward and confess their involvement as well. A spirit of healing and forgiveness came into the church in a way never experienced before, and spiritual revival was occurring. The church had become what the body of Christ should be– a place of forgiveness, reconciliation, and healing. And this all happened because one very brave woman made herself vulnerable and shared a deep, dark secret from her past.

I strongly suggest that every church in America undertake the following in order to address the issue of the sanctity of life with both their members and their communities:

1. **Adopt a prolife Pregnancy Resource Center (PRC) or Medical Clinic (PMC)**: Every community in the nation has a PRC/PMC. The National Institute of Family and

Life Advocates (NIFLA) has a membership network of more than 1,350 such agencies in all fifty states. The PMCs operate as medical clinics providing ultrasound confirmation of pregnancy to abortion minded mothers. Statistics show that the vast majority of mothers considering abortion will choose life if they see an ultrasound image of their babies during a visit to a prolife PMC. (10)

The ministries of PRCs/PMCs provide opportunities from members of churches to volunteer in different capacities such as client advocacy, board membership, material resources coordinators, and other means of involvement. They are in constant need of both financial and material assistance. In short, these life-affirming ministries are ready made for serious church involvement.

I want to emphasize that churches need to adopt a PRC/PMC and not just support it. What is the difference? Think of your neighbor's son Johnny who is very active in his high school. You support Johnny by buying raffle tickets for his volleyball team, by going to his band concerts, by going to his special events, and even going to his graduation. However, if Johnny's parents were killed in a tragic accident and you went to court to adopt him, your level of support would be far different. You would make sure that he was fed and clothed. You would provide a roof over his head and a room to sleep in. You would give him loving nurture and counsel as he grows up.

To adopt a PRC/PMC means that a church will consider it one of their own ministries and make sure that it has sufficient resources, both financial and material, to successfully fulfill its mission. It means that a church will supply volunteers, leaders, and money to ensure that its local PRC/PMC brings about an end to abortion in the community. This is far different than just providing support for a PRC/PMC with a periodic check and/or announcement supporting its upcoming events.

2. **Educate Church Members on Life Issues through a Prolife Committee**: Every church should have a recog-

nized prolife committee that provides education materials, resources, and organizes events in which church members can participate. The committee could sponsor monthly meetings which feature a speaker or a movie of importance. It could organize congregational participation in community prolife events such as a March for Life, Life Chain, and a PRC/PMC banquet. It can provide resource material to the pastor to use in sermons and teaching. It can organize materials for use in Sunday school classes. While this committee, as an arm of the church, cannot endorse or oppose candidates for office it can inform the congregation of important life-related issues in the public policy arena and educate them on the positions of candidates for local office on life issues.

3.  **Develop a Post-Abortion Ministry**: There are countless numbers of women and men in every church in America who are suffering guilt and remorse from a previous abortion. Likewise, there are men who have participated in abortion and are suffering in silence. They feel isolated and alone. They need to feel the loving and forgiving hand of Christ in their lives. Every church in America should have an outlet for this kind of healing ministry. There are numerous Bible studies and materials available to help in this process with study guides for small group leaders to effectively use. (11)

4.  **Personal Involvement from the Pastor**: The pastor of every church should find some area for personal involvement to set an example for the congregation. The book of Nehemiah tells us of the miraculous work of God through Nehemiah in rebuilding the destroyed wall of Jerusalem in record time. In order to accomplish this, Nehemiah challenged the people in every part of the city to rebuild the section of the wall in their own neighborhood. In doing so, the city wall was quickly rebuilt. However, the first group of people to go to work on the wall was the spiritual leaders of the city, the priests.

Nehemiah 3:1 (NIV) says, "Eliashib the high priest and his fellow priests went to work and rebuilt the Sheep Gate." This was the beginning of the great rebuilding project, and it was undertaken by the spiritual leaders—the high priest and his fellow priests. The people of Jerusalem followed their examples. There is a nugget of deep truth here. When the *spiritual leaders* lead, the people will follow. Some may grumble and complain. Others may try to undermine. Some will leave the church because they do not like what the pastor says and does. However, the majority of the sheep will follow the leading of their shepherd.

Personal involvement from the pastoral staff of a church can be reflected in various ways. An acknowledgment of Sanctity of Life Sunday in January with a sermon specifically geared to address the sanctity of life issue should be an annual event, and a pastor can address this issue with fellow clergy in the community through personal communications. Serving on a board of a PRC/PMC is another outlet. Each pastor will have his or her own strengths and gifts to use in this regard, but they should understand that if they truly lead by example the congregation will follow.

Such involvement in the sanctity of life issue by every church in America will have a dramatic impact in changing hearts and minds and achieving a culture where the unalienable right to life is protected under the law.

Ultimately the abortion issue must be addressed by the Christian community on the spiritual level. This means that first of all abortion must be acknowledged by our spiritual leads as a violation of God's law against the shedding of innocent blood. As such, it is the denial of the unalienable right to life bestowed upon every human being by our Creator. The community of faith must come to grips with its acquiescence in abortion and, in some cases, its outright endorsement and promotion of it.

The first chapter of the book of Isaiah is a very relevant message to the American church regarding this. This chapter in Isaiah is written to God's people, the children of Israel. It is not a message for unbelievers. Rather, it is an appeal to people of faith who have strayed far from the truth. Pertinent parts of this chapter to the American church today are as follows:

○ "The multitude of your sacrifices – what are they to me?" says the Lord. "I have more than enough of burnt offerings of rams and the fat of fattened animals; I have no pleasure in the blood of bulls and labs and goats" (verse 11).

○ "When you come to appear before me, who has asked this of you, this trampling of my courts?" (verse 12).

○ "Stop bringing meaningless offerings? Your incense is detestable to me. New Moons, Sabbaths and convocations—I cannot bear your evil assemblies" (verse 13).

○ "Your new Moon festivals and your appointed feasts my soul hates. 'They have become a burden to me. I am weary of bearing them" (verse 14).

○ "When you spread out your hands in prayer, I will hide my eyes from you; even if you offer many prayers I will not listen" (verse 15).

So far, this is quite an indictment upon God's chosen people, the nation of Israel. What did they do that was so appalling to the Creator that he would tell them that their religious worship and sacrifices are "detestable" and that when they pray he will hide his eyes from them and not listen? The answer is found in the next part of verse 15 where the Lord says to his people,

○ "Your hands are full of blood." (verse 15).

The children of Israel had adopted the practices of the pagans in sacrificing their own children to pagan gods. (12) And the Lord continues in his chastisement by saying,

○ "Wash and make yourselves clean. Take your evil deeds out of my sight! Stop doing wrong, learn to do right. Seek justice, encourage the oppressed. Defend the cause of the fatherless, plead the case of the widow." (verses 16–17).

The Lord then follows with this classic invitation to come to him. However, keep in mind this invitation is not given to nonbelievers; it is an invitation to the people of God.

- ○ "Come now, let us reason together," says the Lord. "Though your sins be as scarlet they shall be as white as snow, though they are read as crimson, they shall be like wool." (verse 18).

The Creator then issues both a promise and a warning:

- ○ "If you are willing and obedient, you will eat the best from the land;. . . but if you resist and rebel, you will be devoured by the sword." For the mouth of the Lord has spoken (verses 1 and 20).

Many actions and inactions of the Christian church, both Catholic and Protestant, have either promoted abortion or looked the other way refusing to address the moral crisis created by the acceptance of abortion. This is detestable in the sight of the Creator who created humanity in his own image and endowed every human being with an unalienable right to life. His words of indictment to the children of Israel so long ago are being spoken again today to the spiritual and church leaders of America.

The denial to some human beings of the unalienable right to life opens up the door for increasing disrespect for life and an erosion of the unalienable right to liberty. With a loss of liberty comes the inability for individuals to exercise their right to the pursuit of happiness. As these self-evident and unalienable rights erode our government will exercise a growing intrusion into our privacy and personal lives until freedom is completely lost.

Where is America today on this slippery slope, which ultimately leads to tyranny and bondage? An objective look at the American nation reveals an increasing erosion of our fundamental Constitutional rights protected by the Bill of Rights as follows:

1. Freedom of speech is being suppressed by a growing culture of political correctness.
2. Freedom of religion is under fire from the government in an effort to coerce people to go against their deeply held religious convictions against abortion and same-sex marriage.
3. The privacy rights of every individual are now subject to government surveillance under the guise of protecting national security.

And the legal protections for these cherished liberties continue to erode the power of our government to deny such rights grows. As such power grows, the rights of individuals continue to decrease, ultimately making the pursuit of happiness impossible. Let us soberly remember, however, that this cultural slide began when America denied to some human beings made in the image of God the unalienable right to life.

Will Americans someday awaken to a nation that is ruled by men without chests? Will the soul of our nation continue to be destroyed as millions of innocent unborn children are denied their God-ordained right to life? The answers to these questions ultimately rest in the hands of the spiritual leaders of our nation.

Every human being is created equal. Every human being has been given by the Creator an unalienable right to life. No government can legitimately deny this to any human being. To do so means impending peril upon a nation.

May God truly bless America. More importantly, however, may America truly bless God by being obedient to his commands and honoring him as the Creator who bestows upon humanity the unalienable right to life. In doing so, the lives of all will once again be protected under the law, respected throughout the culture, and our fundamental liberties will be preserved.

## Moments of Reflection

1. Do you agree that America is headed towards a nation that is ruled by men without chests? Why or why not?
2. C. S. Lewis refers to a future then the abolition of man has occurred. What does this exactly mean? What kind of society would exist if this were to occur?
3. Does the Christian community in America, both Catholic and Protestant, currently have sufficient influence on the culture to change its current direction and restore a respect for the sanctity of life in our nation? If not, what must be accomplished in the American churches to make such a change in the culture?
4. Practically what should each church do to promote the sanctity of life in their communities?

## Endnotes

1. Richard Wurmbrand, *Marx and Satan* (Bartlesville, OK: Living Sacrifice Book Company, 1986), 42.
2. Mary Shelley, *Frankenstein* (New York: Dover Publications, 1994), 32. A replication of the text of the third edition published in 1831 as originally published by Colburn and Bentley (London) for their Standard Novels series.
3. Much can be discovered and read about the transhumanist movement by doing a Google search. Unfortunately only a brief mention of it is made here but the topic is clearly the subject of a separate book.
   Professor of Philosophy Nick Bostrom, Oxford University says this:

   Transhumanism is a loosely defined movement that has developed gradually over the past two decades. It promotes an interdisciplinary approach to understanding and evaluating the opportunities for enhancing the human condition and the human organism opened up by the advancement of technology. Attention is given to both present technologies, like genetic engineering and information technology, and anticipated future ones, such as molecular nanotechnology and artificial intelligence.

The enhancement options being discussed include radical extension of human health-span, eradication of disease, elimination of unnecessary suffering, and augmentation of human intellectual, physical, and emotional capacities. Other transhumanist themes include space colonization and the possibility of creating superintelligent machines, along with other potential developments that could profoundly alter the human condition. The ambit is not limited to gadgets and medicine, but encompasses also economic, social, institutional designs, cultural development, and psychological skills and techniques.

Transhumanists view human nature as a work in progress, a half-baked beginning that we can learn to remold in desirable ways. Current humanity need not be the endpoint of evolution. Transhumanists hope that by responsible use of science, technology, and other rational means we shall eventually manage to become posthuman, beings with vastly greater capacities than present human beings have. (*Ethical Issues for the 21st Century*, ed. Frederick Adams (Philosophical Documentation Center Press, 2003); reprinted in *Review of Contemporary Philosophy*, Vol. 4, May (2005))

4.  Coalition Members." Religious Coalition for Reproductive Choice. http://rcrc.org/homepage/about/coalition-council/

5.  Mark Tooley, Presbyterians Become the Silly Church: A Dying Mainline Church Speeds its Decline," *The American Spectator,* June 21, 2014.
6.  Dietrich Bonhoeffer, *The Cost of Discipleship* (Touchstone, 1995).
7.  A final Gallup poll, reflecting tracking from Nov. 1 to 4, showed Catholics favoring Obama by 52 to 45 percent.
8.  Alan Guttmacher Institute, *Perspectives on Sexual and Reproductive Health* 34, no. 5, (September/October 2002).
9.  Guttmacher Institute, *Perspectives on Sexual and Reproductive Health.*
10. In 2014 the National Institute of Family and Life Advocates (NIFLA) surveyed its members that operate as medical clinics on the effectiveness of ultrasound upon a mother who is considering abortion. Of its one thousand members that are medical using ultrasound, nearly half responded. These respondents reported that approximately 80 percent of pregnant mothers considering abortion who saw an ultrasound image of their unborn child chose to carry their pregnancies to term and give birth.
11. One highly recommended study is *Forgiven and Set Free* by Linda Cochrane, which can be order on Amazon.com
12. The children of Israel had adopted the child sacrifice practices of the pagan cultures around then. Because of this, God tells his people that their religious practices will not be accepted. Scripture prohibitions against the pagan practice of child sacrifice are numerous:
    *   Leviticus 18:21: You shall not give any of your children to offer them to Molech, and so profane the name of your God: I am the Lord.
    *   Deuteronomy 12:31: You shall not worship the Lord your God in that way, for every abominable thing that the Lord hates they have done for their gods, for they even burn their sons and their daughters in the fire to their gods.
    *   Leviticus 20:1–5: The Lord spoke to Moses, saying, "Say to the people of Israel, Any one of the people of

Israel or of the strangers who sojourn in Israel who gives any of his children to Molech shall surely be put to death. The people of the land shall stone him with stones. I myself will set my face against that man and will cut him off from among his people, because he has given one of his children to Molech, to make my sanctuary unclean and to profane my holy name. And if the people of the land do at all close their eyes to that man when he gives one of his children to Molech, and do not put him to death, then I will set my face against that man and against his clan and will cut them off from among their people, him and all who follow him in whoring after Molech.

- Ezekiel 16:20–21: And you took your sons and your daughters, whom you had borne to me, and these you sacrificed to them to be devoured. Were your whorings so small a matter that you slaughtered my children and delivered them up as an offering by fire to them?

- 2 Kings 17:17–18: And they burned their sons and their daughters as offerings and used divination and omens and sold themselves to do evil in the sight of the Lord, provoking him to anger. Therefore the Lord was very angry with Israel and removed them out of his sight. None was left but the tribe of Judah only.

# APPENDIX A

## The Declaration of Independence

*Author's Comments: The Declaration of Independence established the United States of America as a new nation independent from Great Britain. In doing so, it recites the basis upon which this new nation exists—the conviction that human rights come from the Creator and cannot be legitimately deprived to any person by government. It is this foundation upon which all further governing documents (such as the Constitution) are based.*

## IN CONGRESS, July 4, 1776.

**The Unanimous Declaration of the Thirteen United States of America,**

When in the Course of Human Events, it becomes necessary for one people to dissolve the political bands which have connected them with another, and to assume among the powers of the earth, the separate and equal station to which the Laws of Nature and of Nature's God entitle them, a decent respect to the opinions of mankind requires that they should declare the causes which impel them to the separation.

We hold these truths to be self-evident, that all men are created equal, that they are endowed by their Creator with certain unalienable Rights, that among these are Life, Liberty and the pursuit of Happiness.--That to secure these rights, Governments are instituted among Men, deriving their just powers from the consent of the governed, --That whenever any Form of Government becomes destructive of these ends, it is the Right of the People to alter or to abolish it, and to institute new Government, laying its foundation on such principles and organizing its powers in such form, as to them shall seem most likely to affect their Safety and Happiness. Prudence, indeed, will dictate that Governments long established should not be changed for light and transient causes; and accordingly all experience hath shown, that mankind are more disposed to suffer, while evils are sufferable, than to right themselves by abolishing the forms to which they are accustomed. But when a long train of abuses and usurpations, pursuing invariably the same Object evinces a design to reduce them under absolute Despotism, it is their right, it is their duty, to throw off such Government, and to provide new Guards for their future security.--Such has been the patient sufferance of these Colonies; and such is now the necessity which constrains them to alter their former Systems of Government.

The history of the present King of Great Britain is a history of repeated injuries and usurpations, all having in direct object the establishment of an absolute Tyranny over these States. To prove this, let Facts be submitted to a candid world.

> He has refused his Assent to Laws, the most wholesome and necessary for the public good.
> He has forbidden his Governors to pass Laws of immediate and pressing importance, unless suspended in their operation till his Assent should be obtained; and when so suspended, he has utterly neglected to attend to them.
> He has refused to pass other Laws for the accommodation of large districts of people, unless those people would relinquish the right of Representation in the Legislature, a right inestimable to them and formidable to tyrants only.

He has called together legislative bodies at places unusual, uncomfortable, and distant from the depository of their public Records, for the sole purpose of fatiguing them into compliance with his measures.

He has dissolved Representative Houses repeatedly, for opposing with manly firmness his invasions on the rights of the people.

He has refused for a long time, after such dissolutions, to cause others to be elected; whereby the Legislative powers, incapable of Annihilation, have returned to the People at large for their exercise; the State remaining in the meantime exposed to all the dangers of invasion from without, and convulsions within.

He has endeavored to prevent the population of these States; for that purpose obstructing the Laws for Naturalization of Foreigners; refusing to pass others to encourage their migrations hither, and raising the conditions of new Appropriations of Lands.

He has obstructed the Administration of Justice, by refusing his Assent to Laws for establishing Judiciary powers.

He has made Judges dependent on his Will alone, for the tenure of their offices, and the amount and payment of their salaries.

He has erected a multitude of New Offices, and sent hither swarms of Officers to harass our people, and eat out their substance.

He has kept among us, in times of peace, Standing Armies without the Consent of our legislatures.

He has affected to render the Military independent of and superior to the Civil power.

He has combined with others to subject us to a jurisdiction foreign to our constitution, and unacknowledged by our laws; giving his Assent to their Acts of pretended Legislation:

For Quartering large bodies of armed troops among us:

For protecting them, by a mock Trial, from punishment for any Murders which they should commit on the Inhabitants of these States:

For cutting off our Trade with all parts of the world:

For imposing Taxes on us without our Consent:

For depriving us in many cases, of the benefits of Trial by Jury:

For transporting us beyond Seas to be tried for pretended offences

For abolishing the free System of English Laws in a neighboring Province, establishing therein an Arbitrary government, and enlarging its Boundaries so as to render it at once an example and fit instrument for introducing the same absolute rule into these Colonies:

For taking away our Charters, abolishing our most valuable Laws, and altering fundamentally the Forms of our Governments:

For suspending our own Legislatures, and declaring themselves invested with power to legislate for us in all cases whatsoever.

He has abdicated Government here, by declaring us out of his Protection and waging War against us.

He has plundered our seas, ravaged our Coasts, burnt our towns, and destroyed the lives of our people.

He is at this time transporting large Armies of foreign Mercenaries to complete the works of death, desolation and tyranny, already begun with circumstances of Cruelty & perfidy scarcely paralleled in the most barbarous ages, and totally unworthy the Head of a civilized nation.

He has constrained our fellow Citizens taken Captive on the high Seas to bear Arms against their Country, to become the executioners of their friends and Brethren, or to fall themselves by their Hands.

He has excited domestic insurrections amongst us, and has endeavored to bring on the inhabitants of our frontiers, the merciless Indian Savages, whose known rule of warfare, is an undistinguished destruction of all ages, sexes and conditions.

In every stage of these Oppressions We have Petitioned for Redress in the most humble terms: Our repeated Petitions have been answered only by repeated injury. A Prince whose character is thus marked by every act which may define a Tyrant, is unfit to be the ruler of a free people.

Nor have We been wanting in attentions to our British brethren. We have warned them from time to time of attempts by their legislature to extend an unwarrantable jurisdiction over us. We have reminded them of the circumstances of our emigration and settlement here. We have appealed to their native justice and magnanimity, and we have conjured them by the ties of our common kindred to disavow these usurpations, which, would inevitably interrupt our connections and correspondence. They too have been deaf to the voice of justice and of consanguinity. We must, therefore, acquiesce in the necessity, which denounces our Separation, and hold them, as we hold the rest of mankind, Enemies in War, in Peace Friends.

We, therefore, the Representatives of the United States of America, in General Congress, Assembled, appealing to the Supreme Judge of the world for the rectitude of our intentions, do, in the Name, and by Authority of the good People of these Colonies, solemnly publish and declare, That these United Colonies are, and of Right ought to be Free and Independent States; that they are Absolved from all Allegiance to the British Crown, and that all political connection between them and the State of Great Britain, is and ought to be totally dissolved; and that as Free and Independent States, they have full Power to levy War, conclude Peace, contract Alliances, establish Commerce, and to do all other Acts and Things which Independent States may of right do. And for the support of this Declaration, with a firm reliance on the protection of divine Providence, we mutually pledge to each other our Lives, our Fortunes and our sacred Honor.

**Georgia:**
Button Gwinnett
Lyman Hall
George Walton

**North Carolina:**
William Hooper
Joseph Hewes
John Penn

**South Carolina:**
Edward Rutledge
Thomas Heyward, Jr.
Thomas Lynch, Jr.
Arthur Middleton

**Massachusetts:**
John Hancock

**Maryland:**
Samuel Chase
William Paca
Thomas Stone
Charles Carroll of Carrollton

**Virginia:**
George Wythe
Richard Henry Lee
Thomas Jefferson

Benjamin Harrison
Thomas Nelson, Jr.
Francis Lightfoot Lee
Carter Braxton

**Pennsylvania:**
Robert Morris
Benjamin Rush
Benjamin Franklin
John Morton
George Clymer
James Smith
George Taylor
James Wilson
George Ross

**Delaware:**
Caesar Rodney
George Read
Thomas McKean

**New York:**
William Floyd
Philip Livingston
Francis Lewis
Lewis Morris

**New Jersey:**
Richard Stockton
John Witherspoon
Francis Hopkinson
John Hart
Abraham Clark

**New Hampshire:**
Josiah Bartlett
William Whipple

**Massachusetts:**
Samuel Adams
John Adams
Robert Treat Paine
Elbridge Gerry

**Rhode Island:**
Stephen Hopkins
William Ellery

**Connecticut:**
Roger Sherman
Samuel Huntington
William Williams
Oliver Wolcott

**New Hampshire:**
Matthew Thornton

# APPENDIX B

## The Constitution of the United States of America

Author's Comments: *The Constitution of the United States builds upon the principles of the Declaration of Independence and establishes the legal framework under which the unalienable rights of life, liberty, and the pursuit of happiness are to be protected. The Preamble to the Constitution states that it is established to "secure the Blessings of Liberty to ourselves and our Posterity." Posterity is defined in the dictionary as all future descendants of a person, which would clearly include both born and unborn. Such a proclamation is not surprising when it is understood that the right to life set forth in The Declaration of Independence includes those who reside within their mothers' wombs. Correctly interpreted, the Constitution, as a document coming from the foundation of the Declaration of Independence, is protective of the right to life of all human beings, born and unborn.*

**We the People** of the United States, in Order to form a more perfect Union, establish Justice, insure domestic Tranquility, provide for the common defense, promote the general Welfare, and secure the Blessings of Liberty to ourselves and our Posterity, do ordain and establish this Constitution for the United States of America.

# Article. I.

## Section. 1.

All legislative Powers herein granted shall be vested in a Congress of the United States, which shall consist of a Senate and House of Representatives.

## Section. 2.

The House of Representatives shall be composed of Members chosen every second Year by the People of the several States, and the Electors in each State shall have the Qualifications requisite for Electors of the most numerous Branch of the State Legislature.

No Person shall be a Representative who shall not have attained to the Age of twenty five Years, and been seven Years a Citizen of the United States, and who shall not, when elected, be an Inhabitant of that State in which he shall be chosen.

Representatives and direct Taxes shall be apportioned among the several States which may be included within this Union, according to their respective Numbers, which shall be determined by adding to the whole Number of free Persons, including those bound to Service for a Term of Years, and excluding Indians not taxed, three fifths of all other Persons. The actual Enumeration shall be made within three Years after the first Meeting of the Congress of the United States, and within every subsequent Term of ten Years, in such Manner as they shall by Law direct. The Number of Representatives shall not exceed one for every thirty Thousand, but each State shall have at Least one Representative; and until such enumeration shall be made, the State of New Hampshire shall be entitled to choose three, Massachusetts eight, Rhode-Island and Providence Plantations one, Connecticut five, New-York six, New Jersey four, Pennsylvania eight, Delaware one, Maryland six, Virginia ten, North Carolina five, South Carolina five, and Georgia three.

When vacancies happen in the Representation from any State, the Executive Authority thereof shall issue Writs of Election to fill such Vacancies.

The House of Representatives shall chose their Speaker and other Officers; and shall have the sole Power of Impeachment.

## Section. 3.

The Senate of the United States shall be composed of two Senators from each State, chosen by the Legislature thereof for six Years; and each Senator shall have one Vote.

Immediately after they shall be assembled in Consequence of the first Election, they shall be divided as equally as may be into three Classes. The Seats of the Senators of the first Class shall be vacated at the Expiration of the second Year, of the second Class at the Expiration of the fourth Year, and of the third Class at the Expiration of the sixth Year, so that one third may be chosen every second Year; and if Vacancies happen by Resignation, or otherwise, during the Recess of the Legislature of any State, the Executive thereof may make temporary Appointments until the next Meeting of the Legislature, which shall then fill such Vacancies.

No Person shall be a Senator who shall not have attained to the Age of thirty Years, and been nine Years a Citizen of the United States, and who shall not, when elected, be an Inhabitant of that State for which he shall be chosen.

The Vice President of the United States shall be President of the Senate, but shall have no Vote, unless they be equally divided.

The Senate shall chose their other Officers, and also a President pro tempore, in the Absence of the Vice President, or when he shall exercise the Office of President of the United States.

The Senate shall have the sole Power to try all Impeachments. When sitting for that Purpose, they shall be on Oath or Affirmation. When the President of the United States is tried, the Chief Justice shall preside: And no Person shall be convicted without the Concurrence of two thirds of the Members present.

Judgment in Cases of Impeachment shall not extend further than to removal from Office, and disqualification to hold and enjoy any Office of honor, Trust or Profit under the United States: but the Party convicted shall nevertheless be liable and subject to Indictment, Trial, Judgment and Punishment, according to Law.

## Section. 4.

The Times, Places and Manner of holding Elections for Senators and Representatives, shall be prescribed in each State by the Legislature thereof; but the Congress may at any time by Law make or alter such Regulations, except as to the Places of choosing Senators.

The Congress shall assemble at least once in every Year, and such Meeting shall be on the first Monday in December, unless they shall by Law appoint a different Day.

## Section. 5.

Each House shall be the Judge of the Elections, Returns and Qualifications of its own Members, and a Majority of each shall constitute a Quorum to do Business; but a smaller Number may adjourn from day to day, and may be authorized to compel the Attendance of absent Members, in such Manner, and under such Penalties as each House may provide.

Each House may determine the Rules of its Proceedings, punish its Members for disorderly Behavior, and, with the Concurrence of two thirds, expel a Member.

Each House shall keep a Journal of its Proceedings, and from time to time publish the same, excepting such Parts as may in their Judgment require Secrecy; and the Yeas and Nays of the Members of either House on any question shall, at the Desire of one fifth of those Present, be entered on the Journal.

Neither House, during the Session of Congress, shall, without the Consent of the other, adjourn for more than three days, nor to any other Place than that in which the two Houses shall be sitting.

## Section. 6.

The Senators and Representatives shall receive a Compensation for their Services, to be ascertained by Law, and paid out of the Treasury of the United States. They shall in all Cases, except Treason, Felony and Breach of the Peace, be privileged from Arrest during their Attendance at the Session of their respective Houses, and in going to and returning from the same; and for any Speech or Debate in either House, they shall not be questioned in any other Place.

No Senator or Representative shall, during the Time for which he was elected, be appointed to any civil Office under the Authority of the United States, which shall have been created, or the Emoluments whereof shall have been increased during such time; and no Person holding any Office under the United States, shall be a Member of either House during his Continuance in Office.

## Section. 7.

All Bills for raising Revenue shall originate in the House of Representatives; but the Senate may propose or concur with Amendments as on other Bills.

Every Bill which shall have passed the House of Representatives and the Senate, shall, before it become a Law, be presented to the President of the United States: If he approve he shall sign it, but if not he shall return it, with his Objections to that House in which it shall have originated, who shall enter the Objections at large on their Journal, and proceed to reconsider it. If after such Reconsideration two thirds of that House shall agree to pass the Bill, it shall be sent, together with the Objections, to the other House, by which it shall likewise be reconsidered, and if approved by two thirds of that House, it shall become a Law. But in all such Cases the Votes of both Houses shall be determined by yeas and Nays, and the Names of the Persons voting for and against the Bill shall be entered on the Journal of each House respectively. If any Bill shall not be returned by the President within ten Days (Sundays excepted) after it shall have been presented to him, the Same shall be a Law, in like Manner as if he had signed it, unless the Congress by their Adjournment prevent its Return, in which Case it shall not be a Law.

Every Order, Resolution, or Vote to which the Concurrence of the Senate and House of Representatives may be necessary (except on a question of Adjournment) shall be presented to the President of the United States; and before the Same shall take Effect, shall be approved by him, or being disapproved by him, shall be repassed by two thirds of the Senate and House of Representatives, according to the Rules and Limitations prescribed in the Case of a Bill.

## Section. 8.

The Congress shall have Power To lay and collect Taxes, Duties, Imposts and Excises, to pay the Debts and provide for the common

Defense and general Welfare of the United States; but all Duties, Imposts and Excises shall be uniform throughout the United States;

To borrow Money on the credit of the United States;

To regulate Commerce with foreign Nations, and among the several States, and with the Indian Tribes;

To establish an uniform Rule of Naturalization, and uniform Laws on the subject of Bankruptcies throughout the United States;

To coin Money, regulate the Value thereof, and of foreign Coin, and fix the Standard of Weights and Measures;

To provide for the Punishment of counterfeiting the Securities and current Coin of the United States;

To establish Post Offices and post Roads;

To promote the Progress of Science and useful Arts, by securing for limited Times to Authors and Inventors the exclusive Right to their respective Writings and Discoveries;

To constitute Tribunals inferior to the supreme Court;

To define and punish Piracies and Felonies committed on the high Seas, and Offences against the Law of Nations;

To declare War, grant Letters of Marque and Reprisal, and make Rules concerning Captures on Land and Water;

To raise and support Armies, but no Appropriation of Money to that Use shall be for a longer Term than two Years;

To provide and maintain a Navy;

To make Rules for the Government and Regulation of the land and naval Forces;

To provide for calling forth the Militia to execute the Laws of the Union, suppress Insurrections and repel Invasions;

To provide for organizing, arming, and disciplining, the Militia, and for governing such Part of them as may be employed in the Service of the United States, reserving to the States respectively, the Appointment of the Officers, and the Authority of training the Militia according to the discipline prescribed by Congress;

To exercise exclusive Legislation in all Cases whatsoever, over such District (not exceeding ten Miles square) as may, by Cession of particular States, and the Acceptance of Congress, become the Seat of the Government of the United States, and to exercise like Authority over all Places purchased by the Consent of the Legislature of the State in which the Same shall be, for the Erection of Forts, Magazines, Arsenals, dock-Yards, and other needful Buildings;--And

To make all Laws which shall be necessary and proper for carrying into Execution the foregoing Powers, and all other Powers vested by this Constitution in the Government of the United States, or in any Department or Officer thereof.

## Section. 9.

The Migration or Importation of such Persons as any of the States now existing shall think proper to admit, shall not be prohibited by the Congress prior to the Year one thousand eight hundred and eight, but a Tax or duty may be imposed on such Importation, not exceeding ten dollars for each Person.

The Privilege of the Writ of Habeas Corpus shall not be suspended, unless when in Cases of Rebellion or Invasion the public Safety may require it.

No Bill of Attainder or ex post facto Law shall be passed.

No Capitation, or other direct, Tax shall be laid, unless in Proportion to the Census or enumeration herein before directed to be taken.

No Tax or Duty shall be laid on Articles exported from any State.

No Preference shall be given by any Regulation of Commerce or Revenue to the Ports of one State over those of another; nor shall Vessels bound to, or from, one State, be obliged to enter, clear, or pay Duties in another.

No Money shall be drawn from the Treasury, but in Consequence of Appropriations made by Law; and a regular Statement and Account of the Receipts and Expenditures of all public Money shall be published from time to time.

No Title of Nobility shall be granted by the United States: And no Person holding any Office of Profit or Trust under them, shall, without the Consent of the Congress, accept of any present, Emolument, Office, or Title, of any kind whatever, from any King, Prince, or foreign State.

**Section. 10.**

No State shall enter into any Treaty, Alliance, or Confederation; grant Letters of Marque and Reprisal; coin Money; emit Bills of Credit; make any Thing but gold and silver Coin a Tender in Payment of Debts; pass any Bill of Attainder, ex post facto Law, or Law impairing the Obligation of Contracts, or grant any Title of Nobility.

No State shall, without the Consent of the Congress, lay any Imposts or Duties on Imports or Exports, except what may be absolutely necessary for executing it's inspection Laws: and the net Produce of all Duties and Imposts, laid by any State on Imports or Exports, shall be for the Use of the Treasury of the United States; and all such Laws shall be subject to the Revision and Control of the Congress.

No State shall, without the Consent of Congress, lay any Duty of Tonnage, keep Troops, or Ships of War in time of Peace, enter into any Agreement or Compact with another State, or with a foreign Power, or engage in War, unless actually invaded, or in such imminent Danger as will not admit of delay.

# Article. II.

**Section. 1.**

The executive Power shall be vested in a President of the United States of America. He shall hold his Office during the Term of four Years, and, together with the Vice President, chosen for the same Term, be elected, as follows:

Each State shall appoint, in such Manner as the Legislature thereof may direct, a Number of Electors, equal to the whole Number of Senators and Representatives to which the State may be entitled in the Congress: but no Senator or Representative, or Person holding an Office of Trust or Profit under the United States, shall be appointed an Elector.

The Electors shall meet in their respective States, and vote by Ballot for two Persons, of whom one at least shall not be an Inhabitant of the same State with themselves. And they shall make a List of all the Persons voted for, and of the Number of Votes for each; which List they shall sign and certify, and transmit sealed to the Seat of the Government of the United States, directed to the President of the Senate. The President of the Senate shall, in the Presence of the Senate and House of Representatives, open all the Certificates, and the Votes shall then be counted. The Person having the greatest Number of Votes shall be the President, if such Number be a Majority of the whole Number of Electors appointed; and if there be more than one who have such Majority, and have an equal Number of Votes, then the House of Representatives shall immediately chose by Ballot one of them for President; and if no Person have a Majority, then from the five highest on the List the said House shall in like Manner choose the President. But in choosing the President, the Votes shall be taken by States, the Representation from each State having one Vote; A quorum for this purpose shall consist of a Member or Members from two thirds of the States, and a Majority of all the States shall be necessary to a Choice. In every Case, after the Choice of the President, the Person having the greatest Number of Votes of the Electors shall be the Vice President. But if there should remain two or more who have equal Votes, the Senate shall chose from them by Ballot the Vice President.

The Congress may determine the Time of choosing the Electors, and the Day on which they shall give their Votes; which Day shall be the same throughout the United States.

No Person except a natural born Citizen, or a Citizen of the United States, at the time of the Adoption of this Constitution, shall be eligible to the Office of President; neither shall any Person be eligible to that Office who shall not have attained to the Age of thirty five Years, and been fourteen Years a Resident within the United States.

In Case of the Removal of the President from Office, or of his Death, Resignation, or Inability to discharge the Powers and Duties of the said Office, the Same shall devolve on the Vice President, and the Congress may by Law provide for the Case of Removal, Death, Resignation or Inability, both of the President and Vice President, declaring what Officer shall then act as President, and such Officer shall act accordingly, until the Disability be removed, or a President shall be elected.

The President shall, at stated Times, receive for his Services, a Compensation, which shall neither be increased nor diminished during the Period for which he shall have been elected, and he shall not receive within that Period any other Emolument from the United States, or any of them.

Before he enter on the Execution of his Office, he shall take the following Oath or Affirmation:--"I do solemnly swear (or affirm) that I will faithfully execute the Office of President of the United States, and will to the best of my Ability, preserve, protect and defend the Constitution of the United States."

## Section. 2.

The President shall be Commander in Chief of the Army and Navy of the United States, and of the Militia of the several States, when called into the actual Service of the United States; he may require the Opinion, in writing, of the principal Officer in each of the executive Departments, upon any Subject relating to the Duties of their respective Offices, and he shall have Power to grant Reprieves and Pardons for Offences against the United States, except in Cases of Impeachment.

He shall have Power, by and with the Advice and Consent of the Senate, to make Treaties, provided two thirds of the Senators present concur; and he shall nominate, and by and with the Advice and Consent of the Senate, shall appoint Ambassadors, other public Ministers and Consuls, Judges of the supreme Court, and all other Officers of the United States, whose Appointments are not herein otherwise provided for, and which shall be established by Law: but the Congress may by Law vest the Appointment of such inferior Officers, as they think proper, in the President alone, in the Courts of Law, or in the Heads of Departments.

The President shall have Power to fill up all Vacancies that may happen during the Recess of the Senate, by granting Commissions which shall expire at the End of their next Session.

## Section. 3.

He shall from time to time give to the Congress Information of the State of the Union, and recommend to their Consideration such Measures as he shall judge necessary and expedient; he may, on extraordinary Occasions, convene both Houses, or either of them, and in Case of Disagreement between them, with Respect to the Time of Adjournment, he may adjourn them to such Time as he shall think proper; he shall receive Ambassadors and other public Ministers; he shall take Care that the Laws be faithfully executed, and shall Commission all the Officers of the United States.

## Section. 4.

The President, Vice President and all civil Officers of the United States, shall be removed from Office on Impeachment for, and Conviction of, Treason, Bribery, or other high Crimes and Misdemeanors.

# Article III.

## Section. 1.

The judicial Power of the United States shall be vested in one supreme Court, and in such inferior Courts as the Congress may from time to time ordain and establish. The Judges, both of the supreme and inferior Courts, shall hold their Offices during good Behavior, and shall, at stated Times, receive for their Services a Compensation, which shall not be diminished during their Continuance in Office.

## Section. 2.

The judicial Power shall extend to all Cases, in Law and Equity, arising under this Constitution, the Laws of the United States, and Treaties made, or which shall be made, under their Authority;--to all Cases affecting Ambassadors, other public Ministers and Consuls;--to all Cases of admiralty and maritime Jurisdiction;--to Controversies to which the United States shall be a Party;--to Controversies between two or more States;-- between a State and Citizens of another State,--between Citizens of different States,--between Citizens of the same State claiming Lands under Grants of different States, and between a State, or the Citizens thereof, and foreign States, Citizens or Subjects.

In all Cases affecting Ambassadors, other public Ministers and Consuls, and those in which a State shall be Party, the supreme Court shall have original Jurisdiction. In all the other Cases before mentioned, the supreme Court shall have appellate Jurisdiction, both as to Law and Fact, with such Exceptions, and under such Regulations as the Congress shall make.

The Trial of all Crimes, except in Cases of Impeachment, shall be by Jury; and such Trial shall be held in the State where the said Crimes shall have been committed; but when not committed within any State, the Trial shall be at such Place or Places as the Congress may by Law have directed.

## Section. 3.

Treason against the United States, shall consist only in levying War against them, or in adhering to their Enemies, giving them Aid and Comfort. No Person shall be convicted of Treason unless on the Testimony of two Witnesses to the same overt Act, or on Confession in open Court.

The Congress shall have Power to declare the Punishment of Treason, but no Attainder of Treason shall work Corruption of Blood, or Forfeiture except during the Life of the Person attainted.

# Article. IV.

## Section. 1.

Full Faith and Credit shall be given in each State to the public Acts, Records, and judicial Proceedings of every other State. And the Congress may by general Laws prescribe the Manner in which such Acts, Records and Proceedings shall be proved, and the Effect thereof.

## Section. 2.

The Citizens of each State shall be entitled to all Privileges and Immunities of Citizens in the several States.

A Person charged in any State with Treason, Felony, or other Crime, who shall flee from Justice, and be found in another State, shall on Demand of the executive Authority of the State from which he fled, be delivered up, to be removed to the State having Jurisdiction of the Crime.

No Person held to Service or Labor in one State, under the Laws thereof, escaping into another, shall, in Consequence of any Law or Regulation therein, be discharged from such Service or Labor, but shall be delivered up on Claim of the Party to whom such Service or Labor may be due.

**Section. 3.**

New States may be admitted by the Congress into this Union; but no new State shall be formed or erected within the Jurisdiction of any other State; nor any State be formed by the Junction of two or more States, or Parts of States, without the Consent of the Legislatures of the States concerned as well as of the Congress.

The Congress shall have Power to dispose of and make all needful Rules and Regulations respecting the Territory or other Property belonging to the United States; and nothing in this Constitution shall be so construed as to Prejudice any Claims of the United States, or of any particular State.

**Section. 4.**

The United States shall guarantee to every State in this Union a Republican Form of Government, and shall protect each of them against Invasion; and on Application of the Legislature, or of the Executive (when the Legislature cannot be convened), against domestic Violence.

# Article. V.

The Congress, whenever two thirds of both Houses shall deem it necessary, shall propose Amendments to this Constitution, or, on the Application of the Legislatures of two thirds of the several States, shall call a Convention for proposing Amendments, which, in either Case, shall be valid to all Intents and Purposes, as Part of this Constitution, when ratified by the Legislatures of three fourths of the several States, or by Conventions in three fourths thereof, as the one or the other Mode of Ratification may be proposed by the Congress; Provided that no Amendment which may be made prior to the Year One thousand eight hundred and eight shall in any Manner affect the first and fourth Clauses in the Ninth Section of the first Article; and that no State, without its Consent, shall be deprived of its equal Suffrage in the Senate.

# Article. VI.

All Debts contracted and Engagements entered into, before the Adoption of this Constitution, shall be as valid against the United States under this Constitution, as under the Confederation.

This Constitution, and the Laws of the United States which shall be made in Pursuance thereof; and all Treaties made, or which shall be made, under the Authority of the United States, shall be the supreme Law of the Land; and the Judges in every State shall be bound thereby, any Thing in the Constitution or Laws of any State to the Contrary notwithstanding.

The Senators and Representatives before mentioned, and the Members of the several State Legislatures, and all executive and judicial Officers, both of the United States and of the several States, shall be bound by Oath or Affirmation, to support this Constitution; but no religious Test shall ever be required as a Qualification to any Office or public Trust under the United States.

# Article. VII.

The Ratification of the Conventions of nine States, shall be sufficient for the Establishment of this Constitution between the States so ratifying the Same.

Attest William Jackson Secretary

Done in Convention by the Unanimous Consent of the States present the Seventeenth Day of September in the Year of our Lord one thousand seven hundred and eighty seven.

In witness whereof We have hereunto subscribed our Names,
G. Washington *President and Deputy from Virginia*

### Delaware
Geo: Read
Gunning Bedford jun
John Dickinson
Richard Bassett
Jacob Broom

### Maryland
Jame McHenry
Dan of St Thos. Jenifer
Danl. Carroll

### Virginia
John Blair
James Madison Jr.

### North Carolina
Wm. Blount
Richard Dobbs Spaight
Hu Williamson

### South Carolina
J. Rutledge
Charles Cotesworth Pinckney
Charles Pinckney
Pierce Butler

### Georgia
William Few
Abr Baldwin

### New Hampshire
John Langdon
Nicholas Gilman

**Massachusetts**
Nathaniel Gorham
Rufus King

**Connecticut**
Wm. Samuel. Johnson
Roger Sherman

**New York**
Alexander Hamilton

**New Jersey**
Will Livingston
David Brearley
Wm. Paterson
Jonas Dayton

**Pennsylvania**
B Franklin
Thomas Mifflin
Robt. Morris
Geo. Clymer
Thos. FitzSimons
Jared Ingersoll
James Wilson
Gouv Morris

# APPENDIX C

## The Bill of Rights

Author's Comments: *The first ten Amendments to the U.S. Constitution are more commonly referred to as the Bill of Rights. They establish protection to individuals against an overreaching federal government. The Framers of the Constitution were initially divided on the need for a Bill of Rights. Those opposed simply said that because the Constitution only gives to the central federal government specific enumerated powers this new government cannot exercise such powers to the detriment of individuals unless specifically authorized by Constitution to do so. Thus, they argued that a separate Bill of Rights was not necessary.*

*On the other hand, those arguing for a Bill of Rights spelling out specific individual rights persuasively argued that the liberty of individuals, as spelled out in the Declaration of Independence, must be absolutely protected against a central federal government. Without such specifically defined limitations a centralized federal government could eventually encroach upon individual liberty. Hence, they argued that a Bill of Rights which clearly specified protections for the exercise of rights such as the freedom of religion, the freedom of speech, the freedom of association and the right to be free from unreasonable searches and seizures must be adopted to ensure that in the future the federal government will not deny to some the unalienable rights of life, liberty, and the pursuit of happiness. Clearly, the adoption of the Bill of Rights was the provision of constitutional protections of these unalienable rights set forth in the Declaration of Independence.*

## The Preamble to The Bill of Rights

Congress of the United States begun and held at the City of New-York, on Wednesday the fourth of March, one thousand seven hundred and eighty nine.

**THE** Conventions of a number of the States, having at the time of their adopting the Constitution, expressed a desire, in order to prevent misconstruction or abuse of its powers, that further declaratory and restrictive clauses should be added: And as extending the ground of public confidence in the Government, will best ensure the beneficent ends of its institution.

**RESOLVED** by the Senate and House of Representatives of the United States of America, in Congress assembled, two thirds of both Houses concurring, that the following Articles be proposed to the Legislatures of the several States, as amendments to the Constitution of the United States, all, or any of which Articles, when ratified by three fourths of the said Legislatures, to be valid to all intents and purposes, as part of the said Constitution; viz.

**ARTICLES** in addition to, and Amendment of the Constitution of the United States of America, proposed by Congress, and ratified by the Legislatures of the several States, pursuant to the fifth Article of the original Constitution.

### Amendment I
Congress shall make no law respecting an establishment of religion, or prohibiting the free exercise thereof; or abridging the freedom of speech, or of the press; or the right of the people peaceably to assemble, and to petition the Government for a redress of grievances.

### Amendment II
A well-regulated Militia, being necessary to the security of a free State, the right of the people to keep and bear Arms, shall not be infringed.

## Amendment III

No Soldier shall, in time of peace be quartered in any house, without the consent of the Owner, nor in time of war, but in a manner to be prescribed by law.

## Amendment IV

The right of the people to be secure in their persons, houses, papers, and effects, against unreasonable searches and seizures, shall not be violated, and no Warrants shall issue, but upon probable cause, supported by Oath or affirmation, and particularly describing the place to be searched, and the persons or things to be seized.

## Amendment V

No person shall be held to answer for a capital, or otherwise infamous crime, unless on a presentment or indictment of a Grand Jury, except in cases arising in the land or naval forces, or in the Militia, when in actual service in time of War or public danger; nor shall any person be subject for the same offence to be twice put in jeopardy of life or limb; nor shall be compelled in any criminal case to be a witness against himself, nor be deprived of life, liberty, or property, without due process of law; nor shall private property be taken for public use, without just compensation.

## Amendment VI

In all criminal prosecutions, the accused shall enjoy the right to a speedy and public trial, by an impartial jury of the State and district wherein the crime shall have been committed, which district shall have been previously ascertained by law, and to be informed of the nature and cause of the accusation; to be confronted with the witnesses against him; to have compulsory process for obtaining witnesses in his favor, and to have the Assistance of Counsel for his defense.

## Amendment VII

In Suits at common law, where the value in controversy shall exceed twenty dollars, the right of trial by jury shall be preserved, and no fact tried by a jury, shall be otherwise re-examined in any Court of the United States, than according to the rules of the common law.

**Amendment VIII**

Excessive bail shall not be required, nor excessive fines imposed, nor cruel and unusual punishments inflicted.

**Amendment IX**

The enumeration in the Constitution, of certain rights, shall not be construed to deny or disparage others retained by the people.

**Amendment X**

The powers not delegated to the United States by the Constitution, nor prohibited by it to the States, are reserved to the States respectively, or to the people.

# APPENDIX D

## President Abraham Lincoln:
## A Presidential Proclamation Appointing a Day of National Humiliation, Fasting, and Prayer
### March 30, 1863

*Author's Comments:* *The acceptance of the institution of slavery brought about a tragic war where hundreds of thousands lost their lives. The nation was divided in an unprecedented manner. Such a situation caused President Abraham Lincoln to deeply reflect upon the causes of this war and to turn to God to intercede for an end to the bloody conflict. This remarkable presidential proclamation sets forth a statement of humility and repentance for the nation in order to receive once again the blessings of God.*

Whereas the Senate of the United States, devoutly recognizing the supreme authority and just government of Almighty God in all the affairs of men and of nations, has by a resolution requested the President to designate and set apart a day for national prayer and humiliation; and

Whereas it is the duty of nations as well as of men to own their dependence upon the overruling power of God, to confess their sins and transgressions in humble sorrow, yet with assured hope that genuine repentance will lead to mercy and pardon, and to recognize the sublime truth, announced in the Holy Scriptures and proven by all history, that those nations only are blessed whose God is the Lord;

And, insomuch as we know that by His divine law nations, like individuals, are subjected to punishments and chastisements in this world, may we not justly fear that the awful calamity of civil war which now desolates the land may be but a punishment inflicted upon us for our presumptuous sins, to the needful end of our national reformation as a whole people? We have been the recipients of the choicest bounties of Heaven; we have been preserved these many years in peace and prosperity; we have grown in numbers, wealth, and power as no other nation has ever grown. But we have forgotten God. We have forgotten the gracious hand which preserved us in peace and multiplied and enriched and strengthened us, and we have vainly imagined, in the deceitfulness of our hearts, that all these blessings were produced by some superior wisdom and virtue of our own. Intoxicated with unbroken success, we have become too self-sufficient to feel the necessity of redeeming and preserving grace, too proud to pray to the God that made us.

It behooves us, then, to humble ourselves before the offended Power, to confess our national sins, and to pray for clemency and forgiveness.

Now, therefore, in compliance with the request, and fully concurring in the views of the Senate, I do by this my proclamation designate and set apart Thursday, the 30th day of April, 1863, as a day of national humiliation, fasting, and prayer. And I do hereby request all the people to abstain on that day from their ordinary secular pursuits, and to unite at their several places of public worship and their respective homes in keeping the day holy to the Lord and devoted to the humble discharge of the religious duties proper to that solemn occasion.

All this being done in sincerity and truth, let us then rest humbly in the hope authorized by the divine teachings that the united cry of the nation will be heard on high and answered with blessings no less than the pardon of our national sins and the restoration of our now divided and suffering country to its former happy condition of unity and peace. In witness whereof I have hereunto set my hand and caused the seal of the United States to be affixed.

Done at the city of Washington, this 30th day of March, A. D. 1863, and of the Independence of the United States the eighty-seventh.

ABRAHAM LINCOLN.

# APPENDIX E

## Second Inaugural Address
## Abraham Lincoln
### March 4, 1865

Author's Comments: *President Lincoln understood the serious price that America paid for its denial of life, liberty and the pursuit of happiness to black human beings held in the bondage of slavery. His second inaugural address acknowledges that such disregard of the humanity of others by the institution of slavery brought forth the judgment of God as predicted by Thomas Jefferson.*

*Fellow-Countrymen:*

At this second appearing to take the oath of the Presidential office there is less occasion for an extended address than there was at the first. Then a statement somewhat in detail of a course to be pursued seemed fitting and proper. Now, at the expiration of four years, during which public declarations have been constantly called forth on every point and phase of the great contest which still absorbs the attention and engrosses the energies of the nation, little that is new could be presented. The progress of our arms, upon which all else chiefly depends, is as well known to the public as to myself, and it is, I trust, reasonably satisfactory and encouraging to all. With high hope for the future, no prediction in regard to it is ventured.

On the occasion corresponding to this four years ago all thoughts were anxiously directed to an impending civil war. All dreaded it, all sought to avert it. While the inaugural address was being delivered from this place, devoted altogether to saving the Union without war, insurgent agents were in the city seeking to destroy it without war— seeking to dissolve the Union and divide effects by negotiation. Both parties deprecated war, but one of them would make war rather than let the nation survive, and the other would accept war rather than let it perish, and the war came.

One-eighth of the whole population were colored slaves, not distributed generally over the Union, but localized in the southern part of it. These slaves constituted a peculiar and powerful interest. All knew that this interest was somehow the cause of the war. To strengthen, perpetuate, and extend this interest was the object for which the insurgents would rend the Union even by war, while the Government claimed no right to do more than to restrict the territorial enlargement of it. Neither party expected for the war the magnitude or the duration which it has already attained. Neither anticipated that the *cause* of the conflict might cease with or even before the conflict itself should cease. Each looked for an easier triumph, and a result less fundamental and astounding.

Both read the same Bible and pray to the same God, and each invokes His aid against the other. It may seem strange that any men should dare to ask a just God's assistance in wringing their bread from the sweat of other men's faces, but let us judge not, that we be not judged. The prayers of both could not be answered. That of neither has been answered fully. The Almighty has His own purposes. "Woe unto the world because of offenses; for it must needs be that offenses come, but woe to that man by whom the offense cometh." If we shall suppose that American slavery is one of those offenses which, in the providence of God, must needs come, but which, having continued through His appointed time, He now wills to remove, and that He gives to both North and South this terrible war as the woe due to those by whom the offense came, shall we discern therein any departure from those divine attributes which the believers in a living God always ascribe to Him?

Fondly do we hope, fervently do we pray, that this mighty scourge of war may speedily pass away. Yet, if God wills that it continue until all the wealth piled by the bondsman's two hundred and fifty years of unrequited toil shall be sunk, and until every drop of blood drawn with the lash shall be paid by another drawn with the sword, as was said three thousand years ago, so still it must be said "the judgments of the Lord are true and righteous altogether."

With malice toward none, with charity for all, with firmness in the right as God gives us to see the right, let us strive on to finish the work we are in, to bind up the nation's wounds, to care for him who shall have borne the battle and for his widow and his orphan, to do all which may achieve and cherish a just and lasting peace among ourselves and with all nations.

# APPENDIX F

## The Civil War Amendments: The Thirteenth, Fourteenth, and Fifteenth Amendments to the United States Constitution

Author's Comments: *With the end of the Civil War came the legal constitutional amendments that abolished slavery, established equal protection for all Americans, and established the right to vote for former black slaves. The passage of these amendments was clearly necessary to establish within the Constitutional framework of our nation the unalienable rights of life, liberty, and the pursuit of happiness for all Americans. Query: Legally what must be done today to establish such unalienable rights for those to whom such rights are currently being denied?*

### AMENDMENT XIII
*Passed by Congress January 31, 1865. Ratified December 6, 1865.*

**Note**: A portion of Article IV, section 2, of the Constitution was superseded by the 13th amendment.

### Section 1.
Neither slavery nor involuntary servitude, except as a punishment for crime whereof the party shall have been duly convicted, shall exist within the United States, or any place subject to their jurisdiction.

## Section 2.

Congress shall have power to enforce this article by appropriate legislation.

# AMENDMENT XIV

*Passed by Congress June 13, 1866. Ratified July 9, 1868.*

**Note**: Article I, section 2, of the Constitution was modified by section 2 of the 14th amendment.

## Section 1.

All persons born or naturalized in the United States, and subject to the jurisdiction thereof, are citizens of the United States and of the State wherein they reside. No State shall make or enforce any law which shall abridge the privileges or immunities of citizens of the United States; nor shall any State deprive any person of life, liberty, or property, without due process of law; nor deny to any person within its jurisdiction the equal protection of the laws.

## Section 2.

Representatives shall be apportioned among the several States according to their respective numbers, counting the whole number of persons in each State, excluding Indians not taxed. But when the right to vote at any election for the choice of electors for President and Vice-President of the United States, Representatives in Congress, the Executive and Judicial officers of a State, or the members of the Legislature thereof, is denied to any of the male inhabitants of such State, being twenty-one years of age,* and citizens of the United States, or in any way abridged, except for participation in rebellion, or other crime, the basis of representation therein shall be reduced in the proportion which the number of such male citizens shall bear to the whole number of male citizens twenty-one years of age in such State.

## Section 3.

No person shall be a Senator or Representative in Congress, or elector of President and Vice-President, or hold any office, civil or military, under the United States, or under any State, who, having previously taken an oath, as a member of Congress, or as an officer of the United States, or as a member of any State legislature, or as an executive or judicial officer of any State, to support the Constitution of the United States, shall have engaged in insurrection or rebellion against the same, or given aid or comfort to the enemies thereof. But Congress may by a vote of two-thirds of each House, remove such disability.

**Section 4.**

The validity of the public debt of the United States, authorized by law, including debts incurred for payment of pensions and bounties for services in suppressing insurrection or rebellion, shall not be questioned. But neither the United States nor any State shall assume or pay any debt or obligation incurred in aid of insurrection or rebellion against the United States, or any claim for the loss or emancipation of any slave; but all such debts, obligations and claims shall be held illegal and void.

**Section 5.**

The Congress shall have the power to enforce, by appropriate legislation, the provisions of this article.

*Changed by section 1 of the 26th amendment.*

# AMENDMENT XV

*Passed by Congress February 26, 1869. Ratified February 3, 1870.*

**Section 1.**

The right of citizens of the United States to vote shall not be denied or abridged by the United States or by any State on account of race, color, or previous condition of servitude--

**Section 2.**

The Congress shall have the power to enforce this article by appropriate legislation.

# APPENDIX G

## Roe v. Wade, 410 U.S. 113 (1973)
### (Edited)

Author's Comments: *In* Roe v. Wade *the United States Supreme Court voided the antiabortion laws in all fifty states. In doing so, the Court stated that a general right of privacy exists in the Constitution that is broad enough to encompass a woman's decision whether or not to terminate her pregnancy through abortion. While no specific provision of the Constitution mentions such a right, the Supreme Court stated that this right is inferred from the language of other provisions of the Constitution.*

*Of course, individual privacy should be honored and protected and specific rights of privacy are honored in specific provisions of the Constitution such as the prohibition in the Fourth Amendment of unreasonable searches and seizures by law enforcement. However, a general unspecified right of privacy is not mentioned in the Constitution. By proclaiming that it exists regardless of the clear text of the Constitution, the Supreme Court made itself the final judge on what acts of individuals are protected by this right of privacy and what matters are not. In his dissenting opinion (quoted in full below) Justice Byron White declares this usurpation of power by the Court as an exercise of "raw judicial power."*

*Such a situation creates a clear constitutional crisis. As a constitutional republic, our nation is guided by laws adopted by our officials after vigorous open political debate. If such representatives pass laws with which the people disagree, then such officials may be removed and replaced through the political process and new representatives may pass legislation to repeal and/or modify the laws objected to by the public. This is the democratic process. However, how can such actions be taken by the public if the body that decides such laws is made up of unelected judges, such as the justices of the Supreme Court, who serve for life? The role of the judiciary is to interpret the law according to the Constitution—not to invent new laws that fit into the political preferences of the individual judges. The use of an unspecified right of privacy is a tool to allow the judiciary to do this and the ability of the people to remove federal judges for such a misuse of power is virtually nonexistent.*

*The following are excerpts from the* Roe *opinion:*

**BLACKMUN, J., delivered the opinion of the Court, in which BURGER, C. J., and DOUGLAS, BRENNAN, STEWART, MARSHALL, and POWELL, JJ. joined. BURGER, C. J., DOUGLAS, J., and STEWART, J., filed concurring opinions. WHITE, J., filed a dissenting opinion, in which REHNQUIST, J., joined.**

We forthwith acknowledge our awareness of the sensitive and emotional nature of the abortion controversy, of the vigorous opposing views, even among physicians, and of the deep and seemingly absolute convictions that the subject inspires. One's philosophy, one's experiences, one's exposure to the raw edges of human existence, one's religious training, one's attitudes toward life and family and their values, and the moral standards one establishes and seeks to observe, are all likely to influence and to color one's thinking and conclusions about abortion.

In addition, population growth, pollution, poverty, and racial overtones tend to complicate and not to simplify the problem.

Our task, of course, is to resolve the issue by constitutional measurement, free of emotion and of predilection. We seek earnestly to do this, and, because we do, we [410 U.S. 113, 117] have inquired into, and in this opinion place some emphasis upon, medical and medical-legal history and what that history reveals about man's attitudes toward the abortion procedure over the centuries. We bear in mind, too, Mr. Justice Holmes' admonition in his now-vindicated dissent in *Lochner v. New York*, 198 U.S. 45, 76 (1905):

"[The Constitution] is made for people of fundamentally differing views, and the accident of our finding certain opinions natural and familiar or novel and even shocking ought not to conclude our judgment upon the question whether statutes embodying them conflict with the Constitution of the United States."

The principal thrust of appellant's attack on the Texas statutes is that they improperly invade a right, said to be possessed by the pregnant woman, to choose to terminate her pregnancy. Appellant would discover this right in the concept of personal "liberty" embodied in the Fourteenth Amendment's Due Process Clause; or in personal, marital, familial, and sexual privacy said to be protected by the Bill of Rights or its penumbras, see *Griswold v. Connecticut*, 381 U.S. 479 (1965); *Eisenstadt v. Baird*, 405 U.S. 438 (1972); id., at 460 (WHITE, J., concurring in result); or among those rights reserved to the people by the Ninth Amendment, *Griswold v. Connecticut*, 381 U.S., at 486 (Goldberg, J., concurring).

The Constitution does not explicitly mention any right of privacy. In a line of decisions, however, going back perhaps as far as *Union Pacific R. Co. v. Botsford*, 141 U.S. 250, 251 (1891), the Court has recognized that a right of personal privacy, or a guarantee of certain areas or zones of privacy, does exist under the Constitution. In varying contexts, the Court or individual Justices have, indeed, found at least the roots of that right in the First Amendment, *Stanley v. Georgia*, 394 U.S. 557, 564 (1969); in the Fourth and Fifth Amendments, *Terry v. Ohio*, 392 U.S. 1, 8–9 (1968), *Katz v. United States*, 389 U.S. 347, 350 (1967), *Boyd v. United States*, 116 U.S. 616 (1886), see *Olmstead v. United States*, 277 U.S. 438, 478 (1928) (Brandeis, J., dissenting); in the penumbras of the Bill of Rights, *Griswold v. Connecticut*, 381 U.S., at 484–485; in the Ninth Amendment, id., at 486 (Goldberg, J., concurring); or in the concept of liberty guaranteed by the first section of the Fourteenth Amendment, see *Meyer v. Nebraska*, 262 U.S. 390, 399 (1923). These decisions make it clear that only personal rights that can be deemed "fundamental" or "implicit in the concept of ordered liberty," *Palko v. Connecticut*, 302 U.S. 319, 325 (1937), are included in this guarantee of personal privacy. They also make it clear that the right has some extension to activities relating to marriage, *Loving v. Virginia*, 388 U.S. 1, 12 (1967); procreation,

*Skinner v. Oklahoma*, 316 U.S. 535, 541–542 (1942); contraception, *Eisenstadt v. Baird*, 405 U.S., at 453–454; id., at 460, 463–465 [410 U.S. 113, 153] (WHITE, J., concurring in result); family relationships, *Prince v. Massachusetts*, 321 U.S. 158, 166 (1944); and child rearing and education, *Pierce v. Society of Sisters*, 268 U.S. 510, 535 (1925), *Meyer v. Nebraska*, supra.

This right of privacy, whether it be founded in the Fourteenth Amendment's concept of personal liberty and restrictions upon state action, as we feel it is, or, as the District Court determined, in the Ninth Amendment's reservation of rights to the people, is broad enough to encompass a woman's decision whether or not to terminate her pregnancy. The detriment that the State would impose upon the pregnant woman by denying this choice altogether is apparent. Specific and direct harm medically diagnosable even in early pregnancy may be involved. Maternity, or additional offspring, may force upon the woman a distressful life and future. Psychological harm may be imminent. Mental and physical health may be taxed by child care. There is also the distress, for all concerned, associated with the unwanted child, and there is the problem of bringing a child into a family already unable, psychologically and otherwise, to care for it. In other cases, as in this one, the additional difficulties and continuing stigma of unwed motherhood may be involved. All these are factors the woman and her responsible physician necessarily will consider in consultation.

We, therefore, conclude that the right of personal privacy includes the abortion decision, but that this right is not unqualified and must be considered against important state interests in regulation.

The appellee and certain amici argue that the fetus is a "person" within the language and meaning of the Fourteenth Amendment. In support of this, they outline at length and in detail the well-known facts of fetal development. If this suggestion of personhood is established, the appellant's case, of course, collapses, [410 U.S. 113, 157] for the fetus' right to life would then be guaranteed specifically by the Amendment. The appellant conceded as much on reargument. 51 On the other hand, the appellee conceded on reargument 52that no case could be cited that holds that a fetus is a person within the meaning of the Fourteenth Amendment.

The Constitution does not define "person" in so many words. Section 1 of the Fourteenth Amendment contains three references to "person." The first, in defining "citizens," speaks of "persons born or naturalized in the United States." The word also appears both in the Due Process Clause and in the Equal Protection Clause. "Person" is used in other places in the Constitution: in the listing of qualifications for Representatives and Senators, Art. I, 2, cl. 2, and 3, cl. 3; in the Apportionment Clause, Art. I, 2, cl. 3; 53 in the Migration and Importation provision, Art. I, 9, cl. 1; in the Emolument Clause, Art. I, 9, cl. 8; in the Electors provisions, Art. II, 1, cl. 2, and the superseded cl. 3; in the provision outlining qualifications for the office of President, Art. II, 1, cl. 5; in the Extradition provisions, Art. IV, 2, cl. 2, and the superseded Fugitive Slave Clause 3; and in the Fifth, Twelfth, and Twenty-second Amendments, as well as in 2 and 3 of the Fourteenth Amendment. But in nearly all these instances, the use of the word is such that it has application only postnatally. None indicates, with any assurance, that it has any possible pre-natal application. 54 [410 U.S. 113, 158]

Texas urges that, apart from the Fourteenth Amendment, life begins at conception and is present throughout pregnancy, and that, therefore, the State has a compelling interest in protecting that life from and after conception. We need not resolve the difficult question of when life begins. When those trained in the respective disciplines of medicine, philosophy, and theology are unable to arrive at any consensus, the judiciary, at this point in the development of man's knowledge, is not in a position to speculate as to the answer. [410 U.S. 113, 160]

To summarize and to repeat:

A state criminal abortion statute of the current Texas type, that excepts from criminality only a life-saving procedure on behalf of the mother, without regard to pregnancy stage and without recognition of the other interests involved, is violative of the Due Process Clause of the Fourteenth Amendment.

(a) For the stage prior to approximately the end of the first tri-mester, the abortion decision and its effectuation must be left to the medical judgment of the pregnant woman's attending physician.

(b) For the stage subsequent to approximately the end of the first trimester, the State, in promoting its interest in the health of the mother, may, if it chooses, regulate the abortion procedure in ways that are reasonably related to maternal health.

(c) For the stage subsequent to viability, the State in promoting its interest in the potentiality of human life [410 U.S. 113, 165] may, if it chooses, regulate, and even proscribe, abortion except where it is necessary, in appropriate medical judgment, for the preservation of the life or health of the mother.

**MR. JUSTICE WHITE, with whom MR. JUSTICE REHNQUIST joins, dissenting.**\*

At the heart of the controversy in these cases are those recurring pregnancies that pose no danger whatsoever to the life or health of the mother but are, nevertheless, unwanted for any one or more of a variety of reasons—convenience, family planning, economics, dis-like of children, the embarrassment of illegitimacy, etc. The common claim before us is that, for any one of such reasons, or for no reason at all, and without asserting or claiming any threat to life or health, any woman is entitled to an abortion at her request if she is able to find a medical advisor willing to undertake the procedure.

The Court, for the most part, sustains this position: during the period prior to the time the fetus becomes viable, the Constitution of the United States values the convenience, whim, or caprice of the putative mother more than the life or potential life of the fetus; the Constitution, therefore, guarantees the right to an abortion as against any state law or policy seeking to protect the fetus from an abortion not prompted by more compelling reasons of the mother.

With all due respect, I dissent. I find nothing in the language or history of the Constitution to support the Court's judgment. The Court simply fashions and announces a new constitutional right for pregnant mothers [410 U.S. 222] and, with scarcely any reason or authority for its action, invests that right with sufficient substance to override most existing state abortion statutes. The upshot is that the people and the legislatures of the 50 States are constitutionally disentitled to weigh the relative importance of the continued existence and development of the fetus, on the one hand, against a spectrum of possible impacts on the mother, on the other hand. As an exercise of raw judicial power, the Court perhaps has authority to do what it does today; but, in my view, its judgment is an improvident and extravagant exercise of the power of judicial review that the Constitution extends to this Court.

The Court apparently values the convenience of the pregnant mother more than the continued existence and development of the life or potential life that she carries. Whether or not I might agree with that marshaling of values, I can in no event join the Court's judgment because I find no constitutional warrant for imposing such an order of priorities on the people and legislatures of the States. In a sensitive area such as this, involving as it does issues over which reasonable men may easily and heatedly differ, I cannot accept the Court's exercise of its clear power of choice by interposing a constitutional barrier to state efforts to protect human life and by investing mothers and doctors with the constitutionally protected right to exterminate it. This issue, for the most part, should be left with the people and to the political processes the people have devised to govern their affairs.

It is my view, therefore, that the Texas statute is not constitutionally infirm because it denies abortions to those who seek to serve only their convenience, rather than to protect their life or health. Nor is this plaintiff, who claims no threat to her mental or physical health, entitled to assert the possible rights of those women [410 U.S. 223] whose pregnancy assertedly implicates their health. This, together with *United States v. Vuitch*, 402 U.S. 62 (1971), dictates reversal of the judgment of the District Court.

Likewise, because Georgia may constitutionally forbid abortions to putative mothers who, like the plaintiff in this case, do not fall within the reach of § 26–1202(a) of its criminal code, I have no occasion, and the District Court had none, to consider the constitutionality of the procedural requirements of the Georgia statute as applied to those pregnancies posing substantial hazards to either life or health. I would reverse the judgment of the District Court in the Georgia case.

# APPENDIX H

## *Doe v. Bolton*, 410 U.S. 179 (1973)
### (Edited)

***Author's Comments:*** *Most people do not realize that there was a companion decision of the United States Supreme Court to* Roe v. Wade. *In* Doe v. Bolton, *the Court invalidated antiabortion provisions of the law in Georgia and stated clarified what it meant when it said that "for the stage subsequent to viability, the State in promoting its interest in the potentiality of human life may, if it chooses, regulate, and even proscribe, abortion except where it is necessary, in appropriate medical judgment, for the preservation of the life or health of the mother."*

*At first glance this language might indicate that the Court actually was allowing states to at least ban and/or limit abortion in the latter stages of pregnancy after viability. However, notice that it cannot do so when the abortion is necessary to preserve the health of the mother. Instead of defining health in a manner most understand to be as the absence of illness, the Court used a broad expansive definition of health that virtually allows for abortion on demand at any stage in a mother's pregnancy.*

*Chief Justice Warren Burger filed a concurring opinion stating that he supported the two decisions of* Roe *and* Doe *and that they do not amount to an endorsement by the Court of abortion on demand. Certainly history has proven Burger far off the mark in such a statement. As a supporter of the* Roe *and* Doe *decisions, he clearly did not compre-*

*hend the far-reaching impact the language of these opinions would have on the culture.*

*The following are excerpts from the* Doe *opinion:*

**BLACKMUN, J., delivered the opinion of the Court, in which BURGER, C.J., and DOUGLAS, BRENNAN, STEWART, MARSHALL, and POWELL, JJ. joined. BURGER, C.J. and DOUGLAS, J. filed concurring opinions. WHITE, J., filed a dissenting opinion, in which REHNQUIST, J., joined, REHNQUIST, J., filed a dissenting opinion.**

[T]he medical judgment may be exercised in the light of all factors—physical, emotional, psychological, familial, and the woman's age—relevant to the wellbeing of the patient. All these factors may relate to health. This allows the attending physician the room he needs to make his best medical judgment. And it is room that operates for the benefit, not the disadvantage, of the pregnant woman.

The statute's emphasis, as has been repetitively noted, is on the attending physician's "best clinical judgment that an abortion is necessary." That should be sufficient. The reasons for the presence of the confirmation step in the statute are perhaps apparent, but they are insufficient to withstand constitutional challenge. Again, no other voluntary medical or surgical procedure for which Georgia requires confirmation by two other physicians has been cited to us. If a physician is licensed by the State, he is recognized by the State as capable of exercising acceptable clinical judgment. If he fails in this, professional censure and deprivation of his license are available remedies. Required acquiescence by co-practitioners has no rational connection with a patient's needs, and unduly infringes on the physician's right to practice. The attending physician will know when a consultation is advisable—the doubtful situation, the need for assurance when the medical decision is a delicate one, and the like. Physicians have followed this routine historically, and know its usefulness and benefit for all concerned.

### MR. CHIEF JUSTICE BURGER, concurring

I agree that, under the Fourteenth Amendment to the Constitution, the abortion statutes of Georgia and Texas impermissibly limit the performance of abortions necessary to protect the health of pregnant women, using the term health in its broadest medical context. *See United States v. Vuitch,* 402 U.S. 62, 71–72 (1971). I am somewhat troubled that the Court has taken notice of various scientific and medical data in reaching its conclusion; however, I do not believe that the Court has exceeded the scope of judicial notice accepted in other contexts.

In oral argument, counsel for the State of Texas informed the Court that early abortion procedures were routinely permitted in certain exceptional cases, such as nonconsensual pregnancies resulting from rape and incest. In the face of a rigid and narrow statute, such as that of Texas, no one in these circumstances should be placed in a posture of dependence on a prosecutorial policy or prosecutorial discretion. Of course, States must have broad power, within the limits indicated in the opinions, to regulate the subject of abortions, but where the consequences of state intervention are so severe, uncertainty must be avoided as much as possible. For my part, I would be inclined to allow a State to require the certification of two physicians to support an abortion, but the Court holds otherwise. I do not believe that such a procedure is unduly burdensome, as are the complex steps of the Georgia statute, which require as many as six doctors and the use of a hospital certified by the JCAH.

I do not read the Court's holdings today as having the sweeping consequences attributed to them by the dissenting Justices; the dissenting views discount the reality that the vast majority of physicians observe the standards of their profession, and act only on the basis of carefully deliberated medical judgments relating to life and health. Plainly, the Court today rejects any claim that the Constitution requires abortions on demand

**MR. JUSTICE WHITE, with whom MR. JUSTICE REHNQUIST joins, dissenting.**

At the heart of the controversy in these cases are those recurring pregnancies that pose no danger whatsoever to the life or health of the mother but are, nevertheless, unwanted for any one or more of a variety of reasons—convenience, family planning, economics, dislike of children, the embarrassment of illegitimacy, etc. The common claim before us is that, for any one of such reasons, or for no reason at all, and without asserting or claiming any threat to life or health, any woman is entitled to an abortion at her request if she is able to find a medical advisor willing to undertake the procedure.

The Court, for the most part, sustains this position: during the period prior to the time the fetus becomes viable, the Constitution of the United States values the convenience, whim, or caprice of the putative mother more than the life or potential life of the fetus; the Constitution, therefore, guarantees the right to an abortion as against any state law or policy seeking to protect the fetus from an abortion not prompted by more compelling reasons of the mother.

With all due respect, I dissent. I find nothing in the language or history of the Constitution to support the Court's judgment. The Court simply fashions and announces a new constitutional right for pregnant mothers and, with scarcely any reason or authority for its action, invests that right with sufficient substance to override most existing state abortion statutes. The upshot is that the people and the legislatures of the 50 States are constitutionally disentitled to weigh the relative importance of the continued existence and development of the fetus, on the one hand, against a spectrum of possible impacts on the mother, on the other hand. **As an exercise of raw judicial power, the Court perhaps has authority to do what it does today; but, in my view, its judgment is an improvident and extravagant exercise of the power of judicial review that the Constitution extends to this Court.** (Emphasis added.)

The Court apparently values the convenience of the pregnant mother more than the continued existence and development of the life or potential life that she carries. Whether or not I might agree with that marshaling of values, I can in no event join the Court's judgment because I find no constitutional warrant for imposing such an order of priorities on the people and legislatures of the States. In a sensitive area such as this, involving as it does issues over which reasonable men may easily and heatedly differ, I cannot accept the Court's exercise of its clear power of choice by interposing a consti-tutional barrier to state efforts to protect human life and by invest-ing mothers and doctors with the constitutionally protected right to exterminate it. This issue, for the most part, should be left with the people and to the political processes the people have devised to govern their affairs.

It is my view, therefore, that the Texas statute is not constitutionally infirm because it denies abortions to those who seek to serve only their convenience, rather than to protect their life or health. Nor is this plaintiff, who claims no threat to her mental or physical health, entitled to assert the possible rights of those women whose pregnancy assertedly implicates their health. This, together with *United States v. Vuitch*, 402 U.S. 62(1971), dictates reversal of the judgment of the District Court.

Likewise, because Georgia may constitutionally forbid abortions to putative mothers who, like the plaintiff in this case, do not fall within the reach of § 26–1202(a) of its criminal code, I have no occasion, and the District Court had none, to consider the constitutionality of the procedural requirements of the Georgia statute as applied to those pregnancies posing substantial hazards to either life or health. I would reverse the judgment of the District Court in the Georgia case.

# APPENDIX I

## *Planned Parenthood v. Casey*, 505 U.S. 833 (1992)

Author's Comments: *I was privileged to be sitting in the front row of the courtroom of the United States Supreme Court on June, 29, 1992, to listen to the opinion of the Court in this critical decision. The pro-life movement had worked vigorously for years to get to the point where we believed that the high court was ready to overturn its decisions in* Roe v. Wade *and* Doe v. Bolton. *We had worked hard to confirm justices to the Court during the presidencies of Ronald Reagan and George H. W. Bush and were confident that we had at least five votes on the Court to reverse* Roe *and* Doe.

*I arrived very early at the Court in order to secure a place at the front of the line to get in. I also had time to have some breakfast in the Court cafeteria prior to entry into the Court chambers. During breakfast, I saw Justice Harry Blackmun, author of the* Roe *and* Doe *opinions, at a table having breakfast with some of his law clerks. He seemed relaxed and confident. I was unnerved because, if indeed the Court was about to reverse these decisions, then as their author, he should have appeared at least a bit frazzled. He did not.*

*Later that morning, I discovered why Blackmun was so calm. The heart of his opinions in* Roe *and* Doe *remained intact as the Court affirmed by a 5–4 vote the central holdings of these cases by stating that a woman has a constitutional right to secure an abortion. I was stunned at the decision and heartbroken that the years of working toward a reversal of* Roe *and* Doe *failed.*

*The decision of the Court in* Casey *not only upheld the right to abortion but also provided very troubling language defining the meaning of liberty under the Fourteenth Amendment to the US Constitution. If taken seriously, such language, quoted below, provides the legal basis for one to engage in virtually any conceivable deed as an act of protected liberty without government prohibitions.*

*The following are excerpts from the* Casey *opinion:*

**JUSTICE O'CONNOR, JUSTICE KENNEDY, and JUSTICE SOUTER delivered the opinion of the Court with respect to Parts I, II, and III, concluding that consideration of the fundamental constitutional question resolved by Roe v. Wade principles of institutional integrity, and the rule of stare decisis require that Roe's essential holding be retained and reaffirmed as to each of its three parts: (1) a recognition of a woman's right to choose to have an abortion before fetal viability and to obtain it without undue interference from the State, whose pre-viability interests are not strong enough to support an abortion prohibition or the imposition of substantial obstacles.**

After considering the fundamental constitutional questions resolved by *Roe*, principles of institutional integrity, and the rule of *stare decisis*, we are led to conclude this: the essential holding of *Roe v. Wade* should be retained and once again reaffirmed.

It must be stated at the outset and with clarity that *Roe's* essential holding, the holding we reaffirm, has three parts. First is a recognition of the right of the woman to choose to have an abortion before viability and to obtain it without undue interference from the State. Before viability, the State's interests are not strong enough to support a prohibition of abortion or the imposition of a substantial obstacle to the woman's effective right to elect the procedure. Second is a confirmation of the State's power to restrict abortions after fetal viability, if the law contains exceptions for pregnancies which endanger a woman's life or health. And third is the principle that the State has legitimate interests from the outset of the pregnancy in protecting the health of the woman and the life of the fetus that may become a child. These principles do not contradict one another; and we adhere to each.

Constitutional protection of the woman's decision to terminate her pregnancy derives from the Due Process Clause of the Fourteenth Amendment. It declares that no State shall "deprive any person of life, liberty, or property, without due process of law." The controlling word in the case before us is "liberty." Although a literal reading of the Clause might suggest that it governs only the procedures by which a State may deprive persons of liberty, for at least 105 years, at least since *Mugler v. Kansas*, 123 U.S. 623, 660–661 (1887), the Clause has been understood to contain a substantive component as well, one "barring certain government actions regardless of the fairness of the procedures used to implement them." *Daniels v. Williams*, 474 U.S. 327, 331 (1986). As Justice Brandeis (joined by Justice Holmes) observed, "[d]espite arguments to the contrary which had seemed to me persuasive, it is settled that the due process clause of the Fourteenth Amendment applies to matters of substantive law as well as to matters of procedure. Thus all fundamental rights comprised within the term liberty are protected by the Federal Constitution from invasion by the States." *Whitney v. California*, 274 U.S. 357, 373 (1927) (Brandeis, J., concurring). "[T]he guaranties of due process, though having their roots in Magna Carta's '*per legem terrae*' and considered as procedural safeguards 'against executive usurpation and tyranny,' have in this country 'become bulwarks also against arbitrary legislation.' "*Poe v. Ullman*, 367 U.S. 497, 541 (1961) (Harlan, J., dissenting from dismissal on jurisdictional grounds) (quoting *Hurtado v. California*, 110 U.S. 516, 532 (1884)).

The most familiar of the substantive liberties protected by the Fourteenth Amendment are those recognized by the Bill of Rights. We have held that the Due Process Clause of the Fourteenth Amendment incorporates most of the Bill of Rights against the States. See, *e. g., Duncan v. Louisiana*, 391 U.S. 145, 147–148 (1968). It is tempting, as a means of curbing the discretion of federal judges, to suppose that liberty encompasses no more than those rights already guaranteed to the individual against federal interference by the express provisions of the first eight amendments to the Constitution.

See *Adamson v. California*, 332 U.S. 46, 68–92 (1947) (Black, J., dissenting). But of course this Court has never accepted that view.

Our law affords constitutional protection to personal decisions relating to marriage, procreation, contraception, family relationships, child rearing, and education. *Carey v. Population Services International*, 431 U.S., at 685. Our cases recognize "the right of the *individual*, married or single, to be free from unwarranted governmental intrusion into matters so fundamentally affecting a person as the decision whether to bear or beget a child." *Eisenstadt v. Baird, supra*, at 453 (emphasis in original). Our precedents "have respected the private realm of family life which the state cannot enter." *Princ e v. Massachusetts*, 321 U.S. 158, 166 (1944). These matters, involving the most intimate and personal choices a person may make in a lifetime, choices central to personal dignity and autonomy, are central to the liberty protected by the Fourteenth Amendment. **At the heart of liberty is the right to define one's own concept of existence, of meaning, of the universe, and of the mystery of human life. Beliefs about these matters could not define the attributes of personhood were they formed under compulsion of the State** (emphasis added).

# APPENDIX J

*In honor of William Wilberforce, I have over the years produced commentaries regarding the sanctity of human life and related issues. Such commentaries are found on the website of the National Institute of Family and Life Advocates (NIFLA) at www.niffla.org under the section entitled "The Wilberforce Forum." A selection of these commentaries are reproduced here from latest to earliest for reading and reflection about the issue of abortion and related life issues that are currently dividing the nation.*

*Each of these commentaries speaks to the sanctity of human life and the unalienable right to life of every human being. Each can be read separately for reflection and meditation. When reading each of these commentaries, prayerfully consider God's role for you in restoring the sanctity of human life and protecting the unalienable right to life of all human beings.*

# COMMENTARIES FROM THE
# WILBERFORCE FORUM

Albert Einstein and the Unalienable Right to Life
January 23, 2014

The founding of the American Republic resides in these familiar words from our Declaration of Independence, which states,

The uniqueness of America is that it is a nation that was founded upon what was considered at the time to be a radical notion concerning the natural rights of every human being. Such a radical principle stated unequivocally that human rights are gifts from a Creator and therefore, cannot be denied to anyone by a government made up of mere mortals. Since human rights are not granted by a king, ruler, or government, they cannot be taken away at the whim of tyrants.

Succinctly put, America was founded upon the belief that (1) there is a Creator who grants natural rights to human beings emanating from the fact that such humans are created; (2) all human beings are created equal and our nation does not acknowledge a class structure where some are considered superior to others; (3) such natural rights are self-evident. meaning that they are true on their very face and need not be proven through reasoning or logic; and (4) such self-evident truths are unalienable meaning that since they are granted by God alone they are incapable of being transferred, denied, or taken away by anybody else, including the government.

The American concept of the equality of all because they are created equal and are given by a Creator natural self-evident rights was a radical departure from a contrary view held for centuries. The pre-American worldview proclaimed that human rights are granted by the king or government who alone will determine which subjects will be blessed with such rights and which subjects will be so denied.

Prior to the American Revolution, the prevailing view of the rights of human beings could be summed up simply as "the King giveth and the King taketh away." Prior to the American Revolution, nations and cultures recognized various classes of people and gave superior rights and status to a few elite while discriminating against those who belonged to lower classes. The Declaration of Independence was a dawning of a new day in the history of the world where the dignity and equal status of every human being was recognized.

This American view states that the natural rights of life, liberty, and the pursuit of happiness come from a Creator. This is, indeed, a strange concept for today's modern-day American society whose current academic, political, and scientific elite promote the humanistic concept that we are not created but rather exist because of some random cosmic accident that occurred millions of years ago.

Modern American intelligentsia are very uncomfortable with the notion that humanity is created by an intelligent being. To believe otherwise flies in the face of their passionately held view that humankind is simply a higher form of animal life on an evolutionary chain. However, if such a concept of humanity is true then it is impossible for one to persuasively make the case that membership in the human race alone gives one superior rights to other life-forms.

Only a belief in the Judeo-Christian concept that one is created by God and in his image can explain why humanity, as opposed to animal and plant life, is accorded superior rights of life, liberty, and the pursuit of happiness.

Current scientific and academic communities are divided on the issue of the existence of a Creator. Some say that this question is simply a matter for religion and therefore, an answer to it requires speculation and faith. Others argue very persuasively that biological facts show an intelligent design and order to the universe that can only be explained by the proposition that the universe and life itself was created by a superior being.

Ultimately, no matter which view one holds regarding the existence of a Creator such a view requires faith to support it. Those who say there is no Creator and that science has no proof of such are taking a faith position in the same manner as those who believe in a Creator. There is no scientific proof that the universe and life came about by a random cosmic accident where something miraculously appeared out of nothingness, or that the universe has always eternally existed. (These are the only two explanations for the existence of the universe and life outside the belief in a Creator.) Hence, those who hold to such view(s) must also do so by faith.

Was mankind created and thus, granted by its Creator self-evident and unalienable rights? Albert Einstein, perhaps the greatest scientific mind of the twentieth century, said this.

> *[E]very one who is seriously engaged in the pursuit of science becomes convinced that the laws of nature manifest the existence of a spirit vastly superior to that of men, and one in the face of which we with our modest powers must feel humble.*

It would be inaccurate to state that Einstein shared the theological views of many orthodox Christian believers. However, his brilliance led him to conclude that humankind, indeed, cannot exist because of a series of random cosmic accidents. Behind the existence of humankind, according to Einstein, is a spirit "vastly superior to that of men."

It is the belief in a Creator who provides to humankind self-evident and unalienable rights that are the bedrock of the American nation.

177

This foundational belief supplied the rationale and moral fiber for the abolition of slavery and for the ending of the Jim Crow era of discrimination against African Americans. It is also the foundation for the belief in the sanctity of life of all, born and unborn, and thus, provides the basis upon which millions of Americans rely to justify their opposition to abortion, infanticide, and euthanasia.

The belief in the unalienable rights of life, liberty, and the pursuit of happiness has eroded in our nation over the last forty-one years. Since 1973, more than 56 million unborn children have lost their lives to abortion, and this number continues to increase at a rate of 1.2 million each year. Only a return to a commitment to once again protect the natural rights of all human beings will reverse this trend. Such a return requires a reaffirmation throughout our culture that humankind is special among all creation because humankind was created in the image of a Creator.

Is this really such a hard pill for our intellectual elite to swallow and accept? Apparently, it wasn't for Albert Einstein.

## Pregnancy Resource Centers That Offer Ultrasound Are Medical Clinics
### July 8, 2013

Since the mid-1990s, pro-life Pregnancy Resource Centers (PRCs) have been offering ultrasound confirmation of pregnancy to mothers considering abortion. This movement to provide ultrasound has accelerated dramatically over the years to the point that currently more than 860 pregnancy centers are providing ultrasound and other medical services.

Opponents of PRCs have conducted a decade's long smear campaign to slander the work of PRCs claiming that they are "bogus clinics" and that their use of ultrasound amounts to medical malpractice. Even some well-intentioned pro-life people, in attempting to defend the work of PRCs, have stated that these centers are not clinics.

However, in doing this, such pro-life friends have done a great disservice to medical pregnancy centers and have unintentionally aided the enemies of PRCs by confirming their slanderous charges.

Pregnancy centers that provide ultrasound services (and other medical services such as STI testing and treatment) under the supervision and direction of a licensed physician are, in fact, medical clinics and should be acknowledged as such. A medical clinic under its dictionary definition is simply a facility that provides medical services under the supervision and direction of a licensed physician.

Four states—California, New York, New Jersey, and Massachusetts—have detailed regulations on the licensing of medical clinics and such regulations must be complied with in order to be a "clinic." In the other 46 states, a pregnancy center that provides the medical services under the license of a physician who supervises the services is a medical clinic. And this is exactly what medical PRCs do!

All medical PRCs provide their medical services under the direction of a licensed physician. The primary medical service being provided is a diagnosis of pregnancy through limited obstetric ultrasound. (Other medical services provided by some PRC medical clinics include STI testing and treatment, prenatal care, laminaria removal, and provision of prenatal vitamins.) The provision of ultrasound services is always a medical service and, thus, must be supervised by a licensed physician who is the medical director of the clinic.

The provision of pregnancy confirmation through limited obstetric ultrasound is a medical service that requires medical professionals skilled in the implementation of ultrasound. **NIFLA** has since 1998 through its *Institute in Limited Obstetric Ultrasound* trained more than 3,000 nurses and other medical health professionals in the legal and medical "how tos" of ultrasound within the setting of a PRC. This course is based upon legal and medical guidelines issues by the medical profession and the ultrasound medical community. Ongoing onsite training is also provided for such medical personnel to allow them to enhance their skills. All such medical professionals work under the supervision of the medical director—a licensed physician.

Medical PRCs are staffed by both paid and volunteer medical professionals. In addition to the medical director, they also utilize the services of RNs, Physicians Assistants, Registered Diagnostic Medical Sonographers (RDMS) and other licensed health care providers.

The dramatic work of medical PRCs is changing lives and building a culture of life throughout the country. Their credibility is enhanced by professionally providing medical services under medical professional guidelines. The pro-life movement needs to understand and acknowledge that such PRCs are indeed medical clinics and are not bogus as asserted by the abortion industry.

## The Gosnell Murder Trial and the Conscience of a Nation
### May 28, 2013

Abortion is simply the issue that will not go away. Despite the desires of many to ignore this very uncomfortable topic, the reality of its brutality and injustice are becoming more apparent to the public. Evidence of this is found in the recent conviction of Mr. Kermit Gosnell (who masquerades as a physician) for the first-degree murder of three babies who survived his failed abortion attempts.

The gruesome details of Gosnell's abortion clinic, which he operated for years without government inspection, have shocked the conscience of a nation. Even many of those who proclaim to be pro-choice are now openly expressing doubts about the morality of abortion. The grisly evidence presented at Gosnell's trial included details about babies born alive during the abortion procedure and subsequently killed by the snipping of their spines. Testimony from clinic workers included heartbreaking stories of babies surviving the brutal abortion assault and crying for help only to be viciously killed. Evidence included details of remains of infants aborted (and even tiny severed feet of infants) kept in refrigerators for storage. Gosnell was convicted of the first degree murder of three infants born alive, but the evidence showed that hundreds of such killings had occurred over the years at Gosnell's bloody house of horrors.

Pro-choice proponents of abortion, led by Planned Parenthood, have been quick to claim that Gosnell's practices are the exception and not the rule as to how abortion clinics operate around the nation. However, further evidence coming from around the nation indicates that such claims are not well-founded. Indeed, it is becoming more apparent that Gosnell's operations are the rule for abortion providers, not the exception. Consider the following:

- In Alabama, an abortion clinic in Birmingham is being investigated for operating without proper licensure—this same clinic was shut down a year ago for failure to follow basic health and safety regulations.
- The Lt. Governor in Texas is demanding an investigation into an abortionist that may be even worse than Gosnell, according to three of his former employees who have turned whistleblowers on his gruesome operations.
- Maryland officials closed down three abortion clinics recently, two for faulty equipment and poor training to deal with life-threatening complications.
- Illinois state health officials reinvigorated their clinic inspections in the wake of Gosnell, and closed two clinics, including one fined for "failure to perform CPR on a patient who died after a procedure," according to the Associated Press.

And the list goes on and on. The US House of Representatives has now launched a nationwide investigation to determine what actions have been and/or are being taken at the state level to ensure that these types of horrors are not going undetected.

It certainly does appear that there are many more Gosnells operating across the nation, and of course, the public should express outrage at such atrocities occurring under the ruse of a so-called constitutional right of privacy. However, the deeper question that must be faced by our fellow countrymen is the legitimacy of abortion on demand itself.

We must ask—what moral difference is there between snipping the spine of a baby born alive from a failed abortion procedure and killing her, and snipping the spine of a baby still in the womb and killing her? The first is now recognized as first-degree murder. The second is what some refer to as "safe and legal" abortion.

Since 1973, when the US Supreme Court in *Roe v. Wade* decriminalized the prolife protective abortion laws of all fifty states, there have been 55 million legal abortions. Abortion takes the lives of 1.3 million unborn children a year, 3,000 per day, and one every 25 seconds. Unless she turns away from these acts of brutality America seems to be bent on committing demographic suicide killing millions of its future leaders, citizens and tax-payers.

Abortion is not an issue of liberals versus conservatives; of Democrats versus Republicans; of those of religious faith versus those who do not believe. Neither is it an issue of women's rights. (Consider that at least half of the abortions have killed little girls. What become of the rights of these little women?) Rather, it is an issue of humanity versus barbarianism. It is an issue of right versus wrong. It is an issue of life versus death.

Political ideology should be irrelevant to this great issue of morality that now assaults the conscience of a nation. Clearly, the way America chooses to handle this issue in the next few years will undoubtedly determine the future of the nation.

In other contexts America is indeed a compassionate nation. It is now time for her compassion to be unleashed to provide help and support for those women who without such support will be brutalized by the Gosnells of the nation. Currently, over 3,000 prolife Pregnancy Resource Centers and Medical Clinics exist across the nation in every community providing support, medical resources, and encourage-ment to empower mothers considering abortion to choose life.

The lessons of the Gosnell trial are many. However, one lesson appears to be louder and more convicting than the others. It is now time that our leaders—political, civic, religious, corporate, and educational—all come together and support the life-affirming work of those who provide support to mothers in crisis and alternatives to abortion. If they fail to do so then the very soul of America will be lost.

There are alternatives to abortion. There have to be.
National Pro-life Leader Thomas Glessner Applauds Gosnell Verdict

FREDERICKSBURG, Va., May 14, 2013 /*Christian Newswire*/ -- Thomas A. Glessner, J.D., president of the National Institute of Family and Life Advocates (NIFLA), a network of more than 1,250 pro-life pregnancy resource centers and medical clinics, issued the following statement applauding the jury verdict in the Gosnell mur-der trial.

"We rejoice that justice has been served in the verdicts finding abor-tionist Kermit Gosnell guilty of three counts of first-degree murder. However, abortion continues to tear our nation apart. America must come to grips with this evil or lose its soul.

"Our fellow countrymen must ask what is the difference between snipping the spine and killing a baby after she is born and snipping the spine and killing a baby while she is still inside the womb? The first is now recognized First Degree Murder. The Second is called (by some) 'safe and legal abortion.'

"Since 1973 fifty-five million unborn children have suffered the same fate as the victims of Gosnell's serial killings and America pretends that these deaths have never happened. But God sees and knows. Thomas Jefferson speaking of the institution of slavery said, 'I trem-ble in fear for my country when I realize that God is just and his justice will not sleep forever.'

"May America awaken and turn away from this evil and experience God's mercy. If she does not she will experience his awakening justice."

## Abortion is Not Safer for Women than Childbirth
### May 30, 2012

Media outlets such as *Time* Magazine and Reuters have provided extensive coverage to an article recently published as "original research" and entitled, "The Comparative Safety of Legal Induced Abortion and Childbirth in the United States," by Raymond and Grimes in the February 2012 journal *Obstetrics & Gynecology*. The article concludes by stating, "Legal induced abortion is markedly safer than childbirth. The risk of death associated with childbirth is approximately 14 times higher than that with abortion. Similarly, the overall morbidity associated with childbirth exceeds that with abortion."

Is this the truth? **NIFLA** doesn't believe so and recommends that Pregnancy Medical Clinics (PMCs) be aware of the errant methodologies of this study and be able to explain such errors to media-savvy pregnant women who question the safety of childbirth over abortion. In order to comprehend the faulty research in the Raymond and Grimes' article, there is a helpful critique and refutation of it, written by Priscilla K. Coleman, PhD, Professor of Human Development and Family Studies at Bowling Green State University. Coleman says:

> *You need to know that the data reported by abortion clinics to state health departments and ultimately to the CDC significantly under-represents abortion morbidity and mortality for several reasons: 1) abortion reporting is not required by federal law and many states do not report abortion-related deaths to the CDC; 2) deaths due to medical and surgical treatments are reported under the complication of the procedure (e.g., infection) rather than the treat-*

*ment (e.g., induced abortion); 3) most women leave abortion clinics within hours of the procedure and go to hospital emergency rooms if there are complications that may result in death; 4) suicide deaths are rarely, if ever, linked back to abortion in state reporting of death rates; 5) an abortion experience can lead to physical and/or psychological disturbances that increase the likelihood of dying years after the abortion, and these indirect abortion-related deaths are not captured at all.*[1]

To understand why abortion is under-reported with related statistics, review the Guttmacher Institute State Policies on abortion at www.guttmacher.org/statecenter/spibs/spib_ARR.pdf, which provides information on reporting requirements for abortion.

As an example of the faulty statistics used by Raymond and Grimes, one need only consider California, the most populous state where almost 1 in 8 US residents live. California has no reporting requirements for abortion. Additionally, only 27 states require any type of abortion complication reporting, with 3 of the 4 most populous states not requiring this information.

David Reardon, PhD, and researcher on abortion's effects, states:

*Hundreds of news articles appeared this week claiming, once again, that the best medical evidence shows that abortion is safer than childbirth. The rash of articles was all tied to a blatant piece of propaganda published in Obstetrics and Gynecology by Dr. David Grimes, an abortion provider and chief propagandist for "medical proof" of abortion's safety. . . In short, Grimes used a very incomplete record of abortion-associated deaths and compared it to a complete record of deaths associated with non-aborted pregnancies, and found that the death rate is lower. Therefore, he concludes, abortion is safer than childbirth.*"[2]

Further, Reardon provides evidence from research in Finland that clearly contradicts the Grimes article. Finnish researchers found that women are four times more likely to die in the year following abortion than women who give birth. Similar findings were reported in a record-based study of California women. Observe the graph below taken from Afterabortion.org regarding the study from Finland.

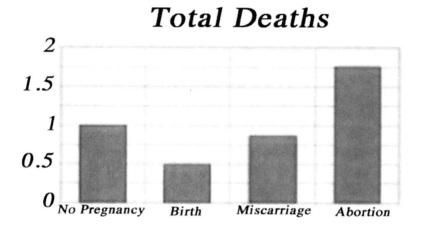

The figure above shows the age-adjusted relative risk of death in the year following a birth, miscarriage, or abortion compared to the rate of death among women not pregnant. The results are from a multi-year study of all women in Finland, linking death certificates to central registries for pregnancy outcomes. It clearly shows abortion is associated with an elevated risk of death, while carrying to term is associated with a lowered risk of death.

Additionally a previous, insightful article written by Reardon and others in the Journal of Contemporary Health Law, 2003, regarding the long-term effects of abortion can be linked from his article. For a complete review of the literature on mortality rates related to abortion and childbirth, Reardon suggests readers should study "Deaths

Associated with Abortion Compared to Childbirth: A Review of New and Old Data and the Medical and Legal Implications." Its graphs (example above) are particularly informative with easy-to-grasp facts about abortion's devastating consequences for women. A copy of this article would be helpful to have in your PMC for reference or to allow clients to read.[3]

Coleman concludes her critique of the Raymond and Grimes study noting that "pregnant women considering their options deserve accurate information about comparative risks."

So, why have Raymond and Grimes chosen to disrespect women and medical professionals by knowingly offering a false impression of the relative risk of death between abortion and childbirth? When one reads several paragraphs of their report that is devoted to a political discussion of state-level informed consent laws, the answer to this question seems pretty obvious."[4]

In the PMC it is important that medical information shared with patients by medical professionals should, when possible, utilize referenced materials, such as the ones cited below. PMCs and PRCs exist to serve mothers at risk for abortion with integrity and providing medical evidence based upon credible information. The Raymond and Grimes article is not credible.

Mothers considering abortion deserve honest information. Providing them with copies of the articles listed here and providing information to access the websites where they are located is strongly encouraged.

References

1.    Coleman, P. A serious misrepresentation of the relative safety of induced abortion compared to childbirth published in a leading medical journal. Retrieved February 6, 2012 from www.wecareexperts.org/content/serious-mis-representation-relative-safety-induced-abortion-com-pared-childbirth-published-l-0.

2.  Reardon, D., (2012, January). Rehash of abortion safety claim ignores all inconvenient evidence to the contrary. Retrieved February 6, 2012, from afterabortion.org/2012/re-hash-of-abortion-safety-claim-ignores-all-inconvenient-evidence-to-the-contrary.

3.  Reardon, D., Straham, T., Thorp, J., Shuping, M., (2004). Deaths associated with abortion compared to childbirth[euro]"a review of new and old data and the medical and legal implications. Journal of Contemporary Health Law & Policy 2004; 20(2);279-327. Retrieved February 6, 2012, from www.afterabortion.org/pdf/DeathsAssocWithAbortionJCHLP.pdf.

4.  Coleman (2012).

## The Hysterical Ranting of Opponents of Ultrasound Legislation in Virginia Amount to a New Low
### March 15, 2012

The recent legislative session in the state of Virginia resulted in the passage of a law that promotes the use of ultrasound to enable abortion-minded mothers to see the image of their unborn children before obtaining an abortion. Indeed, the medical technology of ultrasound has proven over the years to reduce abortions dramatically. The membership of the National Institute of Family and Life Advocates (**NIFLA**) is comprised of nearly 1,250 prolife Pregnancy Resource Centers (PRCs). Of these, more than 800 either operate as medical clinics providing ultrasound confirmation of pregnancy or plan to do so in the very near future.

Anecdotal statistics from **NIFLA** members indicate that, on average, non-medical PRCs see approximately 25% of their clientele choose life, as opposed to abortion, after receiving resources and counseling. However, for PRCs that are medical clinics and provide ultrasound confirmation of pregnancy this percentage increases to nearly 90%.

It is easy to understand why such an increase in the number of pregnant mothers choosing life exists in medical PRCs. When an abortion-minded mother sees on the ultrasound screen the reality of the life within her she understands that she is not carrying a "blob of pregnancy tissue," as asserted by the abortion clinic and its supporters. Rather, she observes with her own eyes that within her is a separate human being with brain waves, moving arms, kicking legs and a beating heart. An anecdotal study in *The New England Journal of Medicine* in February 1983 entitled *"Maternal Bonding in Early Fetal Ultrasound Examinations"* made these astute observations when its authors attempted to discover what impact, if any, the viewing of an ultrasound image would have on the ultimate decision of a mother considering abortion. The authors write:

> *One of us pointed to the small, visibly moving fetal form on the screen and asked, "How do you feel about seeing what is inside you?' She answered crisply, 'It certainly makes you think twice about abortion! When asked to say more, she told of the surprise she felt on viewing the fetal form, especially on seeing it move: 'I feel it is human. It belongs to me. I couldn't have an abortion now."*

> *(T)he mother was asked about her experience with ultrasound. She said, "It really made a difference to see that it was alive." Asked about her position on the moral choice she had to make, she said, "I am going all the way with the baby, I believe it is human."*

Because of this dramatic impact of ultrasound numerous state legislatures have, in recent years, passed legislation requiring that ultrasound imaging be made available to mothers considering abortion before they make their final decision. The state of Virginia is the latest to do this. However, in Virginia abortion proponents descended to a new low in their opposition to such legislation by hysterically claiming that such legislation amounts to "state-mandated rape."

Such ranting was based upon the fact that in the early stages of pregnancy, the standard practice of medicine requires that to obtain a proper ultrasound image a transvaginal ultrasound probe be used.

The use of ultrasound is a medical diagnostic procedure and always constitutes the practice of medicine. As such, it must always be used under the direction of a licensed physician, must be medically indicated, and must follow accepted standards of medical practice. In the Pregnancy Medical Clinic setting the use of an ultrasound is medically justified through medical guidelines from the American Institute in Ultrasound Medicine (AIUM), which state that an indication for ultrasound exists to "confirm the presence of an intrauterine pregnancy." Such information is crucial to a mother considering abortion because until she knows that she is, in fact, pregnant she cannot consider what options, including abortion, exist. The results of a urine pregnancy test cannot tell her if she is pregnant because urine pregnancy tests are not 100% accurate. Thus, the ultrasound is needed to make a proper diagnosis of pregnancy.

In the early stages of pregnancy when the fetus is very small it is many times difficult, if not impossible, to obtain a proper ultrasound image with the transabdominal probe alone. Thus, the medical standard of practice in this area generally requires the use of the transvaginal probe up to eleven weeks gestational age in order to make a proper medical diagnosis. **An important fact to note is that the use of the transvaginal probe must always be consensual.** If a patient refuses to allow it then the doctor must use the abdominal probe and do the best that he or she can in making a proper diagnosis of pregnancy.

It is clear why proponents of abortion and the abortion industry oppose the passage of ultrasound laws, such as the recent bill passed in Virginia. As ultrasound imaging to mothers considering abortion becomes more available fewer such women choose abortion. The stark reality of this to an annual multi-million dollar abortion industry is that when a mother chooses life, as opposed to abortion, an abortion clinic loses revenue. Thus, the industry is desperate to stop the passage of such laws.

In Virginia abortion proponents resorted to a new low in their claims of "state-mandated rape" through the use of ultrasound. They should be ashamed, but undoubtedly are not. By raising the discussion about the merits of such legislation to such an emotional pitch they created a poisonous atmosphere that prevented rational political discourse on the ultrasound proposal. Further, since the use of the transvaginal probe must always be consensual (and opponents of the bill know this) they intentionally made false claims of "rape" in order to attract a sympathetic media. Finally, such tactics not only slandered the noble intent behind the law to provide good reproductive health information to mothers, but also slandered the professional work of physicians across the nation who routinely, as a matter of medical standards, use the transvaginal probe in ultrasound examinations to give mothers the best possible medical information.

The level of hysteria created in Virginia to oppose ultrasound legislation amounts to the lowest tactic yet from an industry and movement that continues to assert that an abortion is merely the removal of a "blob of pregnancy tissue." Ultrasound proves them wrong. No wonder they have to resort to low-level tactics of deceit and slander to prevent such laws from being passed.

## Speaking Out for Chen Guangcheng—a Human Rights Champion
### February 9, 2012

Very few reports can be found in the press these days about the brutal one-child per family population policy of China. Gruesome stories of forced abortion and sterilization happening in China under this policy have been documented for decades and can be found easily through an Internet search. Yet, apparently the mainstream media does not find it tasteful to expose to the public the barbaric nature of the current Chinese regime, which happens to be the largest creditor nation of the United States.

In China, there are 13 million documented abortions every year—more than 35,000 per day. There have been more than 400 million abortions in China since the middle of the last century. That equals the entire population of the United States. And those brave Chinese dissidents who speak out against such a practice have placed their lives and the lives of their loved ones in jeopardy.

One such dissident is Chen Guangcheng, a blind human rights lawyer who dared to help victims of forced abortion in his country. In 2005, Chen published the results of an investigation he undertook into the coercive family planning practices in Linyl County, Shandong Province. In this report he exposed the fact that there had been 130,000 forced abortions and sterilizations in Linyl in 2005. Among the many stories in the report there are accounts of:

- a woman forcibly aborted and sterilized seven months into her pregnancy;
- villagers sleeping in fields to evade the brutal family planning officials;
- family planning officials breaking three brooms over the head of an elderly man;
- forcing a grandmother and her brother to beat each other; and
- detailed discussions of the practice known as "implication"—the detention, fining and torture of those who violate the One Child policy.

To read this report go to www.womensrightswithoutfrontiers.org/chenreport.pdf.

For speaking out in this manner, Chen received a four-year jail sentence where he was beaten, tortured and denied essential medical care. When finally released in September of 2010, he was sent to a larger prison—his home village. Here he was put under police surveillance 24/7 and the entire village was put under strict police supervision and examination. He remains under house arrest where he has been tortured and denied medical treatment.

While under such scrutiny, Chen produced a video depicting the treatment he was receiving and exposing the brutality of the One Child policy. He had the video smuggled out of the country knowing full well that once this was discovered he would again be beaten and tortured. Indeed, after discovery of the video both he and his wife were beaten senseless and left on their bed without medical treatment.

Human Rights attorney, Reggie Littlejohn, president of Women's Rights Without Frontiers, an organization dedicated to exposing and ending the tortuous One Child policy in China states: "Chen is suffering for doing what we are doing: exposing the truth behind forced abortion and sterilization in China... The spirit of the Cultural Revolution lives on in China's family planning death machine. We have chosen to release the names of the perpetrators of these crimes against humanity, so that they can be held accountable before the world."

President Obama is scheduled to meet the likely new leader of China, V. P. Xi Jinping on February 14. He has been made aware of the plight of Chen, but will he speak up? If his past conduct towards China is an indicator (he has denounced past US-China policies that saw China as a dangerous enemy of freedom), then this is highly unlikely. But Americans must speak up for this man who represents the freedom aspirations of all human beings made in the image of God.

Littlejohn's organization has given us tools to speak up for Chen and all those dissidents in China who are suffering because they dare question the criminal conduct of their nation's leaders. Go to www. womensrightswithoutfrontiers.org, and you can sign a petition on behalf of Chen and his family demanding humane treatment and release from his home prison.

Will you join me on behalf of freedom and speak up for Chen by signing the petition?

## Thirty Nine Years and Still Waiting
### January 25, 2012

January 22, 2012 marked the 39th anniversary of *Roe v. Wade*—that infamous decision from the United States Supreme Court that removed legal protection from unborn children and opened the door for abortion on demand in this country. Since then more than 54 million unborn children have died from abortion and the lives of millions more, both men and women, have been forever scarred from trauma suffered due to the fateful exercise of their so-called "right to choose."

This last week I was a participant in Washington, D.C., with over 100,000 people, both young and old, at the annual March for Life. This event is held yearly to commemorate the horrendous and fateful decision of *Roe* and to pray for an end to abortion on demand. I left this event more encouraged than I have been in a long time and hopeful that perhaps America is on the verge of a great turnaround on this issue.

In attendance were thousands of young people under the age of thirty protesting what abortion has done to their generation. One young couple with three small children shared with me how abortion had impacted the lives of their families because several siblings had undergone abortions. They talked about the pain, sense of loss and grief that they felt for their siblings who continue to suffer emotionally because of the choices they made. As they talked with me I knew that their story was not unique and thousands upon thousands of other participants in the march could share similar stories.

The March was attended by members of virtually every Christian denomination who oppose abortion as a matter of their faith commitment, as well as by others who have no particular religious faith but oppose abortion on secular grounds. Further, in attendance were members of virtually every ethnic minority group showing that opposition to abortion is not limited to any one particular group of people. Abortion does not discriminate. It takes the lives of babies of every color and race.

The day after the March I moderated a forum of national prolife leaders who meet quarterly in Washington, D.C., to exchange information and encourage one another. Topics discussed included not only issues relating to the practice of abortion across the nation, but also the upcoming presidential election this November. The foremost question on the minds of everybody at this meeting was simply which candidate is the most likely to replace President Obama and show true leadership that will bring us closer to the day when America becomes an abortion free nation. The determination to succeed in this great quest that was shown by these leaders at this meeting gives me further cause to be optimistic and hopeful.

Thirty nine years have passed since a culture of abortion was thrust upon our nation. And our nation continues to wait for the day when true liberty reigns in America and the lives of all, both born and unborn, are protected under the law. From what I witnessed this last week in Washington, D.C. I believe that this day of liberation is closer at hand than anybody can possibly imagine.

## A Life Worthy to Be Lived
### January 17, 2012

The Supreme Court's 1973 decision of *Roe v. Wade* not only opened the door for abortion on demand throughout all nine months of pregnancy, but it also provided very troubling language which suggests that some human beings are not worthy of life. In this decision the Court stated that laws could only protect unborn human life after the time during pregnancy when the unborn child is deemed viable. Viability is medically defined as the point when the unborn can live independently outside of the womb, albeit with artificial means of support.

The Court stated that it is at this point of viability when an unborn child is capable of "meaningful life outside the womb" and thus, can be protected by law. In making this statement the Court clearly infers that some human lives are not "meaningful" and not worthy to be protected by law.

While viability of an unborn child is generally accepted to be around 24 weeks gestational age, there are reported cases of babies younger surviving after premature delivery. Further, the accepted point of viability is only a reflection of the state of medical technology. As medical technology improves the accepted point of viability for a premature baby becomes earlier in pregnancy. In other words, the concept of viability is purely a subjective one that changes with advances in technology. Yet, the Court used this subjective concept as a measuring rod to determine which human lives are meaningful and which lives are not.

Apparently, the Court believed that viability is an important point in pregnancy to make such a distinction because prior to viability the unborn child is completely dependent upon his mother for survival. If this is the criterion to determine whether a life is worthy to be lived then what about children, born or unborn, with severe handicaps and/or terminal conditions? Are their lives not "meaningful" and thus, should be ended because of the perceived burden they place upon society?

Due to the current state of medical technology we now can detect various genetic handicaps of children within the womb. This ability to determine whether a child will be born with such a handicap also provides parents with information from which they can choose abortion if they determine that the child is too severely handicapped to have a "meaningful life outside the womb."

One of the most tragic results of abortion on demand can be seen in the plight of children who have a condition known as Down Syndrome. Abortion statistics tell us that currently 9 out of 10 children diagnosed in the womb with Down Syndrome are aborted. Apparently, the decisions to abort such children are made from a determination that, if born, their lives will be overwhelming burdensome and will lack sufficient meaning to be worthy of living.

With the acceptance of abortion on demand and the edict in *Roe v. Wade* American culture has indeed adopted a utilitarian ethic that states some human lives lack meaning and thus, are not worthy to be lived. Yet, parents who have children that are afflicted with Down Syndrome declare the exact opposite. They assert that these children bring joy and purpose to their families and are blessings to many.

No better case can be made for the value a Down Syndrome child brings to his parents and family than the following story about Noah, a child born with Down Syndrome who brings great joy to all who meet him. See www.myfoxdfw.com//dpp/video/dad-working-to-change-down-syndrome-attitudes.

Noah was fortunate to have parents who valued his life regardless of its physical limitations. Many other children diagnosed with Down Syndrome in the womb are not so fortunate. Yet, Noah speaks for these children and clearly is a life worthy to be lived.

In contemporary American culture, life is cheapened and devalued. And those who are afflicted with certain physical "defects," such as Down Syndrome, are seen not as blessings, as clearly exemplified by Noah, but as burdens that should be eliminated prior to birth.

Noah's life teaches us something much different from what American societal norms dictate. Like all children born or unborn Noah has a life worthy to be lived.

# In Honor of Baby Corrine—a Life Lived with Purpose
## December 30, 2011

This is written in honor of baby Corrine, whose short life on earth was well lived and blessed others. Her short life on earth was full of purpose and value. She reminds us that all life, regardless of condition of dependency or physical "imperfection" has meaning and purpose and can bless others.

Much has been said over the years by some about the need for abortion so that parents will be able to terminate a pregnancy when the condition of the unborn child is terminable and "incompatible with life." They argue that since such a child will not survive long after birth that her life should be ended to prevent her parents from suffering trauma due to her condition.

Baby Corrine's life is a response to this argument. This obituary taken from the *Free-Lance Star*—a newspaper in Fredericksburg, Virginia— should cause those who hold to this position to think again.

## *Free-Lance Star*, Fredericksburg, Virginia
### Corrine C. Stryker, December 22, 2011

Corrine Catherine Stryker, infant daughter of Richard and Paula Stryker, passed away Saturday, Dec. 17, 2011, at Inova Fair Oaks Hospital. Corrine Catherine was born the same day, Dec. 17, 2011, at 12:27 p.m.

Corrine Catherine started bringing people closer to God the day her parents knew she was inside her mommy. When she was diagnosed in the womb as "incompatible with life," it did not stop her family from loving her or valuing her place in their lives.

Through the love her family received from her presence, even in the womb, Corrine opened people's eyes to the beauty of life. For someone so frail, she lifted mountains of stone and rock that once had encrusted the hearts of people unable to see the potential for her beauty and meaning. Without uttering a word, she communicated the meaning of unconditional love, directed people closer to their faith, and explained the redemptive power of suffering.

In only an hour and a half, Corrine Catherine shared her special grace with all of her family, giving each of them special moments and memories that they will always treasure. She received a sacred birthday party while being passed around in loving arms. After one final embrace by her mother, Corrine Catherine peacefully fell asleep for her final rest. Corrine Catherine was called back by her heavenly Father after what, for her family, will be an eternity of love.

Her parents and family are comforted to know that she will continue to bring people closer to the Father, and they look forward to being united with her again in their heavenly home.

## Jumping for Joy—Merry Christmas 2011
### December 21, 2011

Christmas time is here and once again our nation is busy in the hustle and bustle of the Holiday season. Millions of dollars will be spent on gifts for the special people in our lives as it is a wonderful thing to take time and express love to those who are important to us. And, of course, the magic of the Holiday excites children who anxiously await the pretend arrival of Old St. Nick on Christmas Eve.

Christmas, however, is so much more than gifts and Santa Claus. As believers, we have based our entire lives on the truth found in the little baby who slept his first night on earth in a manger in the presence of farm animals. Emmanuel (God is with us) has come to earth and, in doing so, has provided for us eternal life and a relationship with the Creator of the universe.

The Christmas story also has profound prolife meaning. Mary, an unwed pregnant teenager at the time, clearly was faced with the embarrassment of the situation and accusations from the gossip mongers in her community. Yet, she placed her situation in the hands of God trusting that in his infinite wisdom and sovereignty all would be well.

My favorite part of the Christmas story comes from the gospel of Luke where Mary visits her cousin Elizabeth who, though in her elder years, is also pregnant with a special baby—John the Baptist. Scripture tells us that when Mary enters the home of Elizabeth a very interesting exchange takes place as Elizabeth proclaims: "Why am I so favored, that the mother of my Lord should come to me! As soon as the sound of your greeting reached my ears, the baby in my womb leaped for joy" (Luke 1: 43–44).

It is interesting to note that Luke, the author of this passage, was a physician. As such a professional in his day he obviously had delivered quite a few babies. It is profound to note that Dr. Luke refers to John who resides at this time within his mother's womb as a baby and, as a medical doctor, makes no distinction between unborn and born human life. Further, his description of this event, while inspired by the Holy Spirit, also reads much like a medical observation of prenatal life. Indeed, through the modern technology of ultrasound we now can actually get a glimpse of what this may have looked like within the womb of Elizabeth.

See www.youtube.com/watch?v=5CdYYzK47X0&feature=mfu_in_order&list=UL.

We have much to be thankful for this Christmas season. Because of Emmanuel, God is truly with us and, like John within the womb of his mother Elizabeth, we too should be jumping for joy. We should jump for joy because of the gift of life, both physical and spiritual, that the child of Bethlehem has given us. Merry Christmas to all.

## It Is Not Just the Economy Stupid!
### December 9, 2011

Across the political spectrum we hear continuous lamentations about the state of the economy and how voter's economic concerns will determine the political direction of the nation in the next election. Both the Tea Party on the right and Occupy Wall Street on the left show great discontent and anxiety over our economic future.

What role, if any, will social issues (and particularly the abortion issue) play in the upcoming election of 2012?

While expressing prolife sentiments, leaders of the Tea Party movement have been adamant that social issues, i.e., abortion, will not be given any place of importance in the current public debate. They assert that such issues are divisive and, if emphasized, will weaken the impact of their demands for pro-growth economic policies and fundamental reforms of our political system.

These pundits fail to realize, however, that in addition to the millions of American who want to only discuss economic woes are millions more who care about the moral fabric and decay of the country. Such social conservatives deeply care about the killing of 3,500 unborn children a day—1.2 million a year through abortion. They intensely care about the emotional devastation that abortion brings to both men and women. And they profoundly care about the cultural loss of respect for life that has engulfed our culture after 38 years of abortion on demand in America.

These people will also vote, unless their heartfelt concerns are not addressed. Accordingly, if such matters are not discussed in the public square as critical issues then such voters will stay home on Election Day.

These heartfelt concerns cry out for our nation to choose a different path from the one upon which it is currently traveling. The millions of unborn human beings who now are subject to abortion and their mothers who have been told that ending the life of their pre-born is their only solution are truly the voiceless in our nation. They need political leaders to courageously step up and advocate their cause of life.

Such life advocates do exist through the work of charitable Pregnancy Resource Centers and Medical Clinics (PRCs). These voices for the voiceless are in every community providing life-affirming resources to empower mothers to choose life. With the help of PRCs and the support of caring communities of faith many women choose life and are given hope for the future.

President Bill Clinton was elected in 1992 in the midst of a difficult economic recession. He campaigned on economic issues with the slogan "It's the economy stupid." As in 1992 we can also agree that the state of the economy is critical to our national future.

But we must also assert loudly and clearly that "It is not just the economy stupid!"

## The *Life Choice* Election of 2012
### November 29, 2011

The state of the economy continues to be the issue that political commentators and the media proclaim as the number one concern facing Americans in the upcoming election of 2012. Indeed, all of the current Republican candidates for president are emphasizing economic issues as they challenge President Obama's reelection. The economic situation of our nation is not good. Unemployment is high and the nation is suffering from large numbers of unemployed and larger numbers of underemployed who are struggling to support their families.

The state of the economy is, of course, an issue of vital concern. However, abortion and related life issues are absolute critical issues that will define the future of America. Yet, they are barely visible on the media's radar screen. The state of the economy will undoubtedly determine how millions of Americans vote in November 2012, but the future of the nation will ultimately be determined by how Americans decide the abortion/life issues.

President Abraham Lincoln said that our nation cannot continue to exist half slave and half free. President Ronald Reagan said, in the spirit of Lincoln, that our nation cannot continue to exist where the lives of some human beings, i.e., the unborn, are not protected under the law while others are granted such protection. Indeed, current abortion statistics are sobering. Since 1973 nearly 55 million unborn children have been killed by abortion. Abortion takes the lives of 1.3 million unborn children a year, 3,300 per day and one every 25 seconds.

Can this nation survive when it is in fact committing demographic suicide and killing our posterity? The results of the upcoming election may well answer this question.

The next President and Congress will have the ability to bring an end to this tragic era of abortion on demand. Not only can they pass meaningful legislation that will protect the unborn but they ultimately will determine the future of _**Roe v. Wade**_ and its legal license of unlimited abortion.

The future direction of the United States Supreme will undoubtedly be determined by the next president. A look at the current justices and their ages clearly shows that the results of this upcoming election will likely decide for the next generation whether _**Roe**_ and its edict of abortion on demand remains the law of the land.

Legal commentators tend to categorize the current makeup of the Court as 4-1-4. That is to say, there are four justices—Chief Justice John Roberts, Antonin Scalia, Clarence Thomas and Samuel Alito— who vote the conservative position on social issues; there are four justices—Bader Ginsberg, Stephen Breyer, Sonia Sotomayer and Elena Kagan—who vote the liberal position on issues; and one justice—Anthony Kennedy—who is generally conservative but remains the swing vote on social issues, particularly abortion and the future of *Roe v. Wade*.

It is generally believed that the four conservative justices would, in the appropriate case, vote to overturn *Roe* and the four liberal justices will vote to uphold it. While he has voted to uphold prolife protective provisions it is unclear as to how Justice Kennedy would vote on the future of *Roe*.

Kennedy, a Roman Catholic, was appointed to the high court in 1988 by President Ronald Reagan. At the time it was hoped that he would be the fifth vote on the court to reverse and correct the tragedy and colossal judicial blunder of *Roe*. Sadly, however, Kennedy was a major disappointment in 1992 when he voted with the majority as the fifth vote in *Planned Parenthood v. Casey* to uphold the central and faulty premise of *Roe* that a constitutional right of privacy exists that includes a right to choose an abortion.

Despite his vote in *Casey*, there is some speculation that Justice Kennedy might have undergone a change of view and would change his vote on the constitutionality of *Roe*. While such an assumption is impossible to make, Kennedy is a reliable vote to uphold abortion restrictions. He wrote the majority opinion in *Gonzales v. Carhart (2007)*, the decision that upheld the Congressional ban on the brutal practice of partial birth abortion.

A look at the ages of the current justices indicates that the next president will have the opportunity to appoint one or more justices to the high court. Such appointments will clearly tip the balance when it comes to abortion and *Roe v. Wade*. On the conservative wing of the court Chief Justice Roberts is 56, Justice Scalia is 75, Justice Thomas is 62 and Justice Alito is 60. On the liberal wing Justice Ginsberg is 78, Justice Breyer is 73, Justice Sotomayer is 57, and Justice Kagan is 51. Justice Kennedy, the swing vote, is 75.

Any, or all, of the four oldest justices—Ginsberg, Scalia, Kennedy, and Breyer—could retire in the next four years. Ginsberg, in particular, has suffered from cancer and the speculation is that she is remaining on the court only to prevent her replacement to come from a conservative prolife president.

The political ramifications of this next election are clear when it concerns the makeup of the Supreme Court and the future of abortion on demand. President Obama has said that in his view abortion is a fundamental right and that he will accordingly appoint justices who will uphold ***Roe v. Wade***. Thus, if he is reelected and either Scalia or Kennedy is replaced by him the future of ***Roe*** will be secured and millions more unborn will die. On the other hand, if a prolife President is elected in 2012 and Ginsberg, Kennedy, and/or Breyer is replaced then clearly ***Roe v. Wade*** will be discarded and take it's deserved place alongside the ***Dred Scott Decision*** of 1857 as the one of the most divisive Supreme Court decisions in our nation's history.

Perhaps the challenge for America in 2012 can be summed up in Deuteronomy 30:19, which says: "I call heaven and earth to record this day against you, that I have set before you life and death, blessing and cursing: therefore choose life, that both you and your descendants may live."

The election of 2012 is the "Life Choice Election" of our time. Will America choose life in 2012 and secure a future for our descendants? Or will this great nation continue on its slippery slide down a path that will leave us in ruins and eliminate our posterity?

The call to our nation today is simple—*choose life so that you and your descendants may live.*

## Ronald Reagan and Crisis Pregnancy Centers
**February 9, 2011**

This year the nation remembers President Ronald Reagan on the 100th anniversary of his birth in 1911. The Reagan presidency was indeed a unique time in American history when the spirit and confidence of the nation was revived. Reagan's sunny optimism and belief that America's best days were ahead along with his steadfast leadership based upon unshakable core values pulled our nation out of the dark spiritual malaise that had engulfed it during the 1970s.

For the prolife movement President Reagan's leadership was inspiring. His presidency started eight years after the Supreme Court's decision of *Roe v. Wade*. At that time the nation had begun to grasp the grisly implications of *Roe*, which resulted in the annual destruction of 1.5 million unborn children a year from abortion on demand. (More than 53 million abortions have occurred since 1973.) Mr. Reagan, first as a presidential candidate and then as president, was unwavering in his prolife convictions and advocacy for the right to life. His administration led the way with policies that banned the funding of tax dollars to organizations that promote abortion as a method of family planning and his appointments to federal agencies and the federal courts were of highly qualified people who shared his foundational prolife beliefs.

Few people are aware, however, of Ronald Reagan's admiration for the work of prolife crisis pregnancy centers. These centers began to flourish across the nation in the 1980s as a response to the proliferation of abortion clinics and the rise of a multi-million dollar tax-supported abortion industry. Crisis pregnancy centers or CPCs, as they were called then, began to spring up in every community of the nation offering alternatives to abortion to women in problem pregnancies. The services provided included free pregnancy testing, material assistance, referrals for medical care and legal help, and temporary housing assistance. Today this movement has flourished and there now are more than 3,000 such centers nationwide (now referred to as Pregnancy Resource Centers) and hundreds of them operate as medical clinics providing pregnancy confirmation through ultrasound, STI testing and Treatment and even prenatal care.

I became aware of President Reagan's support for the work of CPCs in 1983. Earlier that year Laura, my wife, had written the president to thank him for his prolife commitment and to tell him of our work in opening the first CPC in the Northwest in Seattle. Neither of us expected a response. I was pleasantly surprised; however, when an unsolicited letter from the President addressed to my wife came in November. The letter reads in part:

> *I was pleased to learn recently of the valuable and important work performed by the Crisis Pregnancy Center. The time and energy you devote to providing special services for women facing a problem pregnancy are a vital community resource.*
>
> *The need for services provided by organizations like yours is great, and there are few challenges to the well-being of our society which call for more sensitivity and selflessness. By helping to meet this challenge, you have demonstrated to thousands of individual women that there is indeed, a place to turn for strength and assistance. More importantly, you have served as a beacon of light to the community at large, demonstrating that positive solutions to difficult problems are available if we work together.*
> *You can be sure that you have my wholehearted support and my prayers for the heightened public awareness your activities so richly deserve. God bless you.*
>
> *Sincerely,*
> *Ronald Reagan*

Two years later in 1985 the President sent another letter to address the attendees at the annual fund raising banquet for the Crisis Pregnancy Center of King County in Seattle. In this letter he states:

> *The CPC of King County, along with other centers like it across the country, shows Americans that the civilized, morally defensible response to problem pregnancies is not the cynical surrender of abortion, but the life-affirming alliance of all sectors of the community to overcome our problems. You have my admiration, my prayers, and my full support for your beautiful work. God bless you.*

In 1987 I left Seattle to come to the Washington DC area and work full time as an attorney for the prolife cause. While I was honored to be in two meetings with President Reagan unfortunately, due to the size of the group in both meetings, I did not have the chance to personally shake his hand and tell him how much his support meant to us. I do have, however, both of these letters framed and hanging in my office as priceless reminders of a president who truly cared for the weak and vulnerable of this great nation.

Today, as in1980 our nation faces perilous times and is confronted by issues of which the ultimate outcome will determine the destiny of this republic. The issue of the protection of innocent human life continues to confront the conscience of the nation. That is why Ronald Reagan knew that the work of prolife CPCs embody the highest of American principles and ideals.

In 2012 we will once again go to the polls and select a President to lead us in perilous times. Will this person truly believe, as Ronald Reagan did, in the foundational principle of America that all human beings, born and unborn, are made in the image of God and as such are endowed with the unalienable rights of life, liberty and the pursuit of happiness?

As we celebrate the 100th anniversary of the birth of Roald Reagan let us as a nation recommit ourselves to the ideals that e believed in regarding the sanctity of human life. And let every community support with great pride, as he did, the work of its local prfe preg-nancy counseling centers as such agencies work day in and y out.

## The Economy and Abortion
### September 21, 2010

Abortion is a moral and spiritual issue. It is an intense political social issue. It is also a constitutional and legal issue that has divi the nation, splintered political parties and emotionally devasta millions of people, both men and women.

Abortion is also an economic issue. The economic crisis we now fac is caused by numerous factors that all relate to flawed governmenta policies. However, the current economic crisis and, indeed, our eco-nomic future as a nation are impacted by the very uncomfortable fact that since 1973 (when the Supreme Court gave us constitutionally mandated abortion-on-demand), more than 52 million unborn chil-dren have been killed by abortion.

What impact has this massive destruction of human life had on our current economic situation? A very interesting study called *The Cost of Abortion* (www.thecostofabortion.com) gives some insight to this question. The conclusions of this study are staggering and should be taken into consideration by all political leaders who see the state of the economy as the primary issue motivating voters in the upcoming election.

This study begins with the figures for the total number of surgical abortions carried out in the United States from 1973 to 2007. An assumption is made that one-half of these aborted children would be female and, based upon figures from the Centers for Disease Control, each female—at age 25—would have an average of a single child. The study then combines these calculations to generate a number of "missing persons" from the USA from 1973 to 2007. The Gross Domestic Product per capita for each year is then multiplied by the number of "missing persons." Accordingly, the sum of lost GDP from 1973 to 2007 due to surgical abortion is nearly $37 trillion.

It does not take a rocket scientist to understand that a loss of $37 trillion to our economy since 1973 has taken a big toll. Because of abortion, we have 52 million fewer taxpayers who would have provided a strong economic foundation for the nation. Because of abortion, we have lost millions of successful entrepreneurs, inventors, business owners, physicians, lawyers, teachers, venture capitalists, investors, and, of course, mothers and fathers who would have birthed children whose descendants would have become productive citizens contributing to a robust economy.

Abortion is an economic issue. America's most valuable natural resources are human beings who through the creative genius of the human spirit create innovative ways to overcome problems. Abortion has destroyed a large portion of this natural resource.

Today, the state of the economy is a major issue of concern. As our national debt skyrockets and increased taxation and regulations are placed upon small businesses, our unemployment rate rises. These economic concerns have fueled the Tea Party movement, which has galvanized grass-roots political protest against our current political leaders who want to impose bigger government, higher taxation and restricted freedom. The political polls indicate that this protest movement is gaining strength and is expected to have a major impact in this next election upon the political direction of the country.

There is a raging debate among Tea Party leaders regarding the role social issues, such as abortion, should play in their agenda. Many argue that these issues are divisive and should be downplayed in order to attract the broadest coalition possible to bring about economic change. While most participants in the Tea Party movement express prolife sentiments, they do not apparently make the connection between abortion and our economic plight—but they should.

The next two election cycles will determine the ultimate fate of our nation. Our elected representatives will make decisions on the critical issues of taxation, individual liberty and the role of government. In making these decisions they must understand that abortion is an issue that cannot be ignored. If we truly want to restore economic health to the nation then this wanton destruction of innocent human life must end.

## At Last—A Rational Judicial Decision that Protects Human Life
### September 9, 2010

Recently federal judge Royce Lambert issued a preliminary injunction barring the federal government from funding scientific research that uses stem cells derived from human embryos. The law suit was brought against the federal government by stem cell researchers who said the Obama executive order allowing federal funding for such research from the National Institutes of Health violates federal law prohibiting funding of the destruction of human embryos through scientific research.

Judge Lambert's ruling cited the Dickey-Wicker Amendment, passed by Congress in 1996, which bars the use of federal monies for "research in which a human embryo or embryos are destroyed, discarded or knowingly subjected to risk of injury or death." Unfortunately, the U.S. Court of Appeals in Washington has put on hold this injunction saying that it was not ruling on the merits of the law suit but only to give Judge Lambert "sufficient opportunity to consider the merits of the emergency motion for stay." The appellate court emphasized that its decision "should not be construed in any way as a ruling on the merits of that motion."

The removal of embryonic stem cells from an embryo for research purposes, of course, means that the embryo is killed in the process. Thus, the clear intent of this law is to protect embryonic human life. However, in the early days of his administration President Obama issued a presidential executive order that attempted to circumvent the Dickey-Wicker restrictions and allow federal funding for such research, as long as the actual killing of the embryo is paid for with private funds. The administration argues that under the Obama executive order federal funds only pay for experimenting with stem cells taken from embryos—not for experimentation on the embryos themselves. Therefore, the administration asserts that since such research only deals with stem cells already available, and not with human embryos, it should be allowed.

Judge Lambert saw this fine line distinction unpersuasive and issued a preliminary injunction against the funding saying, "(Embryonic stem cell) research is clearly research in which an embryo is destroyed. . . Embryonic stem cell research necessarily depends upon the destruction of a human embryo."

An injunction of this nature is issued by a court only if the prevailing party shows that there is a strong likelihood of success on merits when the matter goes to trial. Thus, in the judge's opinion, there is a strong likelihood that this injunction will become permanent after trial.

I was ecstatic in reviewing this decision because finally a federal judge has made a ruling based upon the clear reading and intent of the law, as opposed to his or her own personal political preferences. Nobody knows what the personal views of Judge Lambert are on the issue of fetal embryonic research. However, such views are totally irrelevant. It is the role of the judiciary to interpret the law as it is clearly intended and not to base decisions upon political biases and what they think the law should be. The language and intent of the Dickey-Wicker Amendment are clear. Judge Lambert's ruling merely abides by this intent, as unmistakably expressed by a bi-partisan Congress in 1996.

This apparent judicial philosophy of Judge Lambert is not adhered to by other federal judges. In fact, activist judges who have a political agenda to achieve would probably have rendered an opinion in favor of the Obama administration's desire to expand federal funding of fetal embryonic research.

When I was in law school my constitutional law professor emphasized how the law was a tool to be used to achieve a more just society. A judge, in his opinion, has a duty to interpret the written law—both constitutional and statutory—in a manner that corrects societal injustices, as he or she perceives them. The proper role of a judge in this scenario is to make sure that those who, in the opinion of the judge, are aggrieved victims of injustice are compensated by the courts for their sufferings. If, according to my professor, the law inadequately provides remedial help to such victims then the judge must stretch the law and make necessary adjustments so that justice prevails. In other words, a judge, under this view, should serve as a legislator and create rules of law that will achieve a just result (as defined by the judge), as opposed to merely applying the law as written to the situation at hand.

To left-wing political activists this view of the role of the judiciary is essential to achieve their political ends. If they fail in passing their agenda through legislative means they resort to the courts arguing that the law, adopted by the representatives of the people, is unjust and unconstitutional. Unelected life-time appointed federal judges then are encouraged to change the law based not upon its clear wording or intent, but rather upon their own political views. Under this scenario judges are viewed as super-legislators who are much wiser than the elected representatives of the people and thus, can overrule the decisions of the people made through the electoral process.

The greatest example of this kind of judicial mischief is found in the infamous 1973 decision of **_Roe v. Wade_**, which overturned the laws of all fifty states that prohibited and restricted abortion. The word "abortion" does not appear in the U.S. Constitution and prior to 1973 the act was regulated and prohibited by the criminal laws of each state. Yet, the high court somehow found a way to decriminalize abortion and by making it a constitutional right it voided the laws of each state adopted by their elected representatives. The

Court did this by stretching a previously found constitutional and unspecified general right of privacy (which also does not appear in the Constitution) to include a right to terminate a pregnancy. In so acting, the Court arrived at a political result that the political advocates of abortion on demand could not have achieved through the legislative process.

Since this decision more that 52 million unborn children have died from abortion and the nation has been divided in a manner not seen since the days of slavery. This so-called superior wisdom of the judiciary has wreaked havoc upon our nation.

America is a constitutional republic. We elect representatives of the people to pass laws for the betterment of society. If such elected representatives pass laws and regulations that do not accomplish a more just society then the public has the ability to change their elected representative through the ballot box. This is clearly what government of, by and for the people means. The role of the judiciary is not to create laws but to properly interpret them and apply them to the situation that they are reviewing.

A judge must not arrive at a decision based upon what he or she desires politically, but instead solely upon the clear meaning of the law in question. This is exactly what Judge Lambert did in his decision to enjoin federal funds from being spent on embryonic research. It is also what he is being criticized for by the Obama Administration and by those who desire to have the law used to achieve their political agenda. To such people it is irrelevant that the Dickey-Wicker Amendment was passed by elected representatives and signed into law by President Clinton. Rather, since they do not like this law they want the judiciary to circumvent the political process and come up with their desired result of expanding federal funding of fetal embryonic research.

The decision of Judge Lambert is an example of correct judicial reasoning and logic. Further, it protects human life from destruction. If this decision is upheld at trial and on appeal it will open up avenues for federal funding of research using adult stem cells, which has shown great promise in finding cures for certain diseases.

The issue of the judiciary and its role in our system of government is not an issue being discussed much these days by candidates for political office but it should be. The example of Judge Lambert in this recent decision is a model for politicians to endorse and support once they are in elective office.

## Will The Tea Party Remember the Genius of the Three-Legged Milking Stool?
### August 31, 2010

Political change is blowing in the wind but it is not the change promised by Barack Obama when he ran for the presidency. For sure, Obama has brought political change to the nation, but his transformational policies have meant bigger government, higher taxes, federal subsidies of abortion on demand, and greater governmental control over the lives of American citizens.

Hundreds of thousands of citizens across the nation have raised their voices to protest Obama's policies of change. They are crying out for a different change that will honor the integrity of each individual and create an atmosphere where true liberty in all spheres of life—economic, cultural, and spiritual—reigns. Political pollsters are now predicting a huge seismic shift in the political landscape this November. The recent Glenn Beck sponsored rally in Washington, D.C., attended by thousands upon thousands of grass roots activists, indicates that this public outcry of protest is real and powerful.

The Tea Party movement is comprised of Republicans, Democrats, and Independents from all walks of life. The political ruling elite, the corporate world, and the media have completely failed to comprehend this populist movement dismissing it as marginal, extreme and even racist. However, this movement is not composed of ignorant and bigoted individuals, as suggested by the political class. Rather, it is an authentic grassroots movement of thoughtful and patriotic people demanding real change from an out-of-touch political establishment.

The Tea Party movement, for the most part, centers its protest on economic issues and concern about the loss of freedom that an ever-growing federal government brings. These concerns are valid and appropriate. Most leaders of this movement also believe in the sanctity of life and the need to halt the wholesale destruction of innocent human life through abortion and other life related issues such as embryonic stem cell research. However, many in the Tea Party movement have made it clear that while they are sympathetic with the prolife cause, the abortion issue is not formally part of the Tea Party agenda.

Economic issues are a vital concern; as is the growing size of the federal government and its overreaching into the lives of ordinary citizens. The overwhelming burden of excess regulation and taxation upon businesses and individuals is alarming. In the same manner, however, the killing of 1.25 million unborn children annually from abortion must be a grave concern. Accordingly, a failure by the Tea Party to incorporate the serious prolife concerns of millions of Americans into its agenda will be fatal to achieving success.

Perhaps, the Tea Party should take a lesson from the old fashioned three-legged milking stool. When I was a child I visited my aunt and uncle on their dairy farm and was intrigued watching my uncle milk the cows while sitting on a three-legged stool. I asked him why he used such a funny chair to milk the cows. He explained that a four legged chair can be unbalanced if one of its legs is a different length than the others and it could even tip over if you leaned backwards. A three legged stool, on the other hand, balances evenly and won't tip over even if one of its legs is longer.

We should learn something from the old-fashioned milking stool. There are three legs to a successful agenda that will change America for the better. Each leg is critical and the current grassroots movement for change in America will collapse if any of these legs is ignored. These legs are:

1. **Revival of the Economy:** This leg requires the establishment a strong robust economy that creates full employment and does not burden small businesses with taxes and oppressive regulations that hinder job development. Limited government and reduced taxation are at the core and are necessary to bring the nation out of the serious economic recession/depression in which we find ourselves.

2. **Maintaining a Strong National Defense and Protecting Homeland Security:** This leg requires a serious commitment by the government to win the war on terror and protect our country's borders from those who would illegally enter and do us harm.

3. **Protecting the Family Unit and Restoring the Right to Life for All:** The social issues—protecting the sanctity of marriage and restoring the right to life—are issues of equal importance. Millions of Americans, including myself, have placed these issues at the top of the priorities list for the next generation of political leaders to seriously address.

To date, while it appears that most Tea Party leaders verbally support all three legs of this "milk stool" some, such as Indiana Governor Mitch Daniels, assert that the social issues (and specifically abortion and the right to life) must take a back seat to the other two legs, which are seen as more important. A further example of this viewpoint was shown in a recent interview of Sarah Palin with Sean Hannity of *Fox News*. Gov. Sarah Palin, a committed prolife leader, was asked to name the top five issues facing the country today and the deaths of 1.25 million unborn annually from abortion was not on her list. If, indeed, this is the approach a new Congress takes after the November mid-term elections, then the agenda of the Tea Party movement will fail.

America must be forewarned. A nation that fails to protect the lives of its most vulnerable members has set a course for itself that will lead to its eventual destruction from within. The killing of future generations through the act of abortion has already taken a toll on the demographical future of the nation and the Western world. Unless this trend is stopped then, notwithstanding the impact of the Tea Party movement, our culture and way of life will have effectively committed suicide.

The invention of the three legged milking stool was ingenious. Will the current populist movement for change understand this and formally incorporate the life issues into its agenda? Time will tell and the future of America hangs in the balance.

## Will Republicans Put "First Things First"?
### August 11, 2010

Public opinion polls and the political pundits seem to now agree that if the November elections were held today the Republican Party would win an historic landslide victory. Indeed, the agenda of the Obama administration has been dominated by far left policies that have deepened the current economic recession and has pursued a radical social agenda, which includes a steadfast commitment to abortion on demand.

Public discontent with these policies is intense and the winds of political change are blowing mightily throughout the nation. The Tea Party movement has galvanized political dissension against the Obama agenda from all segments of society, and political commentators are telling us that the stage is being set for a political tsunami in November that sweeps out the old and brings in the new.

The Republican Party is confidently gearing itself up for taking over the reins of power in Washington, D.C., and thus, bringing about corrective change that will reverse the present course of the country. However, the pro-life movement must inquire of the Republicans if legal protection for the fundamental right to life will be on the forefront of these political changes to come. Will the Republicans who are swept into power because they espoused correct political rhetoric turn their backs on the pro-life movement once political power is obtained?

Recent comments from Indiana's Republican governor Mitch Daniels leaves one with an unsettling feeling that a Republican assent to power may not guarantee significant changes to protect innocent human life from abortion and euthanasia. Daniels is a successful conservative governor who is being mentioned by the pundits as possible presidential timber in 2012. Indeed, his current record from a conservative standpoint is impressive.

Limited government, decreased government spending, and lower taxation on businesses and individuals are clearly being achieved in the Hoosier state under Daniels' watch. His commitment to a sane economic policy is clear and he seems to have an economic game plan to save the country from its current ruinous advance towards economic collapse. And, of course, his public political rhetoric has clearly been on the pro-family/pro-life side of the moral issues including abortion. Yet, recent comments from Daniels raise serious questions about his commitment to the moral issues—particularly on the right to life.

Daniels was recently quoted as saying that there needs to be a "truce" in the country on moral issues such as abortion. When asked a few days later in an interview with Fox News anchor Chris Wallace to explain these comments Daniels defensively emphasized that his pro-life credentials should not be questioned. He went on to say that because our economic situation is in such dire straits the government must put "first things first," downplay our differences on moral issues like abortion, and come together for the good of the country on economic policy.

Such a position amounts to a surrender to the status quo that favors abortion on demand and results in the deaths of 1.2 million unborn children a year. To call such a truce, as Daniels suggests, not only guarantees the deaths of millions of more children to abortion, but also means that the abortion industry will have achieved final victory in this cultural battle.

How can we in good conscience ever agree to such a truce? And how can we ever support a candidate for president who advocates such a position? One who truly believes that abortion is the ultimate atrocity occurring in this nation today, as I do, cannot call a truce on the issue in order to put "first things first."

In 1980 the nation elected President Ronald Reagan in the midst of a deep inflationary recession. Reagan was brought into office through the votes of millions of concerned prolife citizens who wanted to see an end to the abortion madness. Once in office, however, Reagan's advisors told social conservatives that work on the life issue would have to wait because reviving the economy was the top priority of the administration. To his credit President Reagan fought as a leader for the right to life throughout his presidency despite the advice he received from advisors to downplay social issues, particularly abortion, and put "first things first."

President Reagan was a true hero to the prolife movement and did much to advance the cause of life. But many of his advisors, like Governor Daniels, viewed the prolife movement as simply part of a political coalition that only need be placated with political rhetoric but not with solid political action. Reagan disagreed and his administration accomplished much on behalf of the right to life, notwithstanding the advice he was receiving.

As we approach the upcoming mid-term elections and the 2012 presidential sweepstakes the prolife movement must not budge on its fundamental principles. We must insist that all political candidates whom we endorse be committed to ending abortion in the country once they are elected. Candidates of the Governor Daniels stripe must be wholeheartedly rejected.

Of course, the state of the economy is critical to our survival. However, a commitment to the pursuit of a sane economic policy should not preclude a strong commitment to simultaneously ending abortion. Forty million abortions have occurred since President Reagan was elected. Calling a truce in this matter will guarantee that millions more unborn children will be added to this grim statistic. This is simply unacceptable.

Putting "first things first" should clearly mean that the destruction of innocent human life in our nation must come to a screeching halt. The question to ask the Republican Party and its candidates in the coming elections is simply: "If elected, will you put first things first?"

### Thomas Paine, Common Sense, Abortion and the United States Supreme Court
August 2, 2010

The American patriot Thomas Paine helped to fuel the American Revolution with his classic essay *Common Sense*. In this essay, Paine proclaims:

> *"[A] long habit of not thinking a thing wrong, gives it a superficial appearance of being right, and raises at first a formidable outcry in defense of custom. But the tumult soon subsides. Time makes more converts than reason."*

Paine, of course, was talking about the abuses that the American colonists suffered under the crown of England, and he was bemoaning the fact that many colonists had become so used to these abuses that over time they accepted their plight instead of rising up and overthrowing tyranny.

Perhaps Thomas Paine was prophetically observing twenty-first century America and the acquiescence of the public at large to the judicial tyranny that has imposed upon America abortion on demand. When the United States Supreme Court issued ***Roe v. Wade*** in 1973 it invalidated the laws of all fifty states that prohibited abortion. At that time an outcry was heard from some segments of society, most notably the Catholic Church, but for the most part the public at large was silent. The decision was accepted by many as an advancement of an increasingly secular and humanistic culture that views moral values as relative and changing over time.

In 1992 the United States Supreme Court had an opportunity to correct its *Roe* decision but upheld it by one vote. In ***Planned Parenthood v. Casey* (1992)** the Court's decision argued that *Roe* could not be reversed. Under the judicial doctrine of *stare decisis* legal precedent, according to the Court, should be given great respect and requires that precedents not be overturned except for compelling reasons. According to the Court in *Casey,* a generation of Americans have come to rely upon the right to abortion given by *Roe* and thus, a reversal of this decision would create intolerable havoc in the social structure of our nation. Thus, the Court continued to give the horrendous *wrong* of abortion the superficial appearance of being a *right,* and over eighteen years have passed since this decision with the abortion edict of *Roe* still intact.

Since 1973 Americans have lived with abortion on demand as part of the culture. To be sure many have risen in protest to *Roe* and public opinion polls indicate that now a majority of Americans call themselves "pro-life." However, this rising opposition to abortion has not yet reached a level where true societal change and the abolition of abortion has been achieved. It appears that still many members of the public, as described by Paine, have for too long not thought of abortion as a *wrong* and thus, have given it a superficial appearance of being a *right.*

Supreme Court Justice Ruth Bader Ginsberg recently commented on the status of *Roe* and made it clear that, in her opinion, the decision would never be corrected because the American public has come to rely upon it. Participating in a discussion during the Aspen Ideas Festival in Colorado, Ginsburg said the infamous decision won't be overturned because women and society have become accustomed to abortion as a convenient solution to unwanted pregnancies.

"Over a generation of young women have grown up, understanding they can control their own reproductive capacity, and in fact their life's destiny," Ginsburg said. "We will never go back to the way it once was. If people realize that, maybe they will have a different attitude."

It appears that Justice Ginsberg is saying that over time the *wrong* of killing innocent unborn children has taken on the "superficial appearance of being *right*" and thus, will continue. Can she possibly be correct in this assessment? After all, since 1973 more than 52 million legal abortions have occurred. Is this staggering number of deaths not enough to cause the public to rise up and demand an end to the killing? Apparently not. If the public had truly grasped the moral, ethical, spiritual and demographical implications of this number then **Roe v. Wade** and the annual multi-million dollar abortion industry that it birthed would have disintegrated by now.

The great challenge to the leaders of the prolife movement today is to successfully convict the conscience of the nation so that the necessary critical mass of public opinion is developed to bring about an end to abortion. This will take committed efforts on all fronts of our society. The church, the schools, the business community, and the political arena all must be impacted by the passionate cries of those who stand for an end to the killing of the innocent and for the establishment of a nation that truly embraces life, liberty and justice for all. Until then abortion will continue to be a *wrong* with the superficial appearance of being a *right*.

Dissatisfaction with the status quo is in the political winds and public dissension on a host of critical governmental policies is evident in the growth of the Tea Party movement. This movement is demonstrating that when sufficient numbers of the public demand a change in government policies such change can take place. We will not know until the November elections how successful the Tea Party currently is in galvanizing support for its issues. But it must be emphatically stated that those who oppose abortion must galvanize this same level of support and intensity for the life issues in order to achieve an abortion free America.

Thomas Paine successfully challenged his fellow countrymen to throw off the chains of tyranny and achieve a more just society through common sense and a commitment to truth. Eventually the American colonists banded together in a revolution not seen before in the history of the world. The American Revolution was based upon the foundational belief that all human beings are made in the image of God and thus, are afforded the inalienable rights of life, liberty and the pursuit of happiness. The value of each life comes not from what one achieves but rather from the Creator who breathes his image into each human life. A passionate and unshakable conviction of this truth propelled the birth of this nation. And this foundational truth laid the groundwork for the eventual abolition of the institution of slavery which, like abortion, denied the image of God in certain human beings.

Our Constitution was established to form a more perfect union. Perfection is something that never will be completely achieved because society is made of fallen and imperfect individuals. Yet, the American experiment in representative democracy shows that throughout history our nation continues to strive towards perfection by correcting injustices and wrongs that exist in our fallen world.

Today the greatest *wrong* (which has the superficial appearance of a *right*) is the denial of the right to life to millions of unborn human beings who yearn to breathe free and live out the blessings of liberty promised to our posterity by our Constitution. History was forever changed when common sense took hold and the American colonies threw off the chains of oppression. Likewise, may those who are fighting the good fight for the sanctity of human life continue in this noble struggle and through common sense and a commitment to truth also forever change history.

## Nice Shot Mr. President
### July 8, 2009

On June 16 during an interview on CNBC President Obama swatted at and killed a fly. The matter was treated with good humor by most. I, for one, wanted to say, "Nice shot, Mr. President." However, the animal rights group People for the Ethical Treatment of Animals (PETA) felt differently and publicly chastised the President for his apparent cruelty to the insect.

"We support compassion for the even the smallest animals," says Bruce Friedrich, VP for Policy at PETA. "We support giving insects the benefit of the doubt." Friedrich says PETA supports "brushing flies away rather than killing them." Later PETA sent to Obama a fly catching device that traps flies and then allows for their safe release back into nature.

Upon hearing of the compassion PETA has for the smallest of creatures, I wondered what position they took on abortion. After all, if this organization believes in the protection of the lives of flies surely they would be adamantly opposed to the killing of the unborn. Hence, I immediately did a search on the Internet to find an answer to my question. I found out that PETA's compassion for unborn human babies falls far short of its compassion for flies.

In regards to abortion, PETA's official statement reads:

> *PETA does not have a position on the abortion issue, because our focus as an organization is the alleviation of the suffering inflicted on nonhuman animals. There are people on both sides of the abortion issue in the animal rights movement, just as there are people on both sides of animal rights issues in the pro-life movement. And just as the pro-life movement has no official position on animal rights, neither does the animal rights movement have an official position on abortion.*

Now let me understand this clearly. To PETA the life of a fly deserves to be respected and must be treated with dignity, but the life of an unborn child subject to abortion is apparently of no concern. One can be a member of PETA and support the killing of the unborn as long as that person supports the right to life of a fly.

Even if one believes that humans are no more than a higher evolved form of animal life they must surely oppose the killing of unborn children if they oppose the killing of flies. But this logic escapes PETA. Apparently, it is politically correct to PETA for people to have compassion for animals (even flies), but it is not politically correct to stand against the killing of unborn children.

This kind of logic borders on insanity but exists today because American culture no longer accepts the sanctity of life ethic upon which our nation was founded. This ethic, embodied in our Declaration of Independence, proclaims that all human beings are made in the image of God and as such are afforded the inalienable right to life. The Creator bestows this inalienable right upon humanity because humanity is made in His image. In accepting abortion on demand and the killing of 52 million unborn children since 1973 the American nation has departed far from the principles of its founding.

I do believe that most Americans do not accept PETA's dogma that the lives of insects are more important than the lives of human unborn children. Yet, the American public tolerates the ongoing killing of 3,300 unborn children in abortion clinics every day. How many more unborn will needlessly die until the American nation wakes up and demands an end to this carnage?

PETA boldly stands in the public arena for the protection of the life of a fly. When will the majority of Americans who call themselves prolife stand up boldly in the public arena for the protection of the lives of the unborn? Until this happens the killing of the unborn will continue.

## When a Celebrity Dies the Nation Mourns, But When . . .
### June 16, 2009

Recently the nation has seen a wave of deaths of celebrities—Ed McMann, Michael Jackson, Farah Fawcett and Billy Mays. Very few people in the general public had personal relationships with these departed public icons. Yet, the intensity level of mourning that the nation has exhibited upon the news of these deaths shows that millions of people identified with these celebrities in a very personal way.

The public mourning for the death of Michael Jackson has been particularly intense. For several days after his death the news concentrated on both the details of his death and of his life. His music was replayed on both television and radio broadcasts and video images of him dancing to his music were shown over and over again to a grieving public. Likewise, the deaths of Farah Fawcett, Ed McMann, and Billy Mays brought forth many special broadcasts on television to commemorate their lives.

Indeed, when a cultural icon passes away we all feel sadness. We all feel that even a part of our lives has also died, and the grieving families of these celebrities should be recipients of our prayers and compassion.

If we contrast, however, the public show of grief to these celebrity deaths with the public response to the deaths of 3,300 unborn children that occur from abortion every day we will have to make a disturbing observation about our nation.

It appears that when a celebrity dies the entire nation mourns but when 50 million unborn children die the nation pretends it didn't happen. Abortion has since 1973 taken the lives of over 52 million unborn children. Abortion today takes the lives of 1.3 million unborn children every year. 3,300 every day. One every 25 seconds.

Where is the public mourning for these lives?

Each life taken by abortion was a unique person made in the image of God. Abortion has destroyed the lives of future doctors, lawyers, artists, authors, missionaries and others who could have contributed greatly to the quality of life we all enjoy.

Where is the public mourning for these lives?

Abortion has not only taken the lives of 52 million children, but it also ends the generational lines that would have followed such children had they been allowed to live. Millions of human beings who would have loved and been loved and provided so much joy and fulfillment to others will never exist because of abortion.

Where is the public mourning for these lives?

As a nation we mourn the passing of celebrities whom most of us did not know personally. But we ignore the deaths of millions because the manner in which they died is a topic that is not politically correct to bring up in social circles.

I suspect that the topic of abortion is to most Americans an uncomfortable topic that one does not enjoy discussing. Certainly, the passion of people on both sides of this issue makes for stress at your everyday dinner party. Yet, continued silence about this issue will not hide the fact that innocent lives are being taken every day.

Who is to mourn for the lives of the innocent taken by abortion every day?

Until true public awareness of abortion and its ramifications is achieved then there will be no mourning for the deaths of these little ones. Only continued public silence will ensue.

Let us work for an America where this public silence is ended and is replaced by an outcry that will usher in a time period where every human life, born and unborn, is respected and the death of every person, whether a celebrity or an unborn baby, is mourned.

## The Sotomayor Nomination and Abortion
### June 16, 2009

Speculation abounds over President Obama's appointment of judge Sonya Sotomayor to the United States Supreme Court and her position on the issue of abortion. There currently is a very sensitive balance on the Court on some high profile social issues such as abortion, and many cases on these issues are decided by a vote of 5–4. Sotomayor, as a Supreme Court justice, will undoubtedly provide the deciding vote on a variety of such issues.

Judge Sonya Sotomayor, if confirmed by the U.S. Senate, is expected to vote with the liberal wing of the Court. Since her nomination replaces one of the most liberal justices—David Souter—the current balance on the Court is not expected to be disturbed by her confirmation. However, there has been some conjecture by activists in the prolife movement (and some anxiety expressed by pro-choice proponents) that Judge Sotomayor might vote with the prolife side on cases impacting abortion.

These suppositions are based upon three rulings of Judge Sotomayor that have been in favor of the prolife position. One such case upheld the constitutionality of the Mexico City policy, which prevents U.S. tax funds from going to international family planning organizations, i.e., Planned Parenthood, that promote abortion as a method of family planning.

At first glance Sotomayor's rulings in these cases provide some hope that perhaps she might be the fifth vote to reverse *Roe v. Wade*, notwithstanding her clearly liberal view of the Constitution and the role of the judiciary. However, after reviewing the current public information about Judge Sotomayor's record I am doubtful that she will be a vote in favor of life once she sits on the Court.

An assessment of Sotomayor's position on abortion should first start with the political realities of her appointment. It is not likely that Obama would ever consider an appointment to the Supreme Court who did not share his far-left pro-abortion views. When campaigning for the presidency Obama made it very clear in a speech to Planned Parenthood that on the issue of abortion there would be no compromise on his part. He called such an issue fundamental and promised to sign into law the radical Freedom of Choice Act. Since taking office he has relentlessly pursued a pro-abortion agenda through his appointments to his cabinet as well as through his policy initiatives that include overturning of the Mexico City policy and moving to end conscience protections for healthcare professionals who oppose on moral grounds referring patients for abortion services. It is highly improbable with such a deep personal commitment to abortion that Obama would nominate to the Supreme Court a judge who did not share his beliefs. Further, the appointment of Sotomayor has not created concern among key Senators who have stated that a commitment from a judge to preserve abortion and *Roe v. Wade* is paramount to their favorable vote. After interviewing Judge Sotomayor several pro-abortion senators, including Diane Feinstein from California, announced that they are very comfortable with Sotomayor's position on abortion.

A deeper examination of Sotomayor's judicial philosophy indicates that she most likely will vote against the prolife position. She has stated that she believes that the federal judiciary correctly makes public policy as opposed to interpreting the Constitution. This, of course, is the exact judicial philosophy that brought us *Roe v. Wade* in the first place. Further, she has additionally made it known that she thinks factors such as gender and ethnicity should play a role in the decision making process of a judge, as opposed to an objective reading of the Constitution. Again, such superlatives are indicative that Sotomayor will make decisions not upon her reading and interpretation of the Constitution, but rather upon which party before the Court has her empathies and understanding. This manner of decision-making by a federal judge means that objective standards of judging and the clear meaning of the Constitution are trumped by political correctness and emotions. This is the exact judicial philosophy that birthed *Roe* and its constitutional sanction of abortion.

Background information on Judge Sotomayor past professional associations gives us additional clues that she will be a pro-abortion vote on the Court. From 1980 until October 1992 she served on the board of directors of the Puerto Rican Legal Defense and Education Fund. During this time the fund filed many friends of the court briefs in the Supreme Court in cases involving abortion, and such briefs were always in favor of expanding abortion rights. Sotomayor served during part of this period as chairman of the fund's litigation committee and was fully aware of the briefs filed in the Supreme Court in these cases. The *New York Times* reported on May 28 about this fund that "[t]he board monitored all litigation undertaken by the fund's lawyers, and a number of those lawyers said Ms. Sotomayor was an involved and ardent supporter of their various legal efforts."

There is no question that the United States Senate will confirm Judge Sotomayor. The votes in favor of her confirmation exist. While her replacement of Justice Souter will not change the current balance on the Court, I have to conclude that on abortion Sonya Sotomayor will be a vote in continuation of abortion on demand.

Despite her certain confirmation prolife Senators must fight this nomination. The confirmation hearings must show Judge Sotomayor's position on abortion and if, as expected, such information confirms our greatest fears then such testimony should be used to educate the public on the radical pro-abortion agenda of the Obama Administration.

We need some feistiness from prolife Senators on this one. Defeating the nomination of Sotomayor is going to be virtually impossible. But standing on principles and exposing the nature of the Obama agenda will reap great benefits in the future.

# The Foundational Issue of Our Times
## June 11, 2009

I was encouraged recently by the results of a Gallup public opinion poll on abortion taken in May. The poll found 51% of Americans calling themselves "pro-life" and 42% "pro-choice." This is the first time a majority of U.S. adults have identified themselves as prolife since Gallup began asking this question in 1995. Even more astounding is the fact that a recent national survey by the Pew Research Center recorded an eight percentage-point decline since last August in those saying abortion should be legal in all or most cases, from 54% to 46%.

These results, obtained from Gallup's annual Values and Beliefs survey, represent a significant shift from a year ago, when 50% were pro-choice and 44% prolife. Prior to now, the highest percentage identifying themselves as prolife was 46%, in both August 2001 and May 2002.

It would appear that the dedicated work of those involved in the prolife movement is having an impact in shaping public opinion. The work of Pregnancy Resource Centers using ultrasound to show the humanity of the unborn child certainly tops the list of prolife activities that have affected this change in public opinion. The work of prolife activists in the public and political arenas has also clearly impacted public opinion.

These findings are good news, and we should be optimistic about the future. However, succeeding in the task of achieving an abortion free America is going to require heightened and intense efforts on the part of those who believe in the sanctity of life ethic. While our viewpoint may now be the majority opinion it is not the ruling ethic that dominates our public policy. Until current public policy changes abortion will continue unabated.

President Obama and members of his majority Democrat Party are unabashedly pro-abortion, and the president has moved quickly to establish abortion on demand as an official policy of the United States government. So we must ask ourselves this one question.

How can we reconcile the fact that a public that is increasingly prolife elected the most pro-abortion president and Congress in our history?

I believe that while a majority of the public is prolife a majority of the voters are not yet willing to base their vote for any office on this one issue. People do not want to be identified as "single issue" voters and when many who are prolife are asked how such convictions influence their vote they reply: "Of course I am against abortion, but I am not a single issue voter. Other issues are important as well." Accordingly, many of these voters vote for a pro-abortion candidate because they determine that while the position of such candidate on abortion is wrong they agree with him or her on a host of other issues that they also deem important."

This kind of reasoning occurs because the public has allowed the media to tag prolife voters as "single-issue voters" who do not care about other crucial matters that are impacting the nation.

Of course, we all are concerned about the economy, the environment, education, taxes and other critical issues. However, abortion is not just a single issue—one among many of which we are concerned. Rather, abortion is a fundamental issue upon which all other issues depend.

We are not single-issue voters. Rather, our vote is based upon whether or not a candidate is correct on the fundamental issue of our time— the right to life. Without the right to life all other issues are meaningless. The right to life is a fundamental issue upon which we judge the worthiness of any candidate for public office. The importance of other issues pales in comparison, and any candidate who denies this basic principle is not qualified to hold office.

Our nation was created on a sound belief in the sanctity of human life.

The founding document of our nation, the Declaration of Independence, states that all humans are endowed by our Creator with certain unalienable rights with the first of such rights being the right to life. Likewise, our Constitution in the Fifth and Fourteenth Amendments protects the taking of the life of a person without due process of law. Again, life is the first right mentioned in the Constitution ahead of the rights to liberty and property.

Until the majority of Americans who hold prolife convictions understand that abortion and life related issues are fundamental to the continued existence of the American republic we, unfortunately, will continue to elect representatives who do not share such a view. Until the majority of Americans insist that all who represent us in the political arena stand firmly in favor of the foundational issue of life abortion will continue.

It is good news that the majority of Americans now classify themselves as prolife. We must now translate such public sentiment into the political arena so that a majority of our public officials hold such a view.

The right to life is the fundamental issue of our time. When the majority of Americans insist that this fundamental right must never be denied to any class of human beings then abortion will end in America.

## The Sotomayor Nomination: Rule of Law, Not Empathy, is the Standard
### June 3, 2009

When running for the presidency Obama made it very clear what standards he would rely upon, as President, in making appointments to the United States Supreme Court. He made it clear that "empathy" is the character he seeks in a judicial nominee.

> *The empathy to understand what it's like to be*
> *poor, or African-American, or gay, or disabled, or*
> *old. And that's the criteria by which I'm going to be*
> *selecting my judges.*

Obama criticized Chief Justice John Roberts for saying that he saw his role as a Supreme Court Justice like an umpire who calls balls and strikes.

> *But the issues the come before the courts are not*
> *sports. They're life and death. We need somebody*
> *who's got the empathy to recognize what it's like to*
> *be a young teenage mom.*

Obama further said that while 95 percent of the cases that come before the Supreme Court can be judged on intellect the other five percent should be scrutinized differently:

> *In those five percent of cases, you've got to look at*
> *what is in the justice's heart, what's their broader*
> *vision of what America should be.*

It would appear that President Obama's first judicial appointment to the Supreme Court, federal judge Sonya Sotomayor, meets the criteria set forth by the president. Judge Sotomayor grew up on the poor side of town in the Bronx. As such she worked hard and struggled to succeed in life. Through her hard work and motivation she has advanced in the legal world to where she now is ready to take her place as a justice on the highest court in the land. Clearly she comes from a social position that gives her a lot of empathy for those considered less fortunate in our society.

As a judge Sotomayor readily agrees with Obama's assessment of the need for empathy in judging and she believes that someone with her background has far superior wisdom in making just rulings. Her comments that a "wise Hispanic women", such as her, would undoubtedly make wiser judicial decisions than a white male indicate that she believes that not only empathy but also one's race and background are qualities that should affect the outcome of cases.

So whatever happened to the Constitution?

Having empathy with others is, of course, an admirable quality. And it perhaps is one quality we would look for in electing a president, a Congressman or others to political office. But as a quality that impacts the decisions one makes as a Supreme Court justice having empathy towards others should be totally irrelevant to deciding a case before a court. The role of the judiciary in our constitutional system is to decide cases solely upon what is dictated by the Constitution. If a justice decides cases not upon his or her interpretation of the law but rather, upon their ability to empathize then clearly there are no objective constitutional standards upon which to rely.

Judging by one's heart and one's ability to empathize with others means that the judging won't be neutral and justice will not be blind. Rather, some parties who have the empathy of the majority of justices will always win while others no matter how compelling their case is under the law will always lose. Judging by the heart, as opposed to the dictates of the Constitution, means that the one doing the judging will only make a decision based upon the pull of his or her emotions. A Supreme Court decision decided in such a manner is correct as long as the "hearts" of the justices are in the right place.

Whatever happened to the Constitution?

Contrary to the common understanding of the nature of our government America is not a democracy. Rather, it is a Republic ruled by officials who are elected by the populace to carry out the will of the body politic. As a Constitutional Republic our nation has imbedded in our political DNA a system of checks and balances that prevent one branch of government from becoming too powerful. Without such checks a particular branch can overpower the others and create tyranny upon the nation.

The public has the ability to check its elected representatives when they rule contrary to the will of their constituents by voting such people out of office. No such check, however, exists as far as the public being able to control the influence of a federal judiciary that is made up of unelected judges appointed for life. Because of this, the federal judiciary, and particularly the Supreme Court, is to exercise restraint and not make public policy. The making of public policy is the sole responsibility of our elected officials.

The federal judiciary was set up in the Constitution as a co-equal branch of government. However, its role is to make decisions solely upon its understanding of the meaning of the Constitution. It is not to imbed its own social biases into its rulings. If the public determines that the Constitution needs changing to meet unique challenges of our times then the Constitution has an amendment process for the people to undertake through their elected representatives. The judiciary is not to impose its public policy preferences upon the people. It is to rule according the clear meaning of the Constitution. That is the rule of law.

It is a commitment to this rule of law that must be paramount in the mind of every justice who serves in the federal judiciary, and this is particularly so with the Supreme Court. Once the high court renders a decision it becomes very difficult to change such a ruling. If justices ignore the Constitution in making decisions and, instead, rule upon the dictates of their hearts and where their empathies are to be found our Constitution is rendered meaningless.

The upcoming confirmation hearings of judge Sotomayor must clearly determine how she views her role as a Supreme Court justice. If she agrees with Obama that her ability to empathize is a critical component to how a decision should be rendered then her confirmation should be declined.

It is a commitment to the rule of law, not the ability show empathy, which is the standard to use in determining whether one should sit as a justice on the highest court in the land. Preliminary information on judge Sotomayor indicates that she falls short of this standard.

## NARAL Smear Tactics Distort the Truth about Crisis Pregnancy Centers
### March 24, 2009

(Note: This commentary was written in response to a negative commentary by the National Abortion Rights Action League (NARAL) that was published on March 20, 2009, in the *Free Lance Star*, a newspaper in Fredericksburg, Virginia. The *Free-Lance Star* has agreed to publish this response. While it is in specific response to the allegations made by the Virginia chapter of NARAL it is appropriate for all other areas of the country since NARAL and other organizations in the abortion industry have for years been active in a nationwide smear campaign against pro-life pregnancy resource centers.)

The recent commentary by Jessica Bearden from the National Abortion Rights Action League (NARAL) entitled "Crisis Pregnancy Centers. The Zeal is Unreal" is the latest in a sad history of NARAL attacking the integrity of prolife Pregnancy Resource Centers (PRCs). A strong response is required.

PRCs (also called "crisis pregnancy centers") are prolife in philosophy and have operated in every community for more than twenty-five years. Currently, over 3,000 PRCs provide free to hundreds of thousands of women a year material assistance, legal help, pregnancy testing/diagnosis, and medical services. Currently, nearly 700 PRCs operate as licensed medical clinics that are supervised by licensed physicians and staffed by medical professionals. One such medical clinic in Fredericksburg—Bethany Pregnancy Services—provides ultrasound as well as other support services to empower pregnant mothers to be able to carry their pregnancies to term.

No other agencies—certainly not abortion providers and abortion advocates like NARAL—are providing free support services to help mothers in problem pregnancies. Instead, NARAL opposes PRCs as scandalous only because they are prolife and do not provide abortions or referrals for abortions. To NARAL this requires a smear campaign. However, because NARAL cannot substantiate its accusations it couches them in general terms with a broad brush slandering every PRC.

NARAL's attack is the latest from a multi-million dollar abortion industry that wants to close down PRCs. In the mid-1980s Planned Parenthood of New York launched a national negative campaign against PRCs accusing them of deception—the very same things spewed in Bearden's commentary. Dr. Marvin Olasky, a professor of Journalism at the University of Texas, uncovered this campaign in an extensive study published in *Public Relations Review*, Autumn 1987. This study states:

*"The majority of (prolife) counseling centers offer free pregnancy tests to draw clients, as many pro-choice groups and abortion businesses do, but they tell callers that they do not perform abortions... Interviews show that in order to obey one commandment against killing (with the implication that Christians should attempt to save the lives of others) most prolife volunteers are not willing to disregard the commandment about bearing false witness."* (Pp 14-15)

Indeed, the three major national organizations that have a combined membership comprising nearly 90% of all PRCs—the National Institute of Family and Life Advocates (**NIFLA**), Heartbeat International, and Care Net—all are insistent that their affiliates provide services with integrity, truthfulness and honesty. These organizations have endorsed for their membership a national code of conduct entitled *Commitment to Care*. A review of this national code clearly shows that PRCs operate under the highest principles of integrity.

I was amused with the one specific example in Bearden's commentary concerning an investigative report compiled by NARAL Maryland. Such report accused one PRC volunteer of being hostile and aggressive in her counseling session with the NARAL fake client that had come into the PRC "undercover." The accusation, of course, was general and did not give specifics concerning the counselor and the PRC where allegedly this incident occurred. This testimony was given at hearings in both the Maryland Senate and House of Representatives last year over a bill sponsored by NARAL to injure PRCs. I was present at both hearings and testified.

As a former trial attorney I can attest that the credibility of the NARAL staff person who gave this testimony was questionable and ripe for impeachment if she had been cross-examined. At the end of the hearing a pro-choice Maryland Senator apologized to me and said that the bill was dead. Indeed, the predominantly pro-choice Maryland legislature refused to bring the NARAL sponsored legislation to a vote.

America is a nation divided on abortion. However, our United States Supreme Court has stated, "men and women of good conscience can disagree... about the profound moral and spiritual implications of terminating a pregnancy." *Planned Parenthood v. Casey*, 505 U.S. 833 (1992). Yet, to NARAL the compassionate people who work at PRCs cannot be "of good conscience." Rather, NARAL insists on smearing them as "deceptive," "coercive," and "extreme."

NARAL claims to be "pro-choice." However, to have a choice in any matter means that one has more than one option. NARAL supports only one option to a mother in a crisis pregnancy—abortion. And it opposes the work of agencies that are providing support services to empower women to choose life.

It appears that NARAL is really not pro-choice at all but pro-abortion. This is evidenced by its shameless attack on those who sincerely want to provide life-affirming choices to problem pregnancies.

The integrity of those who give of themselves in PRCs is an example of people who live their lives under the highest of ideals, i.e., the "Golden Rule." They should be applauded for their selfless work.

## A Person's a Person No Matter How Small—Part I
### February 25, 2009

(Note: This is the first of a series of commentaries that discusses the concept of personhood and Constitutional protection for all persons.)

The American ideals of equality and justice under the law have over the years inspired many to stand up for the oppressed. Indeed, numerous politicians (including our current president) have run for public office by declaring that they are for "the little guy" who has no voice or representation in our special interest inflicted political institutions. Yet, our president along with most of these politicians (with some notable exceptions) ignore and even work against the interests of the most vulnerable of these "little people"—the unborn.

Dr. Seuss, the beloved children's author, wrote a delightful children's story titled *Horton Hears a Who*. This is a story about a creature named Horton who discovers a tiny microscopic land named "Whoville." Inhabiting this tiny world are creatures named "Whos" that are too tiny for the naked eye to see. However, Horton in making his discovery emphatically states on numerous occasions "a person's a person no matter how small."

The United States Supreme Court clearly lacked the wisdom of Horton when it handed down it infamous decision of *Roe v. Wade* on January 22, 1973. It is too bad that Horton was not present in the courtroom on that day to remind the Justices of the Court that indeed, "a person's a person no matter how small."

At the heart of the *Roe* decision was the declaration that an unborn child is not a person under the Fourteenth Amendment and thus, is not protected by the Constitution. This Amendment clearly states that *"no state shall deny to any person . . . life without due process of law."* And, indeed, Justice Harry Blackmun in writing the *Roe* opinion acknowledged that if an unborn child is a *person* under this Amendment then abortion cannot be allowed because such an act would violate of the Constitutional protections of the Fourteenth Amendment.

To the "average Joe" on the street an understanding of what constitutes a *person* is a no-brainer. The *Merriam-Webster Dictionary* provides an uncomplicated understanding of the meaning of *person*, which it simply defines as "a human being." This definition to most is so obvious that it would be a waste of time and energy to further debate the issue. The Supreme Court, however, did not see it this way and held that although the unborn child may be a human being such a child is clearly not a *person* under the Constitution and thus, is not constitutionally protected.

Contrast the *Roe* decision with a ruling from the Court in the late 19th Century, which held that a corporation is a *person* under the Fourteenth Amendment and thus, is entitled to all of the protections that this Amendment provides. However, because of *Roe* we have a legal system that says some human beings, i.e., the unborn, are not *persons* and are not protected under the Constitution while some nonhumans, i.e., corporations are *persons* and are protected.

At the heart of the cultural debate over abortion and related life issues is this concept of *personhood*. Since legal precedent now declares that unborn human beings are not *persons* are other born human beings also vulnerable to such dehumanization and thus, subject to indiscriminate killing for reasons that society comes to accept as reasonable?

The logic stated in *Roe* to justify the dehumanization of the unborn is that the Court viewed lives *in utero* as not capable of "meaningful life outside the womb." Thus, such lives, according to the Court, are not *persons* and therefore are denied the Constitutional protection of the Fourteenth Amendment.

We should ask the Court a pertinent question that logically flows from its declaration of non-personhood for the unborn. If the life of an unborn child is not meaningful because it is a burden what about the lives of the terminally ill, the infirm, the seriously handicapped, and the retarded? If such lives, like the unborn, have no meaning then are they also not considered *persons* and thus, denied Constitutional protection? And who decides which lives are "meaningful" and thus protected and which lives are not?

There is now a movement across the nation to legislatively address the issue of *personhood* and create a test case to go before the Supreme Court and challenge *Roe v. Wade*. The North Dakota Legislature is considering passage of a law that would define a person to include the unborn. The bill states: "For the purposes of interpretation of the constitution and laws of North Dakota, it is the intent of the legislative assembly that an individual, a person, when the context indicates that a reference to an individual is intended, or a human being includes any organism with the genome of *Homo sapiens*."

This bill has passed the North Dakota House of Representatives and is now being considered by the state Senate. It could be passed and signed into law by Governor John Hoeven, a conservative Republican, within a couple of weeks. Other states are also considering similar measures to define personhood and set up a confrontation with the United States Supreme Court over the precedent of *Roe v. Wade*.

The battle over the sanctity of human life will continue to rage across the nation. As it does this foundational battle over the Constitutional *personhood* of the unborn must be at the forefront if we are truly going to be successful in restoring the sanctity of life ethic in our culture and institutions.

## A Person's a Person No Matter How Small—Part II
### March 10, 2009

(Note: This is the second of a series of commentaries that discusses the concept of personhood and Constitutional protection for all persons.)

Dr. Seuss, the beloved children's author, wrote a delightful children's story titled *Horton Hears a Who*. This is a story about a creature named Horton who discovers a tiny microscopic land named "Whoville." Inhabiting this tiny world are creatures named "Whos" that are too tiny for the naked eye to see. However, Horton in making his discovery emphatically states on numerous occasions "a person's a person no matter how small."

President Obama clearly lacked the wisdom of Horton this week when he issued an executive order allowing for the federal funding of embryonic stem cell research. Stem cells are primal cells found in all multi-cellular organisms. They retain the ability to renew themselves through mitotic cell division and can differentiate into a diverse range of specialized cell types. The three broad categories of stem cells are: 1) embryonic stem cells, which are derived from the inner cell mass of a human embryo and have the potential to develop into nearly all of the tissues in the body; 2) adult stem cells, which are unspecialized cells found in adult tissue that can renew themselves and become specialized to yield all of the cell types of the tissue from which they originate; and 3) cord blood stem cells, which are found in the umbilical cord.

Some in the medical community believe that embryonic stem cell research could lead to therapies to effectively treat diseases such as Parkinson's disease, diabetes and Alzheimer's disease. Due to human reproductive technology there are now many "excess" embryos that have not been implanted inside the wombs of women desiring to bear children. Thus, proponents of this research proclaim that such embryos provide an abundant resource to use. However, such research creates obvious controversy. The end result of removing stem cells from an embryo is the killing of this tiny human being.

President Obama ignored this reality. His executive order not only frees up federal funds for this research but also opens wide the door for the funding of research into the cloning of human stem cells thereby unleashing the probability that the cloning of human beings is around the corner.

Such steps of "scientific advancement" clearly place America down the slippery slope to a brave new world. And such steps have happened because society has since the issuance of the ***Roe v. Wade*** decision accepted the idea that not all human beings are *persons*. Thus, because the Constitution only protects the lives of *persons* such human beings that fail to qualify as *persons* (i.e. the unborn) can be killed for the perceived overall good of society. Under this viewpoint if society can benefit from the killing of human embryos because the stem cells of such tiny humans may serve a useful purpose in curing disease then such research should not only be allowed but should be funded by federal tax dollars.

Unborn life and embryonic life are seen in our culture as meaningless lives—non-persons—that can be manipulated and killed for the perceived betterment of American society. However, scripture does not place higher value on human life already born. To the contrary *personhood* and therefore value on unborn life is clearly seen throughout history.

Psalm 139 remarkably tells us that all human beings are "knit together" by God while in our mothers' wombs. The Psalmist says: "I praise you for I am fearfully and wonderfully made; your works are wonderful, I know that full well. My frame was no hidden from you when I was made in the secret place. I was woven together in the depths of the earth, your eyes saw my unformed body."

This passage clearly states that God's love and concern for the unborn exists at the earliest point of human development. The Hebrew word *golem*, meaning fetus or embryo, is used here and translated as "unformed body." Clearly in the eyes of our Creator unborn live has value and thus, personhood, as He is intimately involved from the beginning of a pregnancy in the development of every human life.

Another powerful scriptural passage that provides insight into the biblical acknowledgment of the *personhood* of the unborn can be found in the gospel of Luke chapter 1. This passage describes the prenatal meeting of John the Baptist who is six months inside the womb and Jesus who has just been conceived. Remember that Luke's was a physician and as such he probably had delivered many babies. Dr. Luke describes this remarkable meeting of the two preborn infants this way:

> At that time Mary got ready and hurried to a town in the hill country of Judea, where she entered Zechariah's home and greeted Elizabeth. When Elizabeth heard Mary's greeting, the baby leaped in her womb, and Elizabeth was filled with the Holy Spirit. In a loud voice she exclaimed: "Blessed are you among women, and blessed the child you will bear! But why am I so favored, that the mother of my Lord should come to me? As soon as the sound of your greeting reached my ears, the baby in my womb leaped for joy. Blessed is she who has believed that what the Lord has said to her will be accomplished! (Luke 1:39–45)

Luke, a man of science and medicine, calls John the Baptist inside the womb a baby. The Greek word used is *brephos*, which can be translated unborn child, baby or infant. It is the same Greek word Luke uses in chapter 2:12, when the angel says to the shepherds, "This shall be a sign to you. You will find a baby (brephos) wrapped in cloths and lying in a manger." In other words the good doctor employs the same word to describe John in the womb as he does to describe Jesus already born. The both are babies.

Does an unborn child have value to God? Does Scripture grant personhood to the unborn? The answer is an impassioned yes! If not, why would God choose an unborn baby, John the Baptist, to be the first person to whom the presence of Jesus the Messiah was revealed?

Scripture is clear on the *personhood* and thus, value of unborn life. In the words of Horton, "A person's a person no matter how small." It is a misfortune that our newly elected president does not understand this. And it is a serious tragedy that in his refusal to accept this truth he has now opened the doors to scientific research that manipulates and kills embryonic human beings for a misconceived notion that the destruction of such lives will bring about great good in society.

Any nation and culture will ultimately be judged not by its military might or economic power. Rather, a nation will be judged by history in how it treated its most vulnerable members. In America today the most vulnerable members of our society are the unborn subject to abortion and now subject to killing for purposes of scientific research.

The doors are now open wide for further manipulation of humanity by science and the emergence of a brave new world where humanity is redefined, manipulated and killed for the perceived betterment of society as a whole. May God have mercy on the soul of this once great nation.

## Obama's Approval of Embryonic Stem Cell Research Will Further Divide the Nation
### February 17, 2009

President Obama ran for president and came into office proclaiming that he was going to bring a divided nation together. He promised to govern in a nonpartisan manner and to seek counsel on the serious issues of the day from a variety of sources who have differing opinions. However, Obama has been in office only four weeks and it appears that such promises were simply empty rhetoric that sounded good on the campaign trail.

Today America is clearly a divided nation. This division runs deep—especially in regards to social issues such as abortion and same-sex marriage. On the life issue the debate intensely rages after years of political activism by both sides. After 36 years of abortion-on-demand (brought about by the edict in *Roe v. Wade*) American society still has not come to terms with the brutal fact that abortion kills 3,300 unborn children a day. Until it finally faces up to this gruesome reality I fear that the culture will continue its slippery slide down the path that led a once great German nation to accept the death camps of Buchenwald and Auschwitz.

The president is blind to this reality as he prepares to issue an executive order allowing for federal funding of embryonic stem cell research. All news accounts indicate that such an order will be signed at any time. If this is done the president will further divide the nation.

Stem cells are primal cells found in all multi-cellular organisms. They retain the ability to renew themselves through mitotic cell division and can differentiate into a diverse range of specialized cell types. The three broad categories of stem cells are: 1) embryonic stem cells, which are derived from the inner cell mass of a human embryo and have the potential to develop into nearly all of the tissues in the body; 2) adult stem cells, which are unspecialized cells found in adult tissue that can renew themselves and become specialized to yield all of the cell types of the tissue from which they originate; and 3) cord blood stem cells, which are found in the umbilical cord.

Some in the medical community believe that embryonic stem cell research could lead to therapies to effectively treat diseases such as Parkinson's disease, diabetes and Alzheimer's disease. Due to human reproductive technology there are now many "excess" embryos that have not been implanted inside the wombs of women desiring to bear children. Thus, proponents of this research proclaim that such embryos provide an abundant resource to use. However, such research creates obvious controversy. The end result of removing stem cells from an embryo is the killing of this tiny human being.

Let us all remember one very important fact—all of us at one time existed as a human embryo! We were human from conception. For those who believe in the sanctity of human life this is a foundational cornerstone of a just society. Innocent human life has an inalienable right to life endowed by the Creator. And history will ultimately judge a nation and culture by how it treats its most vulnerable of the human family. In American society today the most vulnerable of our human family is the unborn, which includes newly conceived human embryos. Medical research, no matter how noble it proclaims itself to be, cannot be allowed to exist if the basis for it is the killing of other human beings. And this is the bottom line on embryonic stem cell research.

President George W. Bush understood the grave consequences of allowing federal funds to be used for medical research on existing human embryos. He accordingly issued an executive order that prohibited such use of federal tax dollars. Now, however, our new president appears desirous of reversing this order thereby allowing millions of tax dollars to be applied to the killing of human embryos in hopes of finding "miracle" cures for human diseases.

The tragedy of such an executive order, if it is issued, is that scientific research appears to be on the verge of discovering promising new therapies using adult stem cells. In November 2007 teams of research scientists reported that they succeeded in reprogramming human skin cells so that they behave like embryonic stem cells. Such cells are referred to as pluripotent stem cells. The new technique uses retroviruses to make the skin cells act like stem cells. Retroviruses insert genetic material into the chromosome of the cells. While it may take years to perfect this new technique to make it workable it does add real promise that a morally acceptable answer to the stem cell research controversy is around the corner.

To date the results of embryonic stem cell research have not shown to be promising. Much more promising has been the results from various adult stem cell research and the possibilities of developing new therapies based upon research such as the one reported in 2007. Yet, the Obama administration appears to be oblivious to these facts and continues to push a radical social agenda that further dehumanizes innocent unborn life.

If president Obama truly wants to unite the nation, as he says he does, then he must not govern in a manner that further ignites the divisions that exist. To issue an executive order that will allow for federal funding of the killing of human embryos certainly does this.

Such an order will bring our country further down a path of cultural decline that will eventually result in the destruction of a once great American nation.

## Watch Out for the Coming Obama Judicial Appointments
### February 10, 2009

Major news this last week came from the United States Supreme Court when we learned that Justice Ruth Bader Ginsberg is suffering from cancer in the pancreas. This is a serious illness and even when detected early, as it has been with Justice Ginsberg, the odds of surviving are not high.

The thought of a vacancy on the Supreme Court in the near future has caused the political pundits to surmise about the kind of judge President Obama would nominate to replace Justice Ginsberg. The deeper concern for conservatives is whether or not such a replacement would disturb the current balance of the Court and thus, affect future rulings on issues of concern such as abortion and same-sex marriage.

The current balance on the court can be described as 4-1-4. That is to say, there are four justices—Scalia, Thomas, Roberts and Alito—who are generally considered to be conservatives on social issues. There are four justices—Stevens, Souter, Breyer and Ginsberg—who favor the liberal side of the spectrum and support abortion rights, gay rights, restrictions on Second Amendment rights and other positions that are part of the liberal agenda.

The middle vote on the Court is Justice Anthony Kennedy who time and again has provided the fifth and determining vote in many controversial decisions. Sometimes Kennedy's vote affirms conservative values, such as his vote and opinion in the decision to uphold the Congressional ban on partial-birth abortion. Other times his vote provides liberals with the victory as it did in *Planned Parenthood v.*

*Casey*, that upheld by one vote the central premise of *Roe v. Wade* falsely concluding that a constitutional right to abortion exists.

President Obama has the constitutional authority to appoint future Supreme Court justices, and it is safe to conclude that such appointments will join the liberal wing of the court thereby possibly tipping the balance of the court on the critical social issues of the day. As long as he does not replace the conservative votes, or the vote of Justice Kennedy the balance will remain as it is today.

Ruth Bader Ginsberg came to the high court with a long resume that showed passionate advocacy of far left political issues. She served as the general counsel for the American Civil Liberties Union and was an advocate for elevating the so-called right to abortion in *Roe* to a position that, if adopted, would place all those who oppose abortion in the same legal position as those who opposed equal rights for African American citizens. Such a position is a dangerous one indeed and, if adopted by the Court, would forever end the debate in political circles about the continuation of abortion on demand as a social policy.

Contrary to popular belief the 1973 decision in *Roe* did not find a new constitutional right to abortion. Rather, it reiterated a previously acknowledged constitutional right—the right to privacy—and expanded such right to include a woman's decision "whether or not" to terminate her pregnancy. (Such a broad right to privacy actually protects a woman's decision to carry her baby to term as well as to abort even though it is almost always couched in terms of a right to abortion.)

Ginsberg's position on abortion, if enacted, would find a right to abortion in the equal protection clause of the constitution. This would mean that the denial to a woman of such a right is a denial to her of equal rights under the law. Thus, those who oppose abortion, under this view, oppose equal rights for women and are misogynists and bigots in the same way as were the racial segregationists in the South during the 1950s and '60s.

In regards to abortion President Obama has made it very clear that he will not compromise his far-left pro-abortion beliefs. While running for president he announced that he would sign into law the radical Freedom of Choice Act (FOCA), which essentially would be a federal codification of the Ginsberg abortion position. Further, his current appointments to head up the Department of Justice indicate that the legal minds of this administration are totally committed to the right to abortion and the Ginsberg view of such a right. Because of this, we simply cannot expect that Obama's judicial appointments are going to be anything but far-left and pro-abortion.

The good news in regards to replacing Ginsberg is, of course, that such a replacement does not change the current balance of the Supreme Court. It merely replaces an older liberal justice with a younger one. The bad news is that Obama will make many judicial appointments to the lower federal courts as well as to the Supreme Court and these appointments are undoubtedly going to be people who are on the far left of the political spectrum.

I believe that the greatest danger to the continuation of the American experiment in representative democracy is the increasing control over our lives being exerted by a federal judiciary composed of non-elected judges who serve for a lifetime. Obama's judicial and political philosophy clearly indicates that under his watch such judicial tyranny is going to increase.

In regards to the Supreme Court and its future decisions I believe that we must fervently pray—"Long live Justice Kennedy." In regards to the future Obama appointments of lower court federal judges we must pray that conservatives in the United States Senate have the political backbone to oppose the nominations of liberal judges who will expand the social agenda of the far left.

## The Sanctity of Life Ethic and the Gospel of Christ
### January 13, 2009

While the election of Barack Obama and the upcoming Presidential Inaugural activities currently dominate the headlines there is another event in January that must not be ignored. On January 18th churches around the nation will celebrate Sanctity of Human Life Sunday. This is the Sunday closest to January 22nd—the day in 1973 when the United States Supreme Court issued its infamous decision of *Roe v. Wade* that ushered in the era of abortion on demand.

Since the *Roe* decision was rendered more than 50 million unborn children have lost their lives from abortion. Today in America abortion kills 1.25 million unborn children per year, 3,425 per day, one every 30 seconds. Can you imagine the reaction of the public if 3,425 Americans were killed in Iraq every day? Or, what would the public response be to a daily 9/11 attack killing this many Americans? Sadly, however, the number of lives lost each day to abortion appears to be a silent holocaust that the public chooses to ignore.

Sanctity of Human Life Sunday is a time for the community of faith to respond and not ignore these tragic numbers. It is a time for the Christian community to come together and pray for an end to abortion and to support the ministries of Pregnancy Resource Centers that provide loving and compassionate alternatives to abortion. It is a time for Christians of every denomination to stand up and be counted and celebrate the sanctity of life by proclaiming that every human being regardless of size, race, age, ethnicity, or condition of dependency is made in the image of God.

The Christian community must proclaim this sanctity of life message because this ethic is a foundational belief of the Christian faith. To separate the sanctity of life ethic from the gospel cuts the very heart out of the gospel message because the scriptural proclamation of salvation rests upon the Biblical teaching that all are made in the image of God.

John 3:16 is possibly the most famous verse in the Bible and lays out the essence of the gospel of Christ. This verse simple sets forth that fallen humanity is so loved by the Creator that he sent to us his son as a sacrifice so that every human being who believes can live forever. "For God so loved the world" does not refer to God's love for the animal kingdom, the mountains, the oceans, the forests, or other magnificent parts of his creation. (Undoubtedly he loves these things because after creation was completed he pronounced "It is good.") Rather, in referring to the "world" scripture is referring to humanity because humanity is made in the image of God.

Without the foundational belief in the sanctity of life ethic the gospel message of Christ's redemptive love is meaningless. If mankind is no different than the animal kingdom then why did Christ have to die?

The American nation is a long way from ending abortion. Recent political developments indicate that the public policy that favors abortion on demand is not going to end in the near future. Therefore, it is imperative now more than ever in our history that the Christian church stand up and be counted on this issue by proclaiming the essential message of the sanctity of human life.

Sanctity of Human Life Sunday is an opportunity for churches to do this. Pastors should preach on this topic and the congregations should spend time in prayer for our nation and those who have been trapped by the snare of abortion. Churches should commit to providing resources for the work of their local Pregnancy Resource Centers, and members of churches should be encouraged to volunteer their time at these centers.

The message of the gospel of Christ is the hope of the world. And the sanctity of life ethic that under girds the gospel must be once again proclaimed and upheld throughout our nation if we have any hope at all of ending the tragic destruction of human life that continues in our land day after day.

## Securing an Abortion-Free America by Opening a Window to the Womb
### December 11, 2008

The election of Barack Obama created shockwaves within the leadership and grassroots of the pro-life movement. Indeed, his assent to the presidency continues to haunt those who have labored years to end abortion in America and restore the God-ordained right to life of all humans being in America—born and unborn.

Over one year ago President-elect Obama spoke to Planned Parenthood officials vowing that the very first thing he would sign as president would be the Freedom of Choice Act (FOCA). If enacted into law FOCA would not only embody in a federal statute the dubious right to abortion found in *Roe v. Wade*, but it would also prohibit states from passing certain restrictions on abortion that *Roe* permits, such as partial-birth abortion bans, state funding of abortion bans, and parental notice requirements. Starting with the appointment of former Senator Tom Daschle at HHS Obama's initial appointments to his administration clearly indicate that he meant it when he told Planned Parenthood that he would not compromise on the issue of abortion.

On other issues the media continues to report that Obama is attempting to modify previous far-left positions to be more "centrist." This is not so on abortion. To our president-elect the right to abortion is a foundational value that must be preserved in our culture.

So now the political winds are blowing against the prolife cause and many are feeling discouragement. Indeed, we must brace ourselves for intense political battles on the issue of life in the next four years. The defeat of FOCA will be a primary focus of prolife activity as will be the defeat of judicial appointments, which are certain to be of judges who unconditionally support abortion on demand and *Roe v. Wade*.

Despite this, however, much is happening in communities across the nation to create a culture of life in America where every life, born and unborn, is respected and given dignity. The ending of abortion will not occur because of political initiatives in Washington, D.C. Rather, an abortion free America will happen because communities across the nation rise and end abortion within their boundaries.

Just such an effort is being undertaken in hundreds of communities through the work of prolife Pregnancy Resource Centers (PRCs). Such small charitable agencies do not exist because of government funding. Rather, they are able to provide loving and caring alternatives to abortion because of the support that they receive from local churches and individual Christians. And recent initiatives regarding the provision of medical services from PRCs are beginning to have an impact in reducing the numbers of abortions in many communities.

After converting to the prolife cause former abortionist Bernard Nathanson (a founder of the National Abortion Rights Action League) lamented that if wombs only had windows that allowed pregnant mothers considering abortion to see their unborn children then abortion would end. Today modern medical technology provides such a "window to the womb" through the tool of ultrasound. Ultrasound provides a visual image of an unborn child to enable a physician to assess and diagnose both the well-being of the child and the condition of the pregnancy.

In PRC settings ultrasound is used, under the supervision of a licensed physician, to diagnose the existence of a viable intrauterine pregnancy. Once a pregnancy is diagnosed in this manner the mother considering abortion has had an opportunity to view in utero her child and observe the child's very human characteristics. Tiny hands, fingers, toes and a beating heart are all made visible to this mother who has been told by others that what is inside her is just a glob of pregnancy tissue. To a pregnant mother considering abortion the impact of looking in this "window to the womb" is remarkable.

The *New England Journal of Medicine* published a study in February 1983 that looked at the impact that ultrasound has upon the choice that a pregnant mother will make concerning abortion. The article entitled "Maternal Bonding in Early Fetal Ultrasound Examinations" observed the following:

> *One of us pointed to the small, visibly moving fetal form on the screen and asked, "How do you feel about seeing what is inside you?" She answered crisply, "It certainly makes you think twice about abortion!" When asked to say more, she told of the surprise she felt on viewing the fetal form, especially on seeing it move: "I feel that it is human. It belongs to me. I couldn't have an abortion now."*

> *"The mother was asked about her experience with ultrasound. She said, "It really made a difference to see that it was alive." Asked about her position on the moral choice she had to make, she said, "I am going all the way with the baby. I believe it is human."*

The physician/authors of this study conclude by saying:

> *Ultrasound examination is likely to increase the value of the early fetus for parents who already strongly desire a child. Viewing the fetal form in the late first or early mid-trimester of pregnancy, before movement is felt by the mother, may also influence the resolution of any ambivalence toward the pregnancy itself in favor of the fetus. Ultrasound examination may thus result in fewer abortions and more desired pregnancies.*

For the last ten years under the leadership of the National Institute of Family and Life Advocates (**NIFLA**) PRCs have been converting their operations to licensed medical clinics in order to use the diagnostic tool of ultrasound. The reported successes are truly stunning. Non-medical PRCs report that 20-25% of their abortion-minded clients choose life after receiving the services offered at the center. However, when PRCs convert to medical clinic status and provide ultrasound confirmation of pregnancy they report that 90% of these clients change their minds and choose life.

**NIFLA**, a legal network of 1,150 PRCs in all 50 states, provides the legal expertise and training to enable a PRC to convert to medical clinic status and provide ultrasound services. Its major initiative—**The Life Choice Project (TLC)**—provides all of the resources needed—legal counsel, medical training of physicians and nurses in the implementation of ultrasound, and ongoing consultation—to enable PRCs to make this transition that can be confusing and somewhat complicated legally.

**NIFLA**'s goal is to eventually have 1,000 PRCs licensed as medical clinics using ultrasound to confirm pregnancy for abortion-minded mothers. (Currently, of **NIFLA**'s membership 650 PRCs are using ultrasound, but many are in the very infancy stage of such a program and have not yet seen the full effects of this endeavor.) **NIFLA** has a further goal to see that the PRCs are developed in their professionalism and marketing skills so that eventually these 1,000 clinics will, on the average, be providing ultrasound services to 1,500 abortion-minded pregnant mothers a year. (Some would see more clientele while others would see less depending upon the geographic area in which they are located.)

If this ambitious goal is achieved then the ultimate results are obvious. Such clinics would be providing ultrasound confirmation of pregnancy to 1.5 million abortion-minded pregnancy mothers a year—that is the exact numbers of annual abortions America is currently experiencing. And the vast majority of these mothers, having looked inside this window to the womb, will choose life and not abortion.

Perhaps ending abortion in America is not as far away as some might believe. And the end to abortion can come despite the hostile political winds being blown our way by an Obama presidency. The abolition of abortion and a restoration of the right to life can be achieved in our country without a change in the law and a reversal of *Roe v. Wade* even though such political goals are earnestly and prayerfully sought.

The incoming Obama administration has nothing but mischief in mind when it comes to dealing with abortion and its related life-issues. However, the life-affirming work of medical PRCs with the use of ultrasound cannot easily be stopped. Perhaps the new administration will try to stop this movement, but they will fail if the Christian community stands firm behind the life work of PRCs with spiritual and financial support.

If you really want to make a difference in this nationwide effort to achieve an abortion free America go to **NIFLA**'s web site at www.nifla.org.

## Why Can't Liberals Be Consistent In Their Compassion?
### August 27, 2007

Let me begin these remarks by emphatically stating that I am an avid dog lover. Shiloh, our family pet beagle, has been a big part of our lives for over a decade now. My four kids have grown up with him. He has been a companion to both my wife and me showing the best attributes of "man's best friend." He cuddles with us at night. He friskily plays with us and even performs a few tricks to our amusement. And Shiloh truly shows deep empathy with his big brown eyes whenever his master is in the dumps and feeling blue.

Being the dog lover that I am you can imagine my outrage over the recent actions of NFL superstar Michael Vick. The details of the dog-fighting ring that Vick was operating are truly shocking and bizarre. Vick's training of these animals to be vicious fighters and his heartless executions of these animals when they didn't produce the desired results in the fighting ring has to disturb the consciences of all who have a sense of decency.

Michael Vick is going to pay a heavy price for his indecent and inhumane actions. Not only will he spend some time in prison, but also he may very well forfeit his promising NFL football career. He is also losing millions of dollars of income in product endorsements, as corporations now no longer want him to promote their products. I shed no tears for Mr. Vick. His disgraceful actions deserve the coming punishment that he is going to receive.

Joining me in my condemnation of Vick are liberals of every stripe. The predictable animal rights groups, such as PETA, are leading the loud public protest, and liberal politicians and liberal commentators in the media such as FOX News commentator Alan Colmes also join them in such denunciations. All of these protestors are expressing sincere voices of compassion as they speak out against the inhumane treatment of helpless creatures that cannot defend themselves.

I join these voices of protest, but I have to ask my liberal friends one question, Why are you so inconsistent in protesting the killing of the innocent?

Yes, Michael Vick's actions in this matter were unspeakably cruel and all Americans of every political persuasion should be appalled and should speak out against such dealings. However, if such cruelty to dogs deserves condemnation from all in society what about the practice of abortion on demand?

Since January 1973, the date of the infamous *Roe v. Wade* decision, more than 46 million unborn children have been destroyed by abortion. Today nearly 4,000 abortions occur every day. Can you imagine the voices of protest that would be heard in liberal circles if it were revealed that 4,000 dogs were being tortured and killed every day through the practice of dog fighting? Think about the loud voices of protest that would be coming from the anti-war crowd if America lost 4,000 soldiers in Iraq every day. Yet, where are the liberal voices protesting the gruesome killing of the unborn in America today?

Since the media was not reluctant to describe the details of Mr. Vick's executions of innocent animals why do they refuse to describe the gruesome details of abortion and the excruciating agony inflicted upon unborn children by this act. The act of abortion, even in the early stages of pregnancy, tears apart and dismembers the body of the unborn victim. Where are the liberal voices of protest?

The gruesome act of partial birth abortion has been publicized over the years to the shock of most of the American public. In a partial birth abortion the baby is pulled out of the birth canal just four inches short of a complete delivery. Surgical scissors are then jabbed into the baby's neck and a vacuum is inserted into the incision thereby sucking out the child's brains and collapsing the baby's skull.

Thankfully, this year the Supreme Court upheld the Congressional ban on partial birth abortion as constitutional. Yet, it was liberals who protested such a ban and hysterically claimed that the Court decision was the beginning of the end for women's rights.

I ask my liberal friends one more question. Should we not have at least the same amount of compassion for unborn children who are subject to the gruesome act of partial birth abortion that we have for the dogs executed by Michael Vick?

Over the years support for abortion-on-demand has become a foundational litmus test in liberal circles to judge whether or not a politician is worthy of liberal support. If any politician dared stray from the liberal party line support for abortion then he/she would be in political jeopardy from their support base. The late Robert Casey, former governor of Pennsylvania, is a case in point.

Governor Casey was a classic domestic liberal Democrat who supported the welfare state and traditional liberal programs, but he committed one act of political heresy to the liberal agenda for which he was never forgiven. He was adamantly and unashamedly prolife. He never wavered in his opposition to abortion and spoke out against it at the national level. Because of his prolife convictions he was denied the opportunity by the leaders in his own party to address the Democrat national convention in 1992.

A fundamental tenet of liberalism today is compassion. Yet, where is the liberal compassion for the tiny lives that are being gruesomely destroyed every day? Where is the liberal compassion for the mothers who aborted but were uninformed about the impact the decision would have upon them and accordingly, are suffering emotionally and spiritually?

Despite the acceptance of abortion on demand I still believe that American society has a conscience. When the details of Michael Vick's treatment of dogs were revealed Americans were shocked and alarmed. I believe that, likewise, if the public becomes educated on the gruesome details about abortion a similar reaction will take place and politicians will be forced to deal with the issue in a manner that will protect innocent human life from destruction.

In the meantime I just have to scratch my head and ask: Why can't liberals be consistent in their compassion?

## Curbing "Raw Judicial Power"
### March 8, 2007

The Presidential sweepstakes for 2008 is underway and the candidates of both parties are scrambling to get the inside track in the minds of the voters. The presidential hopefuls are intensely discussing issues of importance to the future of this nation but, to date, no candidate has clearly spelled out a specific position regarding the appointment of federal judges.

There is no issue more crucial to the future of this country than the issue of who will be appointed to fill vacancies in the federal judiciary. Our nation is a constitutional republic governed by elected representatives. When such representatives pass laws that are not supported by the public at large we have the ability to change such laws through the political process. Indeed, when a legislator acts irresponsible in the execution of his public duties he is subject to recall or defeat at the polls when he runs for reelection. Thus, the public (at least theoretically) has the constitutional ability to reverse bad decisions from our elected officials by engaging in the political process. Such engagement gives "we the people" control over the direction of the nation.

What controls does the public have, however, to check a federal judiciary composed of judges appointed for life who do not face accountability from the public through the electoral process? Indeed, federal courts have over the last few decades shown increasing interference into the lives of ordinary citizens. In regards to this former federal judge Robert Bork states:

> *Courts have all but banished religion and religious symbolism from our public life, created a wholly spurious right to abortion, made discipline difficult to impossible in public schools, required discrimination by judges race in public schools, ordered violent felons back on the streets because of what perceive as overcrowding in prisons, taken over the hiring and promotion of police and fire departments, required drastic changes in the composition of state legislatures, and transformed the First Amendment from a protector of ideas to a protector of self-gratification, so that obscenity and pornography are rife in our culture. Our courts will continue along these lines indefinitely unless we devise a counter.*

In devising our constitutional system the founding fathers ingeniously set up a system of checks and balances to insure that none of the three branches of the federal government—the executive, the legislative and the judicial—would be more powerful than the other two. In addition, the constitution clearly places limits upon the power of the federal government to encroach upon the powers granted to each individual state.

In regards to the power of the federal judiciary it was made very clear by founding father Alexander Hamilton in the Federalist Papers that the judiciary was to be the weakest branch of the federal government. Yet, historically the federal judiciary has usurped for itself increasing power and authority without specific authorization in the Constitution. When the courts do this they in fact become a super legislature overriding the will of the people as reflected in the work of their elected representatives.

How did such an expansion of federal judicial power happen? Beginning in the early 1900s the Supreme Court began to expand the meaning of "liberty" under the 14th Amendment. This Amendment states that no state shall deny to any person liberty without due process of law. Traditionally, this clause was understood to mean that one could not be incarcerated without receiving traditional legal due process rights such as a trial, the right to confront witnesses, freedom from self-incrimination, etc. However, under this expansive interpretation of the liberty clause the Court began to rule that the personal liberty protected under the 14th Amendment meant other things besides freedom from incarceration. Such constitutionally protected liberty also protected, according to the Court, the freedom to contract, the freedom to direct the education of one's child, the freedom to procreate and the freedom to travel.

In a major precedent in the 1960s the Supreme Court further expanded this new understanding of constitutional liberty stating that it provides a right to privacy that allows the purchase of contraceptives for married people. Shortly thereafter the Court found that this constitutional liberty also belonged to unmarried people as well.

In 1973 Court again expanded the meaning of constitutionally protected liberty under the 14th Amendment. In the landmark case of *Roe v. Wade* the Court found the right to privacy under the liberty clause is broad enough to encompass a woman's decision whether or not to terminate a pregnancy by abortion. In making this ruling the Court over ruled the laws of all fifty states that made the commission of an abortion a felonious act.

In ruling that abortion is a constitutional right, as opposed to a criminal act, the Court went far beyond simply expanding the meaning of liberty under the 14th Amendment. The state of Texas, the defendant in the case, argued that abortion was not constitutionally protected liberty because it took the life of a "person." The full text of the 14th Amendment reads: "No state shall deny to any <u>person</u>, life, liberty or property without due process of law." Hence, Texas argued that no liberty exists to take the life of a person for such an act violates the protection of life under the Amendment.

The Supreme Court agreed with this argument of Texas and admitted that if, indeed, an unborn child is a "person" under the 14th Amendment then abortion could not be allowed because it took the life of a "person" without due process of law. This, however, is where the Court made a radical departure from the traditional understanding of the Constitution and the protections it gives to human beings. The Court simply stated that the unborn child is not considered a "person" under this Amendment and thus, abortion is a protected constitutional liberty. The issue of whether or not the unborn is a human being was irrelevant to the Court because it erroneously and foolishly ignored scientific facts and stated that nobody could know when human life begins. Regardless, of the humanity of the unborn the Court said that the unborn cannot be considered persons and thus, are not protected under the 14th Amendment. Hence, the era of abortion on demand was ushered in.

Numerous legal scholars have severely criticized the Court's ruling in *Roe* and many of these scholars are personally supportive of abortion. However, the Court in this decision decided to make public policy and constitutionalize an act that was a felony in all fifty states. Justice Byron White stated in his dissent that this decision was an act of "raw judicial power."

Such "raw judicial power" has divided the American public in a manner not seen since the days of slavery. The Constitution does not mention abortion or a right to privacy. Yet, the Court decided to impose upon the nation a policy of abortion on demand protected by the Constitution by finding such a right. The results of this decision have been tragic—46 million abortions, 1.3 million abortions a year, 4,000 abortions per day and one abortion every twenty seconds.

Raw judicial power from the federal judiciary and the Supreme Court is power that imposes public policy on the nation and imbeds it in the Constitution regardless of whether or not such a policy is specifically mentioned in this fundamental legal document. When such a decision is rendered, as it was in *Roe*, the only clear way to overturn it is through the constitutional amendment process that requires two-thirds (2/3) of Congress passing the amendment and three-fourths (3/4) of the states approving it. Practically speaking the passage of any amendment that would end abortion and reverse *Roe* is politically impossible.

Without a constitutional amendment the only practical way of reversing *Roe* and other decisions of its kind is to have the Supreme Court reverse this decision and begin to render rulings consistent with the text of the Constitution. This means that the justices on the Court must impose upon themselves in judicial restraint. They must not rule in accordance with their own political preferences or biases, but rather must adhere to the intent of the authors of the Constitution. Without such a prevailing philosophy on the Supreme Court and in the federal judiciary we will continue to suffer from rulings handed down by federal judges who believe that they are wiser than the public at large on issues of morality and freedom.

President Bush has had a consistent and impressive track record in the appointment of federal judges. On the Supreme Court he has placed two excellent jurists—Chief Justice John Roberts and Justice Samuel Alito—who clearly believe in judicial restraint and not 'raw judicial power." However, more justices of this kind are needed if our nation is going to stem the tide of judicial encroachment on our liberties and notions of traditional morality.

The upcoming Presidential race will feature a discussion of major issues of concern to our nation. No subject is more important than the topic of judicial appointments by the next President of the United States. Federal judges serve on the bench for life. Their influence on the course of this nation will long outlive the Presidents who appointed them. The next President will make crucial appointments to the judiciary that will once and for all settle in the public arena moral issues like abortion and gay marriage.

The public and general electorate must clearly understand what is at stake in the next election in regards to the make-up of the federal judiciary. Curbing "raw judicial power" through the appointment of federal judges who believe in judicial restraint is an issue that must be foremost in the minds of the voters. Lives are at stake and perhaps the future of our nation, as a true constitutional republic, hangs in the balance.

# ABOUT THE AUTHOR

 Thomas A. Glessner is the founder and President of the National Institute of Family and Life Advocates (**NIFLA**), a public interest law firm founded in 1993 and committed to legal counsel and training for Pregnancy Resource Centers (PRCs) and Pregnancy Medical Clinics (PMCs). **NIFLA** represents more than 1,350 PRCs/PMCs nationwide.

Mr. Glessner is a graduate of the University of Washington, School of Law in Seattle in 1977 and practiced law in the Seattle area for ten years. He was the president and CEO of the Christian Action Counsel (now Care Net) from 1987 to 1992, establishing legal guidelines and programs for the training of hundreds of board members and directors of PRCs/PMCs.

Thomas A. Glessner is the author of *Achieving an Abortion Free America* (Multnomah Publishing 1990), *Destiny's Team: A Story About Love, Choices and Eternity* (Anomalos Publishing 2007), a novel, and *The Emerging Brave New World* (Anomalos Publishing 2008), a nonfiction work. Mr. Glessner is a member of the bar associations for the United States Supreme Court, the State of Virginia and the State of Washington.

Mr. Glessner and his wife, Laura, live in Fredericksburg, Virginia, and have four children — Joshua, SaraLynn, Brannan and Jefferson.